Hush
Little
Babies

Dear Reader:

The book you are about to read is the latest bestseller from St. Martin's True Crime Library, the imprint *The New York Times* calls "the leader in true crime!" Each month, we offer you a fascinating account of the latest, most sensational crime that has captured the national attention. In DEADLY SEDUCTION a prominent attorney thought he'd found the woman of his dreams, until the silky blonde society lady turned into a calculating, cruel seductress whose murderous future was about to rival her sordid past. DEATH CRUISE tells how a dream vacation in Florida turned into a nightmare of death on a tropical ocean for a mother and her two teenage daughters.

True Crime Library is also where readers go to find the classic tales of the most infamous crimes of our times. THE MILWAUKEE MURDERS delves into the twisted world of savage serial killer Jeffrey Dahmer; WHOEVER FIGHTS MONSTERS takes you inside the special FBI team that tracks serial killers; BAD BLOOD is the story of the notorious Menendez brothers and their sensational trials; SINS OF THE MOTHER details the sad account of Susan Smith and her two drowned children; FALLEN HERO recounts the riveting tragedy of O.J. Simpson and the case that stunned a nation.

St. Martin's True Crime Library gives you the stories *behind* the headlines. Our authors take you right to the scene of the crime and into the minds of the most evil murderers to show you what really makes them tick. St. Martin's True Crime Library paperbacks are better than the most terrifying thriller because it's all true! The next time you want a crackling good read, make sure it's got the St. Martin's True Crime Library logo on the spine—you'll be up all night!

Charles Spicer
Senior Editor

There was a mat of blood on the floor, and he saw first one, then two children lying on the floor bleeding. A pale Darlie Routier was screaming hysterically into a cordless telephone while pressing a bloody rag to her neck. Waddell asked her who had done this, and she mumbled incoherently, but pointed toward an open door that led out the rear of the house. Waddell saw Darin drop to his knees and begin trying CPR on one of the boys. The man looked up with pained eyes and told the policeman he could feel air coming through the wounds in the boy's chest. Waddell ordered a stunned Darlie to get some towels and put them on the other boy, but the woman only continued to grip the telephone tightly and scream.

St. Martin's Paperbacks titles
by Don Davis

Hush Little Babies

DON DAVIS

St. Martin's

For Robin

ACKNOWLEDGMENTS

I could almost write another book about all of the people who helped me on this one. Some, however, prefer to stay in the shade of anonymity for personal reasons, and I respect that wish.

The family of Darlie and Darin Routier were most gracious and helpful in allowing me into their inner circle. Their guidance was critical. Special thanks to Darin, Mama Darlie, Sarilda Routier, Dana Stahl, Lou Ann Brown, Sandi Aitken, and Deon and Dana Routier.

In Rowlett, my friends Greg Lynch and Becky Sebastian at the *Lakeshore Times* provided invaluable help and good Mexican food, Estelle Anderson of Back Porch Books became a pal, as did Corrine Wells. Mike Glenn of the *Garland News*, Charlotte Johnson of the Rowlett Chamber of Commerce and Sgt. Dean Poos of the Rowlett Police also were helpful.

In Dallas, Judge Mark Tolle and his staff were more than courteous, and in Kerrville, I enjoyed the assistance of Joe Munoz of Channel 5, Randy Coffey of KRLD, and a few others who know who they are. Thanks to all. My secret weapon was Helen McClure. Much of this book is due to her work.

Robin Murphy Davis provided the original editing and a sense of normalcy while I wrote. Charlie Spicer and Stephen Murphy of St. Martin's Press, and my agent, Jane Dystel, handled the New York end of things with speed and dispatch.

Oh, come, my hand, poor wretched hand,
      and take the sword,

Take it, step forward to this bitter
      starting point,

And do not be a coward, do not
      think of them,

How sweet they are, and how you
      are their mother. Just for

This one short day be forgetful of
      your children,

Afterward weep, for even though
      you will kill them,

They are very dear—Oh, I am an
      unhappy woman!

Medea
Euripides 431 B.C.

Hush
Little
Babies

1

IT WAS ONLY early summer, but already the sun beat down with a fury on the flat anvil that is Texas. On the fifth day of June 1996 the temperature hit 93 degrees and again there was no rain to cool things down. The entire year had been dog-bone dry, and while sixteen inches of rain should have fallen by this time, less than eight had come, leaving the plains dusty and turning the concrete towers and miles of paved road of the big cities into heat-reflecting ovens. A whisper of wet was in the air as forecasters predicted that a front moving in from the west might soon bring afternoon thunderstorms. Thirty percent chance. By the time the sun finally set that day, late, at 8:39 P.M., Dallas had been well-cooked and could look forward only to more of the same. It was, after all, Texas in the summertime. A quarter-moon rose, barely piercing the welcome darkness, which brought a slight reduction in the baking temperature.

Twenty-five miles to the northeast of Dallas, just beyond the I-635 ring road around the city, in a spacious home in the town of Rowlett, Darlie Routier found it was uncomfortable. The temperature for the night eventually would only dip to 70 degrees, leaving Texans reaching for their air conditioners and fans. Heat rises, which meant the upper floor of the two-story brick-fronted house on the sweeping corner at 5801 Eagle Drive would be hotter than the downstairs, even with the air-conditioning. She wore only a light T-shirt and panties. Her husband, Darin, had gone upstairs to put their eight-month-old infant son, Drake, into the crib, brought her down a pillow and light blanket, kissed her good night, and then went up into their master bedroom.

Darlie chose to remain on the cooler lower floor, in the family room, with their two older boys. Everyone had a name that began with the letter *D*. In addition to Darlie and Darin, and the baby Drake, there was Devon, aged six, and Damon, five. The boys, all with the dark hair of their father, were startlingly good-looking kids.

Darin, twenty-eight, was handsome, with a well-trimmed beard and slim body, and twenty-six-year-old Darlie Lynn Routier was a quintessential Texas blonde with a lot of curves to match a dazzling smile. Sweethearts from the moment they met while they were both teenagers, they had been married for eight years. Darin's talents as an entrepreneur provided a more than comfortable lifestyle, and they had talked for a while that night before he went upstairs about the broken Jaguar and that money-sucking boat they planned to sell, one of Darin's business ventures that didn't work out.

Devon and Damon were as boisterous as always that night, still excited by the visit of their aunt, Dana Stahl, one of Darlie's teen-aged sisters, and had splashed almost all of the water out of the hot tub in the backyard after dinner. The brothers' seemingly bottomless pit of energy had led the family area in the big house to be called the ''Roamin' Room.'' Darlie let the boys sack out on the floor and she settled onto the couch against the west wall. All three of them fell asleep that Wednesday night to the mindless muttering of the television set.

*　　*　　*

She had not been asleep long when she felt a tiny push on her shoulder and heard Damon calling weakly to her, "Mommy, Mommy." The words were strained, barely whispered, a tone most unusual from any five-year-old boy. Darlie opened her eyes to find a nightmare.

By the shimmering, lambent light of the television set, she made out the shape of a tall man leaning close to her. It was not Darin, but a stranger, someone she had never seen before. He wore dark clothing from head to toe, blue jeans, a black short-sleeved T-shirt and a dark baseball cap, the bill facing forward, keeping his face deep in shadow. Puzzled as she came out of her sleep, she didn't scream, even when she saw a big knife in his right hand.

Darlie glanced at her boys on the floor, horrified to see that they were surrounded by dark pools of blood. Devon lay quiet and still on his back, his small chest ripped by savage wounds. After awakening his mother, Damon slid back to the floor and Darlie could see he, too, was slathered in blood.

She stared in shock at the mysterious stranger and he moved away, perhaps thinking it was time to leave the awakened, wounded woman. Darlie, frozen in fear, still did not call out. Her mind was paralyzed by the unthinkable sudden violence which had invaded her quiet suburban home in the middle of the night.

It was when the assailant backed away that Darlie snapped out of her stupor. Her bare feet hit the floor and she went after the guy, their arms tangling as she struggled and he slashed at her again and again. She forced him to retreat through the kitchen and into the utility room, then to the garage. There was the sound of breaking glass and her bloodied bare feet tracked a path through the rear of the house as she chased the vicious intruder.

A clatter, and he dropped the knife. It was a long,

white-handled weapon, just like the kind she kept in the kitchen butcher block. She reached down and picked it up. Now that she held the weapon, the intruder wanted no more of this feisty woman. He vanished through a door leading into the garage, and then disappeared, probably going out through a window. Darlie didn't care where or how he had gone, as long as he was gone.

Exhausted, she dropped the big knife on the cement floor and hurried back into the house, each step seeming to take an eternity. A glance in a mirror shocked her, for Darlie, too, had been slashed and stabbed. A torrent of blood gushed from a long wound that went from her throat to her chest, splattering her nightshirt. Her hands were cut, as were her arms and her chin, and her mouth felt raw and sore.

Damon and Devon still lay where they had been attacked, their little bodies motionless and drenched by their own blood. She screamed as loud as she could to awaken Darin. What could she do to help the children?

At 2:31 A.M., Darlie struggled over to the kitchen telephone and dialed the emergency number, 911. The police operator heard an incomprehensible scream as the desolate Darlie begged for help. "Oh, my God! Oh, my God!" The words tumbled out in a tangle, colliding and tumbling in screeching sentences. "My babies have been stabbed! My babies are dying! There's blood everywhere!" Her grief soared into a noise that blurred into an almost electronic range of static. "Hang on, honey. Hang on, hang on," Darlie said.

The keening and incoherence continued, a wave of thunderous portent. Judging by the explosion of emotion, something awful had happened at that house. The emergency communications officer checked a video screen, noted the telephone number from which the call was being made, the computer matched it to a specific address, and she radioed for help at the location.

*   *   *

Darin snapped awake as the tortured screams of his wife filled the dark house. It took but a heartbeat to get from sound asleep to wide awake, knowing in his gut that something awful had happened to make Darlie scream like that. He heard the distant tinkle of breaking glass as he leaped out of the bed and grabbed a pair of blue jeans.

He hit the landing at the top of the curving stairwell at a dead run, grabbing the smooth banister for balance and pounding down the stairs to the first floor, whipping around the corner and dashing through the darkness toward the rear rooms of the house. He saw carnage, and thought one of the boys had shattered the glass-topped coffee table.

"Devon!" screamed Darlie, who was in the kitchen, clutching a bloody towel to her throat and yelling into the telephone. "Devon! Devon!"

Darin looked down at his bloodied boys in horror, and it was as if a cold fist clutched his heart. Both had been brutalized. He dropped to his knees beside Devon and saw huge wounds in the child's chest. The eyes, which were usually filled with wonder, were totally dim and lifeless, looking right up at him without seeing anything. There was no movement, no moan, no sign of life at all in Devon Routier.

Darin spun to check his other son. Damon was face-down with no wounds immediately visible, but the father knew by the stillness and the amount of spilled blood that the boy was badly hurt. He felt for a pulse and thought he detected a flutter of life. His mind whirled. He had no idea what kind of disaster had struck his family, only that his two oldest sons were dead or severely injured and his wife, gushing blood at her neck, was hysterical, fetching wet towels while she talked to police. He guessed that she was calling the police, so help would soon arrive. He could do nothing but work CPR on his little Devon's bloody chest. And pray that Damon could hold on a little longer.

Darlie clung to the emergency line as if to a life preserver. "Baby?" she said softly at one point as she ran out of breath. Then she wailed again. *"Who would do this?"* Darlie was babbling, something about finding a knife, and the police operator told her not to pick it up. It might be evidence. Too late. "I've already touched it," Darlie blurted out. "I picked it up. . . . We could have gotten prints from it, maybe." Her babies lay butchered and bleeding near her feet and she was worrying about fingerprints and telling how someone cut a screen in the garage to enter the house through the utility room. For almost five minutes, she talked with the operator, until a policeman radioed in that he was at the front door of the house. By then, the shrieks had subsided, but not the emotion. Darlie Routier was obviously tumbling from the edge of an emotional cliff, hurtling into a deep and unknown blackness.

The parking lot of the Victory Baptist Church at 7005 Highway 66 was empty at 2:30 in the morning of June 6, except for the patrol car of David Waddell, a thirty-two-year-old officer who had been a Rowlett policeman for more than four years. He had been on duty nearly five hours and was looking forward to getting off at dawn to return home to his wife and two kids. The night had been calm, and he hoped it would stay that way as he watched occasional pairs of headlights slice the blackness along the highway that was one of the few roads in or out of the city.

Waddell was jerked out of any predawn drowsiness by the raucous sound of the fire chimes on his radio, and he switched to the fire channel in time to hear the calm voice of dispatcher Janet Brooks order the paramedics to roll

immediately to 5801 Eagle Drive. There had been a stabbing. The young officer flipped on his emergency lights
and the big patrol car jumped to life, leaving the church
parking lot with a squeal of tires. Eagle Drive was two
miles and two minutes away.

He braked the blue-and-white vehicle to a sudden stop
when he approached the address, a large house on the
corner where Eagle Drive curved to the left. A brightly
lit fountain dominated the front lawn. A bare-chested
man in blue jeans burst through the front door and ran
past the fountain, screaming at the startled officer. David
Waddell had no idea who Darin Routier was, and took
out his pistol as he got out of the car and shouted for the
advancing man to stop. Darin kept coming, staggering,
yelling, loudly enough to wake the neighbors, "Someone
has stabbed my children and my wife!" Weapon at the
ready against his shoulder, Waddell followed Darin
through the big door and into a bloody scene, the worst
he had ever encountered as a policeman.

There was a mat of blood on the floor, and he saw
first one, then two children lying on the floor, bleeding.
A pale Darlie Routier was screaming hysterically into a
cordless telephone while pressing a bloody rag to her
neck. Waddell asked her who had done this, and she
mumbled incoherently, but pointed toward an open door
that led out the rear of the house. Waddell saw Darin
drop to his knees and began trying CPR on one of the
boys. The man looked up with pained eyes and told the
policeman he could feel air coming through the wounds
in the boy's chest. Waddell ordered a stunned Darlie to
get some towels and put them on the other boy, but the
woman only continued to grip the telephone tightly and
scream.

Overwhelmed by the bloody scene, Waddell let his
training take over, remembering that his first duty was
not to render first aid, but to make certain that the suspect

who had made this vicious attack was no longer a danger. Thinking the attacker might still be in the garage, the policeman stepped around an island in the kitchen and peered through a utility room into the garage. He could see nothing at all. Charging blindly into such a situation all alone only happens in TV shows. There was no reason for him to barge into the dark garage by himself, inviting an ambush, for if he was killed, no one would be left to protect the family. The attacker could be anywhere. Upstairs, in the garage, at the back door, at a window, in a closet. He didn't know. David Waddell carefully positioned himself between the family and the rest of the house, keeping both hands on his pistol and trying to talk to Darlie, telling her to sit down to slow the loss of blood that was pumping from a wound in her neck. Each passing second seemed like an hour. Help was on the way, wasn't it?

2

JANET BROOKS, RUNNING the communications console at police headquarters, was having difficulty deciphering the hysterical Darlie. "Ma'am, I can't understand you," Brooks told her on the telephone.

"Yes."

"You're going to have to slow down. Calm down and talk to me."

"I'm talking to my babies. . . . They're dying!"

"What is going on?"

"Somebody came in while I was sleeping. Me and my little boys were sleeping downstairs. Some man came in . . . stabbed my babies . . . stabbed me . . . I woke up . . . I was fighting . . . he ran out through the garage . . . threw the knife down . . . my babies are dying . . . they're dead . . . Oh, my God!"

There was some back-and-forth between Brooks, the caller, and several other people on radios, then, at two minutes and fifty-three seconds into the call, Darlie said, "I feel really bad. I think I'm dying."

Four minutes and five seconds after the call began, Brooks could hear Darlie talking to somebody: "Y'all look out in the garage . . . look out in the garage . . . they left a knife laying on . . ."

Brooks gave a quick instruction—"Don't touch anything"—only to hear Darlie respond, "I already touched it and picked it up."

More crying and screaming came over the open telephone when the first policeman, Waddell, arrived at the house and tried to talk with the woman. Brooks relayed Waddell's call for more assistance, and a ten-channel Dictaphone reel-to-reel tape recorder caught every word of the dramatic call from Darlie Routier to the 911 emergency number.

Sergeant Matt Walling, supervising a shift of five police officers, had been only 3.1 miles away from the murder scene when the call came, and sped onto Willowbrook, which connects with Eagle Drive, right behind ambulance Number 902, containing veteran paramedics Jack Colbye and Brian Koschak, from Shift C at the Rowlett Fire Department's Dalrock station. They had reacted instantly, despite being sound asleep when the alarms rang. Both vehicles stopped in front of the house simultaneously. Walling jumped out and told the paramedics to stay put while he made sure the area was safe. There were at least two kids hurt inside, he said. Get more medical help. Koschak radioed for a fire truck and another ambulance.

Walling found Waddell inside, got a quick explanation from him—the attacker was a male, wearing dark clothes and a baseball cap, and had run out the back of the house. The two officers, both with drawn weapons, edged through the kitchen, toward the utility room. The door to the garage was smeared with blood and partially opened. Walling pushed it wide and went in, his bright flashlight cutting through the darkness. The large rolling door was closed, but Walling saw a window screen with a large slice in it and assumed an attacker may have escaped through it into the backyard. Waddell was right behind, covering him. They found no one. The sergeant summoned the paramedics.

Darin was lost in a maze of bewildered pain, feeling like a stranger in his own house as men in uniforms rushed about shouting, with guns drawn. It was almost as if he were watching some horrible movie. He was in the audience, a viewer, not a participant, and he seemed to move in slow-motion through the rooms. He looked at his hands, which were covered with Devon's blood. Every time he had tried to push on the boy's chest and do CPR, his child's blood had spurted out in carmine jets onto his hands, arms, face, chest, and even on his back. Karen! She was a nurse! She would know what to do! She could help! He ran across Eagle Drive to the home of his neighbors and close friends, Karen and Terry Neal, and pounded on their door.

Terry Neal grabbed a pistol and held it ready until he recognized Darin's silhouette and voice. They threw open their door to find their friend crying, begging. "Help. I need your help. Someone just murdered my children," Darin gasped. "Help me."

Colbye, a paramedic the size of a linebacker, had grabbed his Basic Medical Kit and headed inside the Routier house, with Koschak on his heels. He saw Waddell in the kitchen area, and the officer nodded toward the floor of the nearby den. Following his glance, Colbye found a small child, wearing a dark T-shirt and jeans, facedown on the floor in a pool of blood beside a couch. The big paramedic rolled five-year-old Damon Routier over and the child responded with a single, deep exhale of breath, as if he were ending a foot race. Colbye watched helplessly as the light of life faded from the boy's eyes. The paramedic scooped Damon up in his big arms, as easily as picking up a loaf of bread, and hurried outside, away from Darlie's anguished screaming.

At the rear of the ambulance, he used a knee to prop the boy to his chest while he opened the doors and ducked into the working area. Another paramedic joined him as they launched into CPR, mouth-to-mouth, and other respiration efforts, including starting an IV in the jugular vein to push drugs directly into the system. They worked for fifteen minutes in the back of the ambulance, could not recover a pulse, then sped away to get their tiny victim to a hospital.

Koschak had gone to work on little Devon, who was lying on his back with his chest bare, huge puncture wounds showing as bloody slits in the skin. He checked for vital signs, but could find none. In the vernacular of the paramedic's profession, the child was "black," meaning nonsalvageable, dead. There was nothing Koschak could do for Devon Routier.

He left the small corpse and moved to the third wounded person in the room, Darlie, who was on her knees close to a sliding glass door, holding a rag to a wound on her neck and looking dazed. A mop of disheveled blonde hair topped a pale face, and she was wearing only a blood-covered T-shirt that reached below her hips. Other wounds could be seen on her arms. As he approached, she began to mutter, "Who could have done this?"

The paramedic looked for signs of shock, and noted that her skin color appeared good, and that she seemed to know where she was. The place was becoming chaotic as more police arrived and Koschak coaxed her to come to the front porch, both to find a better place to tend her wounds and to get them out of the way. As she crouched on the porch, he replaced the soaked towel from her neck with a big bandage and called for a stretcher.

*   *   *

While the victims were tended, Sergeant Walling had continued his preliminary check around the property, and went to the backyard through which the intruder was thought to have escaped. A six-foot-high white wooden fence surrounded the yard area, and the gate was closed. He had to lift it slightly to pull it open. As he walked into the dark area toward a structure that he would later learn was a redwood gazebo containing a spa, a motion-sensing detector read his movement and automatically snapped on a light that bathed the yard in brightness. He was able to see clearly enough to observe the cut screen on the rear window of the house.

Satisfied now that no threat still existed, Walling returned to the front of the house and elicited a little information from Darlie while Koschak was afixing the big bandage. Police still had very little information about who might have committed this savage crime and Walling asked the only survivor of the attack to describe the intruder. Darlie basically repeated the same thing she had told the first officer on the scene, Waddell, who had passed the description to Walling earlier. The distraught and wounded woman said she had been sleeping on the couch, and awoke to find a man standing over her. He wore dark clothes, maybe a black shirt and jeans, and a dark-colored baseball cap. It was too dark and things happened too fast for her to remember much more than that. She couldn't tell what race he was.

Their conversation lasted no more than thirty seconds, then Darlie was helped onto the gurney and was rolled to the second ambulance, where her blood pressure was found to be good and an IV was started to replace lost fluids. The blood loss, Koschak thought, did not seem to be severe.

As the ambulance took her away, Koschak went back inside the house to check on Devon once again, then was sent upstairs to look in on a third child. Drake, the baby, was sound asleep in his crib, and the paramedic didn't see any wounds. He radioed the baby's status to his captain, Dennis Vrana, then hurried downstairs and out the front door. Brian Koschak felt that he couldn't get away from that bloody house fast enough.

Two emergency room suites were waiting in the Baylor University Medical Center, a massive 750-bed hospital some forty-five minutes from Rowlett, and teams of doctors and nurses were on alert. They knew that two ambulances with stabbing victims were on the way, one child and one adult.

Dr. Alex Santos had been at work all day, and was tired, but since he was on call, he responded and took charge. The boy came in first and was clearly in trouble. The clothes had been sliced away and Santos saw five major stab wounds on the back. He probed them with a gloved finger and found they reached deep into the body, as nurses checked for a pulse. There was nothing that any medical person could do. Damon Routier was declared dead on arrival.

Another doctor came in and told Santos that an initial examination of the woman showed she needed to go to the operating room, immediately. Someone noted on her chart that she was tearful and frightened. Santos walked over to see her, took one look at the gaping slash wound on the neck, and knew that he didn't have much time. It didn't pay to take chances with a cut like that. Ten minutes after getting to the hospital at 3:40 A.M., Darlie, still bloody, was taken up to the fourth-floor operating theater and put under general anesthetic. Dr. Santos set to work examining and closing the major wound on her neck, minor ones on her shoulder and left arm, a cut on the left side of the chin, and another atop the right forearm. It would take him ninety minutes to finish and release the unconscious Darlie to the Intensive Care Unit at 4:49 A.M.

By then, Darin had tried to return to his house, but was blocked from entering by a police officer at the door. He returned to the Neals, washed away the blood that clung to him, borrowed a fresh T-shirt, and had Terry Neal drive the Routiers' green Pathfinder to the hospital, where Darin learned that his second son had died and his wife was in surgery. He felt the bottom falling out of his world.

On Eagle Drive, police had been busy. As they searched the grounds, a mysterious dark sedan drove past with four people in it, and Sergeant Walling, with his pistol out, ordered it to stop. He was looking for a white male wearing dark clothes and a baseball cap, and ordered the occupants out of the vehicle and made them put their hands on their heads. He counted two white males, one black male, and one white woman. When Walling checked the car and the people, he found no blood, no weapons, and both men wore light-colored shirts and no caps. He carefully looked at their hands, top and bottom, and examined their fingernails. No blood, no cuts. He let them go.

Meanwhile, he had summoned a K-9 unit, then tried, but failed, to get a helicopter. Other officers on his shift had arrived and he posted them on different duties, including one who stood at the door to log in everyone who entered or left the house. Other uniformed officers and detectives fanned out and began to knock on doors in the neighborhood that had come awake to the sounds of sirens and shouts, with cops wanting to get statements before the residents left for work. Walling strung the yellow tape that designated the house as a crime scene, cordoning off an outside perimeter and a tighter one inside that. From that moment on, only people with proper authorization and a reason to be there would enter that house. That did not include the man who lived there.

What, however, was he to do about that baby upstairs? Karen Neal came forward, explained who she was, and Walling escorted her inside to retrieve both the sleeping infant and scoop up the little Pomeranian dog, which had finally awakened and was yapping from the top of the staircase.

Within a few hours of the emergency call, police and paramedics had responded to the scene, paramedics and doctors had tended to the victims, and the big house had been sealed up tight to prevent unauthorized people from tracking through the crime scene. The two boys were dead, the third one in a neighbor's care and being taken to its parents. The mother was being operated on at the hospital and would soon be wheeled into ICU, and the father had gone to be with her.

The crime itself was now a thing of history. It was time for the police to start trying to figure out just what had happened inside that house. Since no suspect had been immediately found, the only person who really knew the answer was Darlie Routier.

Dawn was coming soon, and, although the police didn't know it at the time, some answers would arrive along with the orange sun that was just peeking over the rooftops, ready to bake Texas for another day.

3

THERE WAS NO doubt the murderous attack in a quiet subdivision of a small town outside of Dallas was front-page news, but the timing of the crime played a major role in initial media coverage, which eventually would saturate the case and carry it far beyond the Texas borders.

Darlie's 911 emergency call was made at 2:31 A.M. on June 6, and the middle of the night is much too late for publication in major morning newspapers, such as the ones in nearby Dallas and Ft. Worth. Time is needed to put stories together and get them into print, and this one wasn't important enough for a late-shift editor to stop the presses and delay delivery. Therefore, the Thursday readers of the *Fort Worth Star-Telegram* and the *Dallas Morning News* found not a word about the double murder up in Rowlett.

The same time element had an even worse impact on Greg Lynch, the young publisher of the local weekly newspaper, the *Rowlett Lakeshore Times*, who could only kick a trash can or two at the unfair importance that both the clock and calendar have in the news business. As usual, he worked late on Wednesday night as the deadline approached for the week's edition. When Wednesday, June 5, became Thursday, June 6, he was still in his office, tucked into a Rowlett shopping center not far from the police station. Finally, at 1:30 A.M., Lynch was satisfied with the layout, the stories, and the advertisements for his weekly publication. He closed out the paper, took it over to the printer's shop, and went home. The biggest crime in the history of his town would happen in about sixty minutes, and Lynch would be helpless to publish a story for an entire week.

In the long run, however, this situation would work to his advantage. As the sun rose and the news spread like wildfire over a dry prairie, reporters from the big metro newspapers and crews from television stations herded into Rowlett and began knocking on doors around Eagle Drive. These outside news-gatherers would serve several purposes. They would take the heat when local merchants and officials began to fret that Rowlett's reputation was being tarnished, but they would also become a vital conduit for the police to send bulletins to the community. And, despite the comments that the Dallas reporters were not wanted in Rowlett, the town's residents would buy out the newspaper racks and tune in the TV news every night. Still, advertisers would have no reason to forsake the *Rowlett Lakeshore Times*, something that normally is at stake when a small hometown publication is caught up in a headline crime. After being caught by the clock on the breaking story, Lynch and his editor, Becky Sebastian, would provide solid coverage throughout the case.

A telephone rang insistently in the early morning hours at the home of Sarilda and Leonard Routier, the parents of Darin, who lived far away in Lubbock. Sarilda answered sleepily, but was jolted awake in an electrifying instant when she heard the terrified voice of Darlie Kee, the mother of Darlie, and known to everyone trying to keep the names straight as Mama Darlie. "She was almost incoherent and hysterical," Sarilda would recall of that awful moment. "She just kept repeating that 'Devon and Damon are dead.' She said it over and over."

That wouldn't be the worst of it for Mama Darlie that morning. Shortly after she had notified her in-laws of the tragedy, another of her daughters, Dana Stahl, called her home in Plano, not far from Rowlett. Dana had already been to the house, found it guarded by police, who gave her only garbled information, enough of a mixup to strike even more terror into the hearts of the family.

"Mama," Dana said. "It's not only Devon and Damon. It's Darlie, too. They said Darlie is dead, too."

She was wrong, but confusion reigned on the information front as rumors began to fly through the predawn hours.

Actually, the investigation had already turned up an interesting find.

While it was still dark, Sergeant Tom Dean Ward and another officer walked the long alley behind the house, each shining a flashlight on a single side of the wide, paved pathway. They looked in every backyard, climbed up to look over fences and hedges, pulled plastic bags out of trash containers to search the refuse, peered into storm drains, and looked under boats and vehicles. In the rear of the home at 5709 Eagle, three houses down from the crime scene, they came upon a long white tube sock with an elongated spot on it that Ward thought might be blood. The sergeant called in his find and stood guard over it until another patrolman could come and collect the sock as evidence. In subsequent DNA tests, it would be shown to contain spots of blood from the slain children.

*   *   *

It fell to the electronic media to issue the first reports, follow developments throughout the day, and broadcast updated stories on the evening news. The first television reporter rolled onto Eagle Drive at 3 A.M., and a parade of satellite trucks soon followed. Channel 11 did a live broadcast at 5 o'clock.

Joe Munoz, a dark-haired young reporter for Channel 5 in Dallas, had only been to Rowlett on one other story, a local controversy involving an ancient Indian burial site. Before the Routier story ended, he would be pulled into the murder investigation as an unwitting participant and his name and his work would show up in the murder trial. He eventually would buy a house in Rowlett.

At the Baylor Medical Center, Darlie Routier had been placed under general anesthetic in the operating room at 3:40 A.M., and medical experts would later estimate that it would require some three hours for her to completely shake off the effects of the medicine that induced sleep and eased the pain. As she began to rouse herself from that long sleep at 5:15, a nurse noted that the patient was crying and visibly upset. In addition, Darlie was suffering from nausea, so nurses administered a quarter-milligram of Demerol, a powerful drug that in combination with the lingering effects of the operating room anesthetic, left her groggy and disoriented. That timeline would later assume critical importance.

Jim Cron looks like a lean Texas version of Kentucky's Colonel Sanders, but instead of founding a fried chicken empire, Cron is a veteran lawman whose specialty of many decades is deciphering a crime scene. By his own count, the silver-haired, goateed Cron had a hand with the investigation of some 21,000 crimes during the past thirty-nine years, many of them minor, but some 4,300 of them involving dead people. After retiring from the

Dallas County Sheriff's Department, he turned his knowledge of crime-scene investigation into a successful consulting business, and taught classes not only at the university level but also to police officers. Instead of being just another retired cop, he became a respected professor, and among the places he taught his craft was the Rowlett Police Department, where he had given three seminars in the past few years.

At 5 A.M. on June 6, just as the first media report on the tragedy was being broadcast, the telephone rang on Cron's bedside table, and his presence was requested by the Rowlett police at 5801 Eagle Drive. It was only fifteen minutes away from his home, but Jim Cron took forty-five minutes getting there. He doesn't have to hurry in his line of work. The police had the place secured, and the crime scene could stay just the way it was until the professor arrived.

Meanwhile, Jimmy Patterson, a veteran detective who would become the lead investigator in the case, was on his way down to the hospital, hoping to get some more information from the victim. The paths of Cron and Patterson would converge within a few hours.

If the police were to exert any control over the bewildering situation, they had to straighten out the facts in order to quell the growing rumors, as well as feed the media. Already, word was spreading throughout Rowlett that a vicious child-killer was on the loose. Neighbors who had been questioned earlier by police were now, in turn, asking questions themselves, such as whether it was safe to send their kids off to school that morning. Rowlett trembled in the face of the unknown.

Sergeant Dean Poos, a slender cop with seven years on the Rowlett police force, had done everything from routine traffic to armed special response duties, and was currently saddled with the public information desk. His communications officer, Janet Brooks, dialed Poos at home shortly after the emergency call was logged, and in the coming days, the press spokesman for the police department would become the most well-known man in Rowlett. When he arrived at the office, the first item on his desk was to put out a quick news release, which he did shortly after dawn, giving the bare facts of what had happened during the last four hours.

"At approximately 2:30 A.M. on this morning the Rowlett Police Department received a 911 call from an adult female reporting that she and her children had been stabbed. Officers arrived at the residence at 5801 Eagle Drive and discovered the female caller and two male children, ages 4 and 7, had in fact all been stabbed at the residence. The female adult along with the 4-year-old were transported to Baylor, Dallas hospital for treatment. The 4-year-old was pronounced dead on arrival at the hospital. The 7-year-old was dead at the scene. The mother was treated for multiple stab wounds, has undergone surgery, and has been admitted to the hospital. The father and an 8-month-old infant were also in the home at the time the incident occurred.

"No arrests have been made and no suspect information is available at this time."

It wasn't much, but, at the time, police didn't have much. Poos said a news conference would be held at 10 o'clock at the police station, at which time Chief Randall Posey would brief the media. The chief knew that not only was press interest going to be high in this case, he realized that his small department was about to be tested as never before, and beneath a media microscope to boot. Nothing like this had ever happened in Rowlett.

After receiving the first single-page news release, the media turned to a growing crowd of neighbors, curious passersby and gawkers along Eagle Drive. It wasn't hard to get them to talk, but none had much to contribute.

Most neighbors only knew that when they went to bed, everything in their small town had been just fine. When they woke up, the world had changed, and borders of yellow tape looped around the house on the corner, and police officers were at their front doors with questions.

4

DARLIE, THE ONLY patient in a four-bed pod on the fourth-floor intensive care unit at the huge Baylor Medical Center, was out of danger, but was still a bloody mess. A plastic tube ran into her nose, carrying oxygen. The slashed neck wound, now treated and held together by adhesive strips, was covered with a sterile bandage. Wires led from small round pads on her arm to an EKG machine to measure her vital signs, and an intravenous tube dripped liquids and medicine into her left arm. She had not yet been scrubbed to cleanse the dried blood that caked her arms, her feet, and had even gathered beneath her fingernails. The narcotic effect from the medium dose of Demerol and the general anesthetic administered before the operation had left her sedated and groggy.

But she was not in that secure ICU and under the constant supervision of nurses because her life was still in danger. There was a more pragmatic reason. Dr. Santos and hospital administrators, once aware of the magnitude of the crime, realized that the media would soon be on Darlie's trail and they wanted to isolate her from reporters, television camera crews, and newspaper photographers until she could recover. Dallas already had recorded eighteen murders for the first four months of

1996, and the Baylor hospital was well experienced in dealing with media access on high-visibility cases. With two kids dead and a mother severely wounded, this was one to watch. By daybreak, a hospital administrator was assigned to be in charge of releasing any information, and a uniformed guard was stationed outside the room.

A frantic Darin remained downstairs in Family Room Number One, outside the emergency room, while his wife was being operated on elsewhere in the hospital. Wearing his neighbor Terry Neal's white T-shirt and the bloodstained blue jeans he had jumped into hours before, he was distraught with the news that two of his boys had been murdered and Darlie was fighting for her life. Chris Frosch, a tall young Rowlett detective and Neal's cousin by marriage, arrived at the hospital and talked briefly with him, and at about 4:30 A.M., they were joined by Detective Jimmy Patterson, who would become the lead investigator in the case.

Upon reaching the hospital, Patterson first checked the emergency room and determined that Darlie and the boy had arrived there, and the child was dead. From there, he got directions to the Family Waiting Room and went in to see the distraught husband. After asking Terry Neal to step outside, Patterson questioned Darin for about half an hour. The policeman went off to view the body of the slain little boy, then telephoned police headquarters in Rowlett to get a crime scene unit out to the hospital for photographs. Family members were also arriving at the hospital, and things were getting crowded. He gave permission for the child's grandmother, Darlie Kee, to take a look at the boy. When the police photographer arrived, Darin was escorted to a private area and asked to strip so he could be photographed in the nude. His clothes were seized as evidence and he was handed a set of hospital greens to wear.

At eleven minutes past six, Corporal Phyllis Jackson

of the Baylor Health Care System escorted Patterson and Frosch upstairs to where Darlie rested in the ICU, and the policemen were advised that Darlie had just come out of surgery. In the small room, with Detective Frosch and a nurse, Patterson asked the young, heavily bandaged patient if she felt well enough to talk with him. She replied that she did, and he interviewed her for between twenty and thirty minutes. Emotionally spent, her throat cut, dopey from pain-killing narcotics, Darlie Routier began listening to the questions of the police investigators, only a little more than three and one-half hours after she had made the 911 emergency call. Darlie told the policemen that she had been sleeping on a first-floor couch when she was awakened by an intruder standing over her. She said he had shoulder-length hair, a black baseball cap with no emblem on it, a short-sleeved T-shirt, and blue jeans. She saw a knife in his hand and struggled with the stranger and he ran away through the kitchen, disappearing into the utility room and garage. He dropped the knife in the utility room, and she suddenly realized that she had been stabbed. Darlie said she could not describe the attacker's face. Patterson wondered if robbery might have been a motive for the attack, and Darlie told him of her jewelry and where it might be found. The rings she wore on all ten fingers should be on the countertop where she had left them. He made a mental note to check on that. Patterson, with the first complete interview of the surviving victim, talked a few more minutes with Darin, then left the hospital and headed back to Rowlett to examine the scene of the killings.

About the time Patterson had started questioning Darlie, Jim Cron and a team of three police officers entered the neocolonial house on Eagle Drive to do a visual inspection and try to come up with a game plan for the investigation. His experienced eye would roam everywhere, looking for anything unusual, anything that didn't *belong*, anything that would shed some light on this terrible double murder. As he went through the front door, he saw blood in the entranceway and the hallway, a glass-topped coffee table knocked askew, a lamp shade tilted, but not torn, on a tall, standing lamp.

The kitchen was a mosaic of blood, broken glass, and bloodstained items, with still more blood on the door and floor of the adjoining utility room. A ball cap lay on the floor in there, near the washer-dryer. He had learned what Darlie had told the officers at the scene, and this was the route she had pointed out that her attacker had followed to escape. So far, as he and the officers sidestepped the bloodstains, he had seen nothing to make him doubt that account.

Then he began to see unusual things, facts that did not fit the puzzle coming together in his mind. In the garage, Cron saw the open window with the sliced screen hanging down like wilted leaves. A thick layer of dust lay undisturbed on the low window sill, which came only to his knees. He was searching for a sign of entry, some scuff marks or a footprint or perhaps disturbed vegetation. Making mental notes, he backed away from the garage and led his team out the front door to look in the back yard. Going through the big gate, he again hunted for the unconscious tracks made by the murderer, perhaps a patch of disturbed mulch in a flower bed, some other entrance the man may have used to get inside the house, marks on a doorframe caused by a pry bar, perhaps a skid mark from a foot trying to scale the white fence, maybe a dropped cigarette butt, or patches of blood outdoors. To make sure of his observations, he asked Walling how the sergeant had entered the back yard earlier, so as to eliminate any signs the policeman may have left behind in his quick search. When Walling described having a problem opening the gate, Cron went over and tried it himself, finding that a corner stubbornly dragged on the ground.

Light was showing in the sky as he stood in the yard and examined the fence. Police had been doing this sort of firsthand examination for decades, and in Cron's opinion, the commonsense approach still was the best way to start unraveling the secrets of a crime scene. The legendary fictional detective Sherlock Holmes had pioneered the close, personal examination of a crime scene, and Cron was his twentieth-century disciple. Such a place whispered silently to Cron, little inanimate objects telling him secrets, allowing him to form a picture. Blood samples, fingerprints, and scientific tests would come later, but Cron had already come to a conclusion, made on gut instinct and the experience of seeing thousands of crimes.

He finished his initial walk-through of the house and yard about 6:30 A.M., and although he would remain at the scene more than nine hours that day, nothing he would see would change the important initial opinion he made after only twenty-five minutes of investigation.

Then he conferred with his uniformed colleagues, who listened closely as he explained with a long, low twang what the crime scene had told him. Way it looks, he said, there was no intruder out here.

Cron reached that important conclusion without the knowledge that a white sock daubed with the blood of the two little murder victims had been found in the alley three houses away.

At seven o'clock, Dr. Santos, who had stitched Darlie's slashed neck back together and patched her other wounds, came back for a quick visit and quickly gave her an examination. He looked at the neck wound and recalled how close it came to the vital carotid artery. "You're a very lucky girl," he observed. But Santos was concerned at this point not so much about her physical condition, which seemed to be stable, but about how she might be reacting psychologically. The tragedy and the police questions so closely after the operation, while she was still sedated, had taken a toll on her energy, and her responses came in a slow monotone. Indeed, a nurse made a chart note that the patient was very emotional, crying and sobbing and talking about her family.

Darin was finally allowed in to see his wounded wife and found her on a roller coaster of hysteria, sedated and groggy. When she was shown large pictures of Devon and Damon, she just went to pieces, crying and rocking back and forth in the bed, clutching the framed photos and asking about the baby. Karen Neal brought Drake in, but, as a nurse, recognized the problems her friend was enduring. There was no way that Darlie, hooked up to wires and tubes and emotionally distraught, could take the child, although she wept, "Let me hold him." So one of the duty nurses tucked the baby beside her for a few minutes, and Darlie was able to play with Drake's tiny fingers.

There might have been even more crying if Darin and Darlie had known what was happening back at their house.

Jimmy Patterson was no stranger to death. He had witnessed about fifty cases involving dead people during his more than seventeen years as a cop, more than a half dozen of them murders. As he drove onto Eagle Drive after 8 A.M., he knew the investigation for this one was just starting. He was wrong. Jim Cron, the crafty old crime-scene wizard, was waiting for him with Rowlett policemen who were already gathering evidence at the house. Cron told him there had been no intruder, as the woman claimed.

At that moment, about six hours after the emergency call for help had been made, the investigation changed direction. Instead of spreading a wide net, the focus went inward. The logic was, if there was no intruder, then someone in the house must have killed those kids, and as far as anyone knew, only Darin, Darlie, and the baby, Drake, were home at the time. Certainly, no one else had been flushed out by the police search. Therefore, the killer was probably either the mother or the father, unless further investigation turned up something they didn't already know.

At 10 o'clock in the morning, Chief Randall Posey held his eagerly anticipated meeting with the media in the second-floor conference room at the Rowlett police headquarters. The place was jammed. The chief told reporters that "I understand from the dispatcher that she [Darlie] was understandably hysterical," and added that Darin, the husband, seemed to be in a state of shock.

A police officer for two decades, he had been the chief in Rowlett for almost six years, and openly confessed, "We have never had anything like this."

"It was a pretty bad scene," the chief said, and promised that "our entire detective force is working on it." Actually, calls were also coming in from officers in surrounding towns, even from Dallas, offering assistance. Cops respond when kids are murdered.

Chief Posey was already aware of the early determinations from his on-scene investigators, but could not indicate police were narrowing their scope to the two adults who lived in that house on Eagle Drive. Posey needed this news conference for a larger police purpose, to spin the story so that Rowlett residents would realize some wild-eyed killer was not prowling the streets. In fact, he had instructed his troops to make their presence known to calm people down, and marked patrol cars and uniformed officers fanned out all over town to show people they were safe. He told his police officers that, even if the dispatcher got a call for so much as a strange sound, he wanted a patrol car to respond. "Every time they look up, I want them to see a blue-and-white going past," he decreed. Otherwise, when night fell over an already jittery community, he might have some teenager sneaking home late at night getting smoked by a terrified, gun-toting parent.

By the time his news conference began, a great amount of detail was known to the press about the deep puncture wounds suffered by the two children, but reporters noticed the police seemed to be going light on details of the cuts sustained by Darlie Routier. Now the chief of police clearly seemed to be tap-dancing around vital information, and reporters were beginning to weigh the things that had been said against what was being kept back.

For instance, Mike Glenn, a reporter for the *Garland News*, had more than a newsman's instinct for this story. Prior to getting into journalism, Glenn had been a police officer in another Dallas suburb, and his quick eye for detail noticed the answers from Posey were drifting a little off-center.

"My first question was, 'What kind of wounds did she have?'" Glenn recalled, and Posey gave a vague reply. "Then I directly asked if she had any defensive wounds to her hands and arms," Glenn said, and the chief would not comment on that vital subject at all. "At that point, I thought something was up," observed Glenn. "I couldn't corroborate it, but I told one of my colleagues at the news conference that if her wounds were slashing wounds, then she probably did it."

At 2 o'clock, Sergeant Poos gave still another update. With two press releases and a news conference, the reporters would not be able to say the cops were not sharing information. Poos was to earn his paycheck several times over during the next week, being the departmental spokesman while his comrades did what he wanted to be doing—trying to find a killer.

"The investigation of the double homicide continues. The following release was provided to the Rowlett Police Department by Darlie Kee [sic], mother of Darlie Routier, [the surviving victim of the attack].

"We appreciate everyone's prayers and concerns, but the attention needs to be focused on finding the person that killed these two babies. Anyone who might have seen something, please contact the Rowlett Police Department.

"At a 10 A.M. press conference Police Chief Randall Posey advised that Mrs. Routier had advised officers that she was attacked by a male wearing dark clothes and a baseball cap. That is the only description available at this time. A ground-floor window screen at the home was found to have been cut and may be a possible point of entry for a suspect.

"The 911 tape of this call will be reviewed tomorrow morning by investigators to determine if it contains any additional information of use. After the review, if it is not taken as evidence, we will establish procedures for media release of the call.

"Counseling for neighbors or others affected by this case will be provided by Steven Leatherwood, chaplain for the Rowlett Police and Fire Departments. Mr. Leatherwood may be contacted at his office at this number."

The media had been carefully fed during the day, and had more than enough for their story about the crime. But veteran reporters already were feeling somewhat uncomfortable. Something was missing, although Poos had been very good at burying the problem in legal and bureaucratic terms. The reporters wanted to hear the emergency call Darlie had made, a rather routine item in news stories such as this. The electronic media wanted to splice some of that conversation into their broadcasts. Hadn't the chief himself said the woman sounded hysterical? That would be a terrific sound bite. But Poos had waffled on it, saying the tape had to be "reviewed" the next day before a decision could be made about releasing it, to "determine if it contains any additional information of use."

And the carefully worded news release contained the extraordinary line: *"If it is not taken as evidence!"* Why, some reporters might have wondered, would a 911 call be considered vital evidence? The only people talking on it were the woman who had been attacked and the police dispatcher. Very odd.

Later that afternoon, Dr. Janice Townsend-Parchman was at the Baylor hospital performing the autopsy of Damon Routier for the Dallas County Medical Examiner's Office when a police officer came to her with a special and specific request. He wanted the doctor to step up to the ICU and examine the wounds sustained by Darlie Routier to determine if they may have been self-inflicted. Townsend-Parchman agreed to do so, and when she got there, found a crowd in the small recovery room. She spoke briefly with a surgical resident, then worked her way to the bed where Darlie rested against pillows.

The doctor introduced herself but did not disclose her mission to the woman who had been stabbed, and did a ten-minute examination. Darlie, who now had been given a standard quarter-milligram dose of the drug Xanax, normally ordered to combat anxiety, was compliant. The wounds on her arms had been closed with sutures, and sterile strips of transparent adhesive tape held the edges of the wounds on the left shoulder and the neck. The doctor peeled back the gauze bandages to see the sliced skin. Since she was not the doctor who had performed the operation, she was unaware of all the facts involved, and the report she gave Patterson was based solely on the brief exam. In her opinion, the wounds to Darlie were much different from the wounds suffered by Damon, not very deep or close to vital organs. That was in direct contrast to the finding of Dr. Santos, who had said Darlie was "lucky" to be alive. In the opinion of Townsend-Parchman, the wounds to the woman were superficial and "could have" been self-inflicted.

Since she had been asked to answer only the narrow question of whether Darlie might have intentionally stabbed herself, the doctor was looking for that possibility. She told the policeman what he wanted to hear, and another element was stacked onto the rapidly growing body of evidence against Darlie Routier. Months later, on the witness stand, the doctor would admit that her cursory examination also indicated that someone else may have inflicted the wounds.

The *Dallas Morning News* and the *Fort Worth Star-Telegram* finally were able to splash the story on their front pages on June 7, along with photographs and even locator maps of the house on Eagle Drive.

The newspaper stories were quite complete, containing all the information that was available at the time, and the reporters included comments from neighbors and family acquaintances. The overall impression from the various comments was that the Routiers were just normal people upon whom an inexplicable tragedy had been visited. "This is a wonderful family," the Dallas paper reported neighbor Mercedes Adams as saying. "They are your regular, ordinary family trying to make their living and have a decent place to live," added David Sauerwein, a friend of the family. That impression would be underlined, carefully nurtured, and would steadily grow over the next few days, until the lives of the Routier family assumed almost fairy-tale proportions. And everyone knows fairy tales are not true.

On the answering machine, a sad voice responded to unseen callers.

"This is Darin. Something terrible has happened. We just want to let all our friends and family know that Darlie is okay, but Devon and Damon were stabbed to death yesterday. And we wanted to let everybody know that we understand that everybody loves us. . . . We've had lots of support from a lot of different people." There was a slight pause, then he continued.

"And I just wanted to leave this message so that everybody can understand that we know your prayers are with us. And we need them to be continued for Darlie, because this will be very physically and mentally difficult for both of us. Don't believe everything that the media's saying."

5

BY FRIDAY, JUNE 7, Darlie was feeling better, although her mood swings continued. One person might find her stone-faced and speaking in a monotone, while someone else would see her crying together with her husband as they held hands in her hospital room. But the medical procedures were working for her, and she felt better after having the sticky blood washed from her body. A nurse administered a rape kit examination and said Darlie reported feeling "pressure down there" during the attack.

When her mother arrived at 7:30 A.M., Darlie asked for pain medication and a nurse noted the patient complained of pains in her right shoulder. Dr. Santos came in to check his work and found his patient recovering nicely from her wounds, although he felt she was strangely quiet for a woman who had lost two children in violent murders. Nevertheless, he said she was well enough to be transferred to a general floor of the hospital, and officially upgraded her condition from critical to fair. Darlie was moved out of the intensive care unit.

In the afternoon, she was visited by Barbara Jovell, who had been maid of honor at her wedding and worked for Darin. Embarrassed, Darlie asked everyone to leave the room so she could have a private moment with her friend, who was known by the nickname of Basia, a legacy of her Polish heritage.

Basia sat beside the bed and looked closely at her injured friend, feeling something was amiss. "Darlie, please talk to me," Basia said. "What's going on? Please talk to me." The response startled her, for Darlie confided that when police searched the house, they were going to find some sex toys. "My God!" exclaimed Basia. "You shouldn't worry about those things. The babies have been killed. You've almost been killed. Don't worry about sex toys, lots of people have those things." When she finally left the hospital, Basia realized she had not seen Darlie shed a single tear.

The family, already deep in grief, had a sad task to perform. While Darlie remained hospitalized, they made preparations to bury Devon and Damon. Arrangements were made with the Rest Haven Memorial Park in Rockwall, a town adjacent to Rowlett, for a single grave. The little boys would be buried together. A private viewing for the family and close friends would be held the next day, Saturday, and the funeral would be on Sunday.

Hanging over their preparations, however, was the primary question of who had committed these horrible murders. Neighbors were telling police they saw a suspicious dark car hanging around the neighborhood, and Darin speculated to friends that the murderer was probably someone who had targeted Darlie. God alone knew how many men admired her good looks, and were always following her with their eyes. Officially, the family declined to comment, referring all inquiries to the police, who were being careful with their words.

A Rowlett bank established a memorial fund and a private company offered $10,000 for the arrest and indictment of the person responsible for the double deaths.

*   *   *

The investigation was getting down to nitty-gritty police work, and the house was the center of their attention. Whatever secrets were needed to solve this case, the police felt, lay behind that front door. They could not count on finding any witnesses to the crime, and that meant a circumstantial case would have to be built, brick by brick, until a solid wall of evidence was constructed.

They were not alone. Rowlett cops were getting offers of help from all over, including some FBI personality-profile specialists, and were determined not to block extra assistance. In fact, they eagerly sought it. They wanted to crack this one fast, and felt they had a chance. Patrolmen would pull a regular eight-hour shift, showing the flag throughout the city and keeping people calm, go home and freshen up, and then come back to Eagle Drive to work the crime scene.

Jimmy Patterson's examination of the crime scene and talk with Cron had shown him a couple of things. One point that disturbed him was that Darlie had been asleep on the couch, but there were no bloodstains where her head and shoulders would have rested. With her throat cut and her arms sliced, how could that be? And the route the alleged attacker had taken: There was no blood to be seen in the garage, and none on the white fence or gate. The attacker reportedly had exited through the slit window screen, but the windowsill had an undisturbed layer of dust. Mulch in the backyard flower beds had not been disturbed by running feet. And, most importantly, Cron had already concluded there had not been an intruder at all. Patterson returned to the hospital to interview Darlie again that afternoon and officers carefully combed through the statements made by Darin and Darlie, finding inconsistencies.

One of those statements was on the 911 tape recording. Sergeant Poos had set another afternoon news conference for Friday to play the call for the media, but only two hours before it was to start, the meeting was canceled.

When official police comments were examined later, it was clear that the pieces were not meshing together for them in this puzzle. Few people without a badge knew of the findings of Cron and Patterson at that point, and Sergeant Poos all but spelled it out for reporters. "Everybody is a suspect. Nobody is ruled out," he said late Friday.

Two things were ruled out publicly. Poos said it wasn't a random crime and that it wasn't a burglary. "It was not some crazed lunatic walking down the alley and making some left turn and attacking them," he said. Since no cash or other valuables, such as jewelry lying about in plain sight, was stolen, robbery was stricken as a motive.

When media questions turned back to the tape, which the reporters desperately wanted to hear, Poos tap-danced. Again, he said it might contain "crucial evidence only known by the suspect."

ROBBERY RULED OUT IN ROWLETT SLAYINGS
VICTIMS WERE TARGETED, POLICE SAY

The headlines over the Routier story in the *Dallas Morning News* greeted readers on Saturday, June 8. In retrospect, they seem almost to point an accusing finger at the parents of the slain children. The word was being spread to the rest of Rowlett that they were safe. Indeed, while police officers were working hard at the scene, digging for fragments of clues, they were taking a message of comfort home to their families. They might not be able to say it in public, but they could certainly calm the home front. Relax. There's no deranged killer roaming the town, they whispered in private. Others in Rowlett might still be nervous, but cops' wives slept well.

* * *

Dr. Santos checked on Darlie early Saturday morning, and again found considerable improvement. He thought it best that she remain in the hospital a while longer, but ran into a united front from the family, which wanted just the opposite. The doctor would recall that Darin, in particular, wanted Darlie to be released. Both of the parents wanted to be present that evening for the private viewing of their children at the funeral home. Not only that, but to cheer her up the family had begun planning a special event. Devon's seventh birthday was coming up on June 14, only six days away, and a party was being planned. Santos gave in and signed the papers. Darlie checked out of the hospital at noon.

They could not go home, because the house had been turned into a crime scene and police were not close to letting unauthorized people inside. The owners of the house did not wear badges and were therefore unauthorized. They were also unofficial suspects.

Instead, Darin and Darlie did something that would haunt them in months to come. They cooperated fully with investigators and went straight to police headquarters from the hospital to give formal statements. It would eventually dawn on them that perhaps they should have gone straight to a lawyer instead. The police welcomed them with open arms. They willingly signed papers indicating they were aware of their Constitutional rights, drew diagrams, and wrote out statements. It was as if Darlie and Darin had delivered a pot of investigative gold to the Rowlett police. Now what she had said on the 911 tape and both of their oral statements at the house and the hospital could be compared word by word with the new statements. An investigative Bible was being written and the chief suspects were wielding the pens.

Everyone was getting along so well, in fact, that when it was time for Darin and Darlie to go over to Rest Haven

Memorial Park for the private memorial service, Detectives Jimmy Patterson and Chris Frosch offered to drive them. Sure, said Darlie. Thanks.

The brief time alone with the slain children was shattering. The grieving parents, relatives, and friends slipped gifts into the single casket, just as the Egyptians once provided their kings with golden trinkets, and the ancient Chinese sent deceased rulers into the hereafter with food, wine, and slaves. Instead of gold, the Routier boys would be accompanied by kid things—pocketknives, trick cards, and stuffed animals. A minister, David Rogers, led a brief service, in which everyone placed their hands on the coffin as they prayed for God to have mercy on the children, and grant them peace. When it was over, the couple went home to Plano, moving in temporarily with Darlie's mother, Darlie Kee. As daylight fled, Darlie acted frightened. She was scared of the dark. She wouldn't even go to the bathroom alone. Mama Darlie pointed out how safe the place was—a nine-foot fence, a security system, outdoor floodlights, other people around. It made no difference. Darlie snuggled down beside her husband in a living room where every light burned brightly, but stayed awake until the dawn.

Darlie Kee, an attractive woman, tall and outspoken, became a protective mother bear for her clan of wounded cubs. The family needed a spokesperson, and she was it. Mama Darlie would never be at a loss for words. Rumors and speculation were running rampant that maybe Darlie and Darin were responsible for the crime, and she set about challenging that in a hurry.

"We have to find this guy before he does it to your son or daughter," she declared to reporters. "Somebody is out there doing this. Somebody is very, very sick. He is a demon."

That set off some loud alarm bells in the City of Rowlett Police Department, where Chief Posey was doing everything to avoid this idea of the general population being in danger. *A demon?* Police announced that more officers were being put on the streets. "People in the community are concerned, and we want to make sure we address those concerns," said Sergeant David Nabors. "I got the feeling we are going to crack this open," Dean Poos told the *Morning News*.

More than four hundred people showed up for the Sunday funeral on the flat slab of land in Rockwall County that is the Rest Haven Funeral Home when the two little boys were laid to their final rest. Darlie alternately held her surviving son, Drake, or passed him to other family members when he got too heavy and painful, and clutched teddy bears instead. A printed program stated that "Devon and Damon [are] holding hands through life and into heaven. Now they are Angels playing together and watching over Drake."

"This is a time of celebration," Pastor Rogers told the mourners, although most were weeping over the two lost boys. "You see, as Christians, we celebrate when people go home. Devon and Damon are rejoicing in the streets of Heaven with no sadness and no sorrow."

Randy Reagan, a cousin of Darin's, was the family's press spokesperson for the day. "Darlie wants the public to remember that it could have been any one of their children. They are hopeful that police will catch the person who did it." Reagan shot down the rampant speculation that the parents were somehow involved. "Darin and Darlie have cooperated 100 percent with the Police Department. They have nothing to hide," he told reporters, adding that Darlie particularly wanted people to know she was firm in her total belief that Darin had nothing to do with the crime. Reagan also mentioned that this would not be the last memorial. A birthday celebration was being planned for Devon.

*   *   *

Reagan had unknowingly placed the public relations ball back into the police court. *"Darlie wants the public to remember that it could have been any one of their children"?* The goblin specter was out of the box again and Dean Poos had to stuff it back down. Already the spokesman had changed his routine, and his telephone was ringing so much he couldn't even get out for his daily run that he needed so desperately to relieve stress. He knew a lot of what was going on, but was intentionally staying ignorant of even more. Poos had even stopped attending some pertinent briefings so that if some sharp reporter asked a particularly tricky question, the police spokesman wouldn't have to lie about what had transpired in that meeting. He simply wouldn't know. The job right now was to, once again, reassure the community that they were safe.

For the time being, he had to knock down the fear. The crime, he told the press this time, did not have the marks of "a psycho" or some bloodthirsty "Charles Manson walking down the street."

When asked about the formal statements the Routiers had given police the day before, he sidestepped. Nothing much different from what they had told officers earlier, he replied. In those sessions Poos wasn't attending, the statements were being picked apart like a Thanksgiving turkey.

In Rowlett, a wave of sympathy was turning the house on Eagle Drive into a shrine. People who didn't know the Routier family showed up with balloons and trinkets and symbolic gifts, asking the policemen on duty at the yellow line of tape to add a steady stream of items to the stack of memorials accruing around the big fountain and on the green lawn. Balloons were tied to a wrought-iron bench, a wreath bannered with the children's names leaned on the fountain, and a birthday card was stapled to a large square of particle board, reading: "Dear Devon, You're someone too special to ever forget, so here's a big wish for your best birthday yet." In nearby Richardson, another memorial trust fund was organized to help the stricken family. And ducking under the yellow tape, making his way into the house, was a man unknown to the neighbors, a clean-cut, tall man named Greg Davis, one of the top prosecutors in the office of the Dallas County District Attorney. When an arrest was finally made, he would be the one to take the accused person to trial.

Forensics experts had pieced together a general picture of what had happened, and the conclusion was that Darlie was responsible. However, it was too early for a formal arrest, for one major part of the puzzle was missing. If, indeed, the mother had killed her children, the big question that would have to be answered for a jury was *WHY?* And right now, the investigators simply didn't have that answer.

On Monday, June 10, police brought Darlie in again. They photographed her thoroughly, taking particular notice of the big bruises on her arms, and took prints of her fingers and her feet.

Around the Police Department, as officers talked about the case, speculation began to center on what Darin's reaction would be if and when his wife was arrested. Would he stand by his woman, or say the hell with her and become a witness for the state? It was generally felt that the young man would have a no-win choice. They had talked to him for hours, but they didn't know Darin Routier very well.

Then late one night, as the case was drawing tightly around the prime suspect, a woman television reporter happened into the police station, looking for a source.

When a janitor opened a door to enter the criminal investigation division, she followed him inside, out of the public area of the police station and into the private sanctum where the cops made their decisions, wrote down their suspicions and guesses, and figured out the next step in the the ongoing investigation. Atop one desk, unguarded in the empty room, lay a case file on the murders of the two Routier boys.

A passing cop finally saw her in the off-limits area and hustled her out, pronto. But the mere appearance of a reporter around the case file sent up the storm flags, and officers were summoned in to check and see if anything was missing from their desks, or absent from the files. There was a collective heart attack in the Police Department when she went on the air at ten o'clock with a short teaser that told viewers to stay tuned for the late news, the reporter had new information on Rowlett's famous murder case. Information that was going to turn the case on its ear: Cocaine had been found in the house on Eagle Drive!

Sergeant Poos had been relaxing at home in his T-shirt and shorts when the reporter turned up on his doorstep, looking for confirmation for her hot scoop. He said he didn't know anything about any cocaine being discovered, but no sooner had he shooed her away than his telephone began ringing with assignment editors for other channels and newspapers, who had heard the teaser, now wanted a comment. He had none. In reality, the police had found a small amount of marijuana, not cocaine. The reporter had the wrong drug. While the story was knocked down effectively by Poos, the marijuana was to make another dramatic appearance months later, and became nothing less than the same kind of bombshell the television reporter had predicted.

The investigation stayed on track, and police made a critical decision. By now, everyone who cared to ask knew that a celebration of Devon's birthday was planned at the cemetery in a few days. Investigators, playing *"What if . . ."* scenarios, thought there might be a chance that someone would approach the grave in an emotional and vulnerable moment, and make a confession. *What if we could get that on tape?* So a team of officers carrying electronic equipment was dispatched to Rest Haven in advance of the event. They set up a video camera with a long lens far away by the combination building that housed both offices and chapel at the cemetery, and carefully peeled back some of the deflating balloons and fading cards that covered the grave. No headstone had yet been purchased, but a small marker had been put in place to denote the burial site. Police hid a tiny microphone beneath it to catch every word that would be uttered at the grave site.

Never, not in their wildest imaginings, could the investigators have guessed what was about to happen. The most important development in the case was soon to unfold.

6

FRIDAY, JUNE 14, would render a remarkable and memorable event in the mystery of how Damon and Devon Routier died. The funeral services had already been held, the burial completed, but as the hot sun shone down on the grassy fields of the Rest Haven Memorial Garden, a number of friends and family of the little victims arrived in convoy about 1:45 P.M. for the special service. While police watched and recorded from a hiding place, it was time for a party at Rest Haven.

The event was a postmortem birthday celebration for Devon, who would have turned seven years old on this day. Darlie had been somewhat reluctant to leave the house that morning, so emotionally spent that at one point she lay her head in her mother's lap and cried and cried, but knowing she had to pull herself together. The cops wanted her and Darin to come by for another talk before going to the cemetery. They drove over from the police station in Rowlett, and received what they thought was some good news. By the time Darlie arrived at the grave site, she was all smiles, brightly telling people that the police were saying they were on the verge of solving the case, even making an arrest. The ordeal was almost over!

There was almost no shade on the long, gentle slope where the small group gathered. Tightly mown grass was dried to a brittle brownish-green between the single spindly tree and a low hedge near the single grave. But the arid surroundings were in marked contrast to the burial plot, which was stacked with a cover of bright balloons that were barely stirred by the tiniest whiff of breeze, along with toys, gifts, flags, flowers, poems, pictures, cartoons, and books.

"Happy 7th Birthday" read a white sign. A large square card sporting green, yellow, and purple colors echoed, "Happy Birthday Devon, we love you," and was signed by Uncle Kevin and Aunt Dana. Dana Stahl, one of Darlie's teen-aged sisters, had come to the cemetery prepared to make this a happy occasion. She knew how much Devon had loved surprises, and before she left the house, she picked up some of his favorite toys, surprise poppers, and a can of Silly String. Devon, she believed, could enjoy them one last time.

Also on the grave, Margaret Wise Brown's *The Runaway Bunny* was tenderly signed inside the front cover "We love you, PJ and Ashley." A miniature fleet of Hot Wheels cars in a rainbow of colors rested beneath a pair of small American flags. A book of scary postcards by author R.L. Stine, creater of the popular *Goosebumps* series, lay next to a coiled Slinky. A small plastic fountain with an angel on the side, and a red frog, and a crystal in a clam-shaped bowl stood next to a little potted cactus. Several small gifts still bore price tags. A yellow smiley face button was on the grass, alongside a teddy bear. Balloons of every description imparted an unmistakable air of gaiety, although the many flowers present were obviously there for somber and funereal purposes.

There was a heavy focus on angels, on a pair of good little guys coming back to earth from the afterworld in which only spirits dwell. A child drew a cartoon on white paper that showed three winged figures among the clouds, and named them as "Damon, Devon, and God." The drawing bore a close resemblance to Ninja Turtle warriors. "Rest in peace," an unknown woman wrote on a sympathy card, "I know y'all are two angels now. Love y'all." And a postcard still in a protective layer of plastic and bearing a $6 price marker depicted a pair of cherubs and a poem entitled "Angel Inspiration," which read, in part, that "Angels are everywhere distributed about" to impart their delightful wisdom to the mortal world.

Typically, the celebration drew media interest. Little had occurred that was not covered in detail by newspaper reporters or television crews, and several were present for the gathering. The people of Texas were sharing the grief of the Routier family, and since the press had treated them nicely, why not allow representatives to observe the unique party? Maybe going on TV could help the police catch the killer, they thought.

A quiet, private memorial service was held first, with only adults present, and a minister delivered solemn invocations. After that, Mama Darlie told her daughter that if she didn't stop crying, she might frighten the children who were arriving, and the mini-party that had been forecast for so long began. Several songs were played on a tape deck, starting with the slain children's favorite tune, a rap tune by Coolio called "Gangsta's Paradise," and Whitney Houston's beautiful "I Will Always Love You." Darlie circulated among her family members and friends, happy to be out of the hospital, out in the sunshine. She held the baby, Drake, for a while, passing him off when he got too heavy for her. She smiled and laughed and hugged. So did everyone else. In fact, it seemed that everyone enjoyed the party, which they considered a celebration of life, not death. Some might even say it was classic denial, the parents refusing to admit to themselves that Devon and Damon were dead.

Reporter Joe Munoz of the Dallas Channel 5 station, KXAS-TV, had been working the story hard. He had telephoned Darlie Kee that morning for a routine update on the situation, the part of his news-gathering job that he liked the least. "These people have gone through these horrible things and now we're all standing around them, saying, 'Talk to me, talk to me.'" Munoz was in for a surprise that day. Darlie Kee not only confirmed for him that the graveside ceremony was still planned, she invited him to attend and, when he "respectfully asked to take pictures," Mama Darlie granted permission for Munoz to bring along a cameraman.

Once on the scene, the bereaved parents surprised Munoz by granting him an exclusive question-and-answer session. The reporter recognized a rare opportunity and began asking questions before Darlie and Darin changed their minds. They rarely refused to answer. For forty-five minutes, Darlie and Darin allowed Munoz and several newspaper reporters to interview them. It was the first time that she had been able to comment in public since the awful night of the stabbings eight days earlier. People around Dallas hungered for her account, unfiltered by the unusually careful doses of official information.

Darlie and Darin went out of their way to applaud the Rowlett police, to say they had nothing to hide and to urge the cops to find the killer. "This man is still out there loose. I wouldn't even say a man—he is a coward!" she declared. "The only thing that keeps me going is the hope that they will find that person."

She wore denim shorts and a loose top with a denim collar that was opened wide enough to show the angry red scar and the ugly train of stitches across her throat. A small silver cross was pinned to her collar and she wore small earrings.

"He went to two defenseless children first, and then

he went to me," she said. "I don't know why God spared me." The young mother's mood improved, she smiled a crooked little grin, took the can of Silly String, and pressed the top. More white foam whooshed out in long, thin, wrinkly lines as she waved it over the stacked balloons. The attendees joined in a chorus of "Happy Birthday," and a smiling Darlie went from one person to another with big hugs. The television cameras rolled. A hidden police camera rolled. At one point, she held her only remaining child, eight-month-old Drake, out at arm's length toward a framed picture of his brothers that was held by Darin. What they envisioned as a touching scene was quite jarring to viewers.

Darlie Kee, her mother, said her daughter had been so nervous that she was "hanging by a thread." Darin told reporters that he remained puzzled by the brutal attack. "We are a happy family. We all love each other. We don't have conflicts. We have just never felt unsafe. But if you never feel unsafe, you don't take the precautions." He, too, wore shorts and a lightweight striped pullover shirt.

Darlie was in total agreement. "We don't have marital problems. We don't have a drug problem. We didn't have any type of abuse in our home."

"They were good kids and we tried to teach them right," said Darin. "They didn't see any bad. They still believed in everything we were taught as kids."

"Everything was equal," Darlie added, breaking in before Darin had finished speaking. "They didn't believe that anybody had a different color. They didn't see the world cruelly, as adults have to see it. They saw it as 'Okay, I'm just like you and you're just like me.' And that's really the way they were."

Darin verbally pointed toward the family's great number of possessions. "They knew we were more fortunate than other people," he said.

"They were giving." Darlie nodded. "They were very giving."

Darin recalled one Christmas when he and the family had visited a home that was part of the Rowlett Needy Children's Fund. Damon and Devon wanted to hurry back to their own house and give the less fortunate children "all their old toys" and even some of the new ones that their generous parents had purchased. "They were just a giving type of people. They learned that from us."

Munoz asked them to describe their "sweetest memory of the boys" and Darlie brightly joked that she had so many sweet memories that the correspondent probably would have to "move in" with them if he wanted to hear all of the tales.

They decided to tell the parable of the "Home Alone House."

"When we first bought this house— Oh, this is so sad, but it's sweet, because it's just the way they were. When we bought this house and were having it built, the movie *Home Alone* had come out. And they just loved that movie. They thought that was just the all-time movie. And they kept calling our house the Home Alone House. They were like telling everybody: 'This is our Home Alone house. This is our Home Alone house.' And they said, 'Mommy, when we get in the Home Alone house, we want to get a sled and go down the stairs, like he did in the Home Alone House.' And I was like, 'Oooh, no, you can't do that, you can't do that, you know.' " She paused, shifting emotion, joy to sadness. "If they were here now, I'd let them do it," she added with a quiet sob.

Darin picked up the conversational thread to tell how the boys didn't go down the stairs on a sled, but did try it on a pillow. "They would get a pillow, sit inside with the soft part on the heinie, and they would go *boomp-boomp-boomp*, all the way down the stairs."

"They wanted a sled," Darlie insisted.

"They wanted a sled . . . but it was an angled staircase." Modesty overcame him again, almost as if he were measuring the floor space of his house against the mansion in the movie. "Our house wasn't as big as [the one in] *Home Alone*, but that was how they described it."

Munoz couldn't resist asking about the peculiar backdrop of this interview, at the grave of the children. Why the balloons? Why the birthday song?

Darlie almost chirped a happy answer. "Well, because even though we're sad because Devon and Damon aren't here, we try to hang on to what we can to get us through these times. And if you knew Devon and Damon, you would know they're up in heaven and they're up there having the biggest birthday party that we could ever imagine. They wouldn't want us to be down here bein' sad, even though our hearts are breaking. I know that Devon and Damon would want us to be happy. They wouldn't want us to be crying and they wouldn't want us not to be happy. They would want us to celebrate, as if we were with them, and in a way they are with us because they will always be with us, no matter what we're doin', no matter what we're thinkin', they'll always be a part of all of us and not just Darin and I, but you know they touched a lot of people."

The correspondent from Channel 5 probed further, asking the parents how they felt. How they appeared—relaxed and pleasant and rather unperturbed—contrasted with Darlie's answer.

"We get very sad. We cry a lot. We get sick. We get very angry. We get very angry because this person is still out there and he's doing whatever he wants to do and we're just like in a time warp. It's like we're walking in limbo. We don't know whether we're coming or going, you know? And he's free to do whatever he wants. But

I know that he's not going to be free for long. I feel it, I feel the support, and the hard work that these detectives and police are putting into this is just incredible. It's beyond the call, I mean. . . ."

Darin interrupted with plaudits of his own for the cops. "They're doin' some high-tech stuff on this investigation. Stuff that I wouldn't believe and hadn't even seen in the movies," he said. "They are doin' the best job they possibly can and they are gonna find this person!"

His wife firmly agreed. "They are going to find [who did] it. We're having prayer groups everywhere. Everybody is praying. I said God's hot line must be. . . ."

"Full," Darin interjected, the couple's words tumbling over each other, streams of thought merging into a single, rushing torrent.

"Swamped," Darlie resumed without losing a beat. "Because everybody everywhere is praying. And we can feel it."

There was a slight pause as Munoz attempted to have the couple recall "that night," the time of the murders. "What do you remember?"

Darin's reaction was immediate: "Fear." And Darlie chimed in with another agreement that trailed into question, then into a fast, repetitive sequence in which they finished each other's thoughts and words.

"Fear and pain," she responded. "But you know even with what happened to me, I didn't feel anything because I was in shock. But I wasn't thinking about me. All I was thinking about was trying to save the babies. I mean Darin and I tried to save the babies, but *[a pause, a sigh, a sob]* it was too late, and the babies were gone. But we tried, we tried, and we have to live with that forever."

Darin: "We have to live with what we saw, what we saw in their eyes. . . ."

Darlie: "Nobody could ever imagine. . . .

Darin: "And it happened so fast, that not anybody

could have done anything about trying to save them any faster than what I could. You keep going over it, and you 'what if' it. What if I had done this, and what if I had done that, but if you've never lived in fear, then you'll never think of those things.''

Darlie: ''Never think of those things.''

The correspondent asked how they felt about rumors that perhaps Darin was a suspect in the murders. Darin was understated, deflecting comment, but Darlie jumped on it like a dog on a bone, protecting her husband. People could be evil, she said, and ''gossip is the biggest evil in the world. Unfortunately there is nothing you can do to stop it and we're not going to make an issue out of this because anybody that knows us knows how we were, how we lived, they know the story and we don't have to explain ourselves to anybody.''

Darin flared. ''And everybody else, who cares? It doesn't matter, if they don't know us. They can't damage us any worse than what we are.''

Munoz queried what they would like to say to the mysterious assailant when he was finally captured. Again, Darin wanted to soft-pedal that, but Darlie blurted: ''I think he's a coward because he went after two . . . He went after something that was so innocent and couldn't fight back, then he tried to come to me. But he had to go to them first. And to me that's such a cowardness [sic].''

While others had questioned why an attacker would not have struck the biggest person in the room first, the person most likely to cause him a problem, Darin had a different view. The man was ''like an animal that goes after a weak sheep that is asleep, is completely lifeless and attacks the weakest person in the room first.''

Then, as the long interview drew to a close, he jumped back to the concept of possessions, of their comfortable lifestyle, of inanimate things. Beside the boys' grave, he talked of money and himself. But he also may have been flailing around just trying to find some reason for the awful crime. "I kept hoping and praying that this guy had stolen something out of my house," said Darin. "That he had picked me and my family because I had more than some, or more than this person. That way I could, in my heart, think that living large is the reason why we got targeted."

"Now, you don't know why," Munoz finished.

"Now, we don't know why. Now we know this is a sick individual that took absolutely nothing from our house. But took the two most important things away from us. That's the part we don't understand, that's the part we may never understand. Our goal now in our life is to live our lives the way that God wants us to, so we can be with our boys again and they'll still be five and still be seven and still be playing and fighting."

Darlie added later that the boys would be in Heaven, fighting over who should have which balloon.

Without realizing at the time, Munoz had caught lightning in a bottle. He knew he had a good interview, even a special one, the sort that rarely come along. He didn't know that the rambling conversation would become very important and he had become part of the story he was covering.

For while his primary audience would be Dallas-area viewers whose interest was already hooked by this brutal case, a more interested audience was back at the Rowlett police headquarters. Nobody had been more surprised by the lengthy comments than the investigative team and the cops who had spied on the celebration from their hiding place, hoping to hear their suspect blurt out a confession. Darin and Darlie had gone public with compliments about ongoing police efforts, and with the television interview being broadcast, the cops didn't have to worry about the legality of their own taping. It was now out there for public consumption. Only the police knew at the time they had bugged the grave with hidden microphones, and although many things had been recorded, a confession was not among them.

The group dispersed, family and friends going over to Darlie Kee's house for a more private celebration of Devon's birthday. When police watched their own videotape, they saw several reporters linger behind and steal a few items from the grave. Didn't surprise them at all, for cops consider reporters to be little more than ghouls anyway.

When Munoz put the story on the air, many people simply couldn't believe what they saw and heard.

"I can't think of anybody I talked to, journalists or other people, who were not sort of unnerved by that bizarre birthday party amid the tombstones," said reporter Mike Glenn of the *Garland News*. "Some of the police said it was the oddest thing they had ever seen, and was totally inconsistent with a mother who had lost two children to a murderer."

Greg Davis, the prosecutor who would eventually try the case, said the first time he saw the video, it made him sick to his stomach. Maybe it did. It just as likely made him the happiest man in the office of the Dallas County District Attorney. He could just imagine punching the PLAY button in a courtroom and letting that videotape roll before a jury.

7

TENSION BUILT ALL day Tuesday, June 18. The investigation had been going on for a dozen days and there was a sense that police were about to make a move. Darlie Routier had told television journalist Joe Munoz that afternoon, "They are very close to getting something." Munoz also had the feeling that a break was imminent, so he drove up from Dallas and had his technicians set up their news truck, with its big dish aerial, on the baking parking lot outside police headquarters in Rowlett. He had been on that hot asphalt for five days and was ready for the story to conclude, just so he could find a cooler spot in which to work.

There was one huge clue about the direction of the case. Police still had not released the 911 tape of Darlie's call for help, and pointedly said the call contained information that only the killer would know. Since the call was between Darlie and the police dispatcher, that meant that Darlie was at least a suspect. Perhaps more.

Darlie Routier and her mother had a brief conversation in Plano, about seven o'clock, before Mama Darlie went to work. The mother thought her daughter sounded about as good as the situation would allow. Both were still upset at the reaction to the Munoz tape on television. Comments were made about the way the wounded Darlie appeared as a rather frivolous and heartless person at the graveyard birthday ceremony four days earlier. Everybody was talking about the Silly String and didn't remember that there had been a serious memorial service beforehand, and that she had said, "We don't have anything to hide. We have given everything freely and openly." Mama Darlie thought her little girl was handling the stress as well as could be expected.

Late that day, Darin and Darlie drove again to the police station, because detectives asked them to drop by for still another round of questioning. Once there, they stayed inside. Longer and longer. Back in Plano, someone told Darlie Kee the latest rumor: the police had a suspect. Good, thought Kee. Darin and Darlie had been called down to identify the guy.

Actually, Darin and Darlie had been split up. Detectives Patterson and Frosch asked Darin to take a ride with them back over to Eagle Drive and give them, once again, a walk-through of the house. Maybe your memory might be jogged by something. Maybe we missed something you can point out. We won't be gone long.

Munoz feverishly worked to confirm what was happening inside, but ran into answers that were frustratingly evasive. He had a news break at 10 P.M., and if things didn't come together by then, it would be all over for the night. The first word on whatever was brewing might miss the late newscast and he could be scooped by the morning newspapers. He was determined that would not be the case, and questioned still more of his sources.

As Channel 5 began its 10 o'clock show, Munoz remained cautious, broadcasting a routine update on the story. Then, instead of going home, he continued to work, to dig, and he struck paydirt. A source gave him a vague answer that should have been firmer, and the reporter felt he saw a green light. He was ready to roll the dice. He was going to be a hero or a flop, but he had worked this story too hard and too long—including standing around day after day in the heat—to let someone else take it away from him now. Munoz took a deep breath went on the air.

He announced that police in Rowlett had arrested Darlie Routier for the murders of her two boys. "A chancy story," observed Sergeant Poos, who watched it from inside police headquarters.

Darin and the two detectives had finished the walk-through, which he felt was useless. They weren't paying attention at all, and, in Darin's opinion, seemed to be wasting time, poking listlessly here and there. He was glad to finally take a seat in the rear of their car, getting ready to return to the police station. Darin wanted to get his wife and go on back to Plano. His cellular telephone beeped.

It was Mama Darlie calling, excited, almost incoherent. What she was saying just couldn't be! She was wrong. His mother-in-law was telling him that the Rowlett police had just arrested Darlie! Darin gave a nervous laugh and shook his head, glancing at the two big detectives in the car. "You gotta be shittin' me," he answered, shocked at his own language. "I'm right here with the police. Nothing like that has happened."

"No!" Mama Darlie responded. "It's true! I'm watching it on TV!"

He hung up. Patterson and Frosch confirmed the report. Months later, Darin would say he was stunned and speechless. He didn't believe it, not even when the two cops told him what Mama Darlie had said was true. Darlie was under arrest back at police headquarters. They drove there immediately.

Over the next hours, police would try to convince Darin that Darlie had murdered their boys. He didn't believe a word of what they were saying. Not one single word.

The news spread quickly and cars started arriving at the police station, turning into the parking lot where the reporters had gathered. Ordinary citizens, curious men and women from throughout the community, were dropping by to see exactly what was happening. This was little Rowlett, not Dallas! Things like this don't happen here! Anybody know what happened? Why, it's just like that Susan Smith case over to South Carolina! Other reporters were angry, with questions no one would answer, and Munoz was sweating, far out on a limb. No one else had reported that Darlie was under arrest. Being exclusive on such a dramatic development also meant being uncomfortable.

Twenty minutes later, Munoz could start breathing again. Official word came down that Darlie was under arrest and had been taken before Municipal Court Judge Owen Lokken, who had been called in just to handle this one matter. No bail was set immediately, which meant Darlie was going to jail. It would be her last free day.

She was loaded into a van and driven away, heading toward her first night in the Lew Sterrett Justice Center, as the Dallas County Jail is known in polite circles, located in the Frank Crowley Courts Building on the corner of Commerce and Industrial in downtown Dallas. It is only a stone's throw from Dealey Plaza, the site of one of the most famous murders in American history, the Texas Schoolbook Depository Building where sniper Lee Harvey Oswald fired the shots that assassinated President John F. Kennedy.

Dozens of people had gathered in the gloom of the

parking lot in Rowlett as the small town was caught up in the excitement and drama. They weren't hostile, just amazed. It was the mother, they said. The mother had been arrested!

Darin, who had been the center of so much speculation, was not charged, but felt as if he had been slammed with a sledgehammer. He was stunned and wobbly as he called his parents in faraway Lubbock to tell them what had happened. He was in tears on one end of the line, and his father, Leonard, was crying on the other. "This is crazy," his mother, Sarilda Routier, angrily told reporters who called. "That is not true. I'd lay my life on it. I've never known anyone in my life to love their children like that mother."

In Plano, Darlie Kee watched the news with an incredulous fury. She saw her daughter being led away in handcuffs! "I totally flipped out," Kee said. She instantly staked out a position from which she and the family would never waver for a moment thereafter. "We're going to fight this. This is an unbelievable nightmare," she said. Her daughter was innocent! Without question! The police, she said, were making a rush to judgment, and had arrested Darlie "because they don't have anybody else." And, she confided, what had happened was exactly the opposite of her first thought on the matter. Originally, she had believed that police might arrest Darin. "I never thought they were going to charge Darlie." The possibility never entered her mind. "My daughter is not a murderer," she said.

An hour before midnight, an exhausted Sergeant Dean Poos stepped before the reporters who had assembled for a news conference in the small auditorium on the second floor of the Rowlett Police Department building. His terse comments came in his usual measured and quiet voice, but contained the explosive information to expand on what was already known. He read a news release aloud as reporters scribbled furiously on their pads.

"On the morning of Thursday, June 6th, 1996, an investigation began into the murders of Damon and Devon Routier," said Poos. "A significant event has now occurred in this very intensive investigation.

"At approximately 10:20 P.M. this evening, investigators from the Rowlett Police Department arrested Darlie Routier (white female, age 26). Mrs. Routier was charged with two counts of Capital Murder stemming from the stabbing deaths of her sons Damon (age 5) and Devon (age 6). This arrest is the result of the most intensive and exhaustive investigation ever conducted by the Rowlett Police Department.

"Darlie Routier was arrested at the Rowlett Police Department. She was booked at the Rowlett City Jail and arraigned by Municipal Court Judge Owen Lokken. Judge Lokken ordered Mrs. Routier held without bond. Mrs. Routier was then transferred to the Lew Sterrett Justice Center, where she was placed in an isolated cell under a twenty-four-hour 'suicide watch.'

"I cannot comment on the details of this investigation other than to say we believe that the white male suspect described by Darlie Routier as the man that attacked her and murdered her children never existed. We also believe that the wounds present on Darlie Routier were self-inflicted. As for the father, Darin Routier, at this point we do not believe that he was involved in, or participated in the murders.

"The proper time and place for the details of this investigation to be released is at the time of trial, and in a court of law. The full story will be revealed at that time. Any further questions should be directed to the Dallas County District Attorney's Office."

Chief Posey had very few words, other than to compliment his troops for their hard job. "Everyone has been working on this to some degree or another," he said. "We've had some outside consultants [and] we've had help from several departments. This investigation is still continuing. It is not over.

"The crime scene tells a story. Unfortunately, it's different than hers."

Poos agreed. "On one hand, we had a community thinking that there was a psychopathic killer walking the alleyways at night," he said. "On the other hand, we had a crime scene telling us that what Mrs. Routier was telling us didn't happen."

The police version of the story was spelled out in detail in the lengthy arrest warrant that was released to the media. Inconsistencies in Darlie's story were the key ingredient. First she would tell them one thing, then she would tell them something else. And what she said didn't match up with the physical evidence that had been gleaned over the past two weeks. It was a long and damning document.

AFFIDAVIT FOR ARREST WARRANT
STATE OF TEXAS   COUNTY OF DALLAS

BEFORE ME, THE UNDERSIGNED AUTHORITY, ON THIS DAY PERSONALLY APPEARED THE UNDERSIGNED AFFIANT WHO, AFTER BEING DULY SWORN BY ME, ON OATH STATED: MY NAME IS JIMMY PATTERSON AND I AM A PEACE OFFICER OF THE CITY OF ROWLETT, DALLAS COUNTY, TEXAS. I, THE AFFIANT, HAVE GOOD REASON AND DO BELIEVE THAT ON OR ABOUT THE 6TH DAY OF JUNE, 1996, ONE
    Darlie Lynn Routier, a white female, 26, DOB 1/4/70, 5'4", 130 lbs, blonde hair, hazel eyes,
    DID THEN AND THERE IN THE CITY OF Rowlett [sic], DALLAS COUNTY, TEXAS COMMIT THE

OFFENSE OF *** Capital Murder *** A VIOLATION
OF SECTION 19.03 OF THE TEXAS PENAL CODE,
A Capital FELONY. AFFIANT'S BELIEF IS BASED
UPON THE FOLLOWING FACTS AND
INFORMATION WHICH AFFIANT RECEIVED
FROM:
X̲ AFFIANT'S PERSONAL INVESTIGATION OF
THIS ALLEGED OFFENSE.

My name is Jimmy Patterson, and I am a peace officer
with the State of Texas. I have been a peace officer for
seventeen years. I am presently a detective assigned to
the Criminal Investigations Division, Crimes Against
Persons, of the Rowlett Police Department, and I have
been a detective for more than seven years.

On June 6, 1996, at approximately 2:31 A.M. a call
was made by Darlie Routier to 911 at the Rowlett Police
Department that "they" had just broken in and "stabbed
me and my children" at her home at 5801 Eagle Drive,
Rowlett, Texas, Dallas County. Rowlett Police officer D.
Waddell arrived at the location first. Darlie remained on
the phone with the 911 dispatcher until after officers
arrived, for over 5 minutes. I have reviewed the 911 tape
and talked to Waddell and the other officers and
paramedics at the scene about what they saw and learned.
I arrived at the scene about 1 hour after the 911 call came
in.

From my review of the 911 tape, and my discussions
with Darlie, her husband Darin Routier, and other
officers, I know the following:

Officers and paramedics arriving at the scene found
Darlie Routier, Darin Routier, and their sons, Devon
Routier (6 years old) and Damon Routier (5 years old),
in the downstairs portion of the house in the rear living
area on the southwest corner of the house. Devon had
been stabbed multiple times, including major penetrating
wounds to his chest. Damon had multiple wounds,
including approximately five major penetrating wounds

to his back. Darlie had a slashing wound to her neck, a minor stab wound to her left shoulder, minor cuts to the creases of the last knuckles on the palm side of her left fingers, a minor cut or scrape on the left side of her chin, and a laceration to the top of her right forearm.

When the 911 call began, Darlie referred to the assailant as "they" although she told Sgt. Walling, the second officer at the scene, that the assailant was a single white male, possibly wearing a dark colored ballcap, blue jeans, and a black shirt. Darlie told me later, shortly after 6 A.M. that morning, that the assailant was one male, probably white, with shoulder length hair, a black baseball cap with bill facing front, a pullover, black, short-sleeved tee shirt, blue jeans. Darlie told the 911 dispatcher that "my little boy's dying" and later "my babies are dying." Despite the fact that she knew that one or both of the boys were still alive, Waddell has told me that Darlie never made attempts to stop their bleeding, touch them, or render other first aid. Before going to the garage, Waddell told her twice to take the rag that she was holding and apply pressure to the wounds of the younger child, who had been stabbed in the back, but she never went to the child or attempted to help him (although she said in a later written statement that she put a towel on his back before police arrived). Waddell remarked that Darlie was instead preoccupied with the minor wound on her neck, and she kept the rag pressed to it.

Darlie told Waddell upon his arrival that the assailant had gone out the utility room and into the garage and out of the house through the garage. Waddell went to the utility room and garage to look for the assailant. He saw no one in the garage. While Waddell and Walling were in the garage, they saw that one of the garage windows leading into the back yard of the house was open and that the screen was split.

Darlie initially told officers at the scene, and me at the hospital that same morning, that she was asleep in the family room on the couch, which sits parallel to the west wall of the house, and awoke to find the assailant standing over her with the knife in his hand, she had then struggled with him, and that he then walked away through the kitchen, into the utility room, and out of the house through the garage (which adjoined the utility room); in this story Darlie told us that she saw the assailant drop the knife in the utility room. Darlie told officers at the scene that she realized she had been stabbed while she was on the couch. She told me that she realized that she had been stabbed only after she found the knife. When she gave me a written statement on June 8, 2 [sic] days later, she changed her story to say that she woke with Damon, the younger child, pressing on her shoulder and that the assailant was "standing" down by her feet at the end of the couch "walking away" from her. In the written statement, Darlie said that she "walked after him and heard glass breaking." In the written statement Darlie did not mention the knife until she says she "realized there was a big white handled knife laying on the floor of the utility room" when she followed the assailant there from the kitchen. In the written statement Darlie said she picked up the knife "thinking he was in the garage." When Darlie later drew a diagram of the house for me, which is attached to this affidavit as exhibit A, she told me that the assailant "ran away" and that she "ran" behind him into the kitchen. At that time, Darlie told me that she didn't see the knife on the utility room floor until she went back to the kitchen doorway near the family room to turn on the light, and that she then saw the knife by looking over the kitchen island toward the utility room floor. When I examined the scene after she told me this version of her story, I was unable to see the utility room floor from the vicinity of the light switch by looking across and over the kitchen island because the island is too large, and I am taller than Darlie.

During the 911 call, after about 4 minutes had passed and the first officer had apparently arrived, Darlie said, "Look out in the garage. They left a knife lying on the . . .'' The dispatcher told her, "Don't touch anything,'' to which Darlie replied "I already touched it and picked it up.'' Darlie later told the dispatcher again that she had touched the knife, 5- minutes into the call and while her dying children were still on the floor in front of her, and she said, "I wonder if we could have gotten the prints maybe.''

During the 911 call, there is no mention of, or sound from, Darin (Darlie's husband) until 43 seconds into the call, after which a male voice is first heard. Darlie told the 911 dispatcher that "my husband . . . just ran downstairs,'' but she never asks him, or mentions during the call, her 8-month-old baby, who Darlie and Darin later told us was sleeping upstairs with Darin at the time of this offense.

I know from talking to the officers involved and reviewing their reports that Rowlett patrol officers secured the crime scene and maintained it until crime scene physical evidence officers arrived at the scene within 2 or 3 hours of the 911 call. Sgt. Nabors, Rowlett Police physical evidence supervisor, personally surveyed the scene and made a preliminary report which I have read. Nabors also sought the assistance of Retired Dallas County Sheriff's Lieutenant James Cron to help examine the crime scene because Cron has extensive experience in examination of murder crime scenes. Cron has also sent some preliminary reports which I have reviewed. We also have received assistance from Richardson Police Physical Evidence Supervisor Jeff Craig, who helped obtain blood evidence from the kitchen and other areas. From my own investigation of the scene, as well as my discussions with Sgt. Nabors, Lt. Cron, Mr. Craig, and my review of their reports, I have learned the following facts inconsistent with Darlie Routier's stories to us:

Although Darlie has consistently said that the assailant fled the house through the garage, there was no blood found in the garage, on the window in the garage, or on the white wood fence or gate surrounding the back yard, even though the assailant would have had to leave the back yard over the fence or through the gate. The overhead garage door, the only way out of the garage besides the windows, was closed and latched from inside when police arrived, and Darlie has never told us that she heard that door open or close. The window sills had a layer of dust on them which was undisturbed. Mulch on flower beds between the garage and backyard gate was undisturbed in the morning hours after the offense when Cron examined it.

Although Darlie told us that she followed the assailant through the kitchen and heard him breaking glass ahead of her, the only broken glass found in or around the house was a wine glass which was broken in [sic] the kitchen floor. Bloody footprints were found on the kitchen floor and photographed by physical evidence investigators at the scene. These footprints were all made by a single-size set of bare feet. Darlie was barefoot when officers arrived at the scene. The broken wine glass in [sic] the kitchen floor was found lying on top of one of the bloody footprints—the footprint appeared to have been left on the floor before the glass was broken on top of it. We examined Darlie's feet and took footprints with her consent on June 10th. I have seen the footprints in [sic] the kitchen floor and the footprints taken from Darlie and her husband Darin, and the footprints on the floor appear to me to be the same size as Darlie's prints. Although the broken glass was near and on top of the prints on the floor, Darlie had not injuries to the bottom of her feet four days after the offense. Darin also had no injuries to his feet, and his feet are much larger than Darlie's. All of the bloody footprints in [sic] the kitchen floor lead from the kitchen sink area back toward the family room where the offense occurred. There are no bloody footprints leading into the utility room where Darlie says she followed the assailant. There was also an upright vacuum cleaner overturned in the kitchen with blood on its handle—the vacuum would have appeared to have been overturned in a struggle or by accident, except that it was overturned on top of blood drops and bloody bare footprints leading back into the family room.

Although Darlie at some times has told us that she found the knife on the utility room floor, Cron has examined the floor and told me that he has found no blood splatters or other marks consistent with the bloody murder weapon being dropped on that floor.

Although Darlie has never mentioned to us being near the kitchen sink, which is on the west wall of the kitchen, during or after the offense, the physical evidence investigators examined that area and determined that there had been significant quantities of blood shed or dripped immediately in front of the kitchen sink. Although attempts had been made to clean the counter top and sink, tests with Luminol revealed blood on the top of the counter in front of the sink. Nabors, Cron, other officers, and I have all examined the couch where Darlie says she was sleeping when she was attacked; although there are quantities of blood throughout the room and around the boys, there was no appreciable blood on the couch where Darlie's head, neck and shoulders were located at the time she says she was stabbed by her assailant. Cron's opinion from this blood evidence is that Darlie self-inflicted her wounds while standing at the kitchen sink.

The murder weapon, a wooden block knife-holder from the kitchen, and the cut screen and uncut screen from the garage windows, among other things, were seized at the scene by Rowlett officers and turned over to Charlie Linch, a forensic analyst employed by the Southwest Institute of Forensic Sciences in Dallas. Mr. Linch performed tests on the undamaged screen taken from the garage and compared residue from that screen and residue found on one of the knives taken from the kitchen, and his expert opinion is that the garage screen found cut by Rowlett police, and through which the assailant supposedly exited and/or entered the house, was cut from the outside of the house using a knife from Darlie's kitchen, which knife was recovered from the wood block container after the offense. Linch has also told me that the murder weapon matches the set contained in the wood block container taken from the kitchen, and the murder weapon is consistent with the slot in that wooden block container from which one knife was missing when the block was seized by police.

Although Darlie initially told us that she "struggled" with the assailant, Cron's expert opinion is that the blood splatters in the family room are inconsistent with a violent struggle.

Although Darlie at some points has told us that she chased her assailant through the kitchen, the blood splatters left in the kitchen lack the "high velocity" spread pattern which would be consistent with splatters left behind by someone running through the area.

I spoke today to Mike Bosillo, an investigator with the Dallas D.A.'s office, who spoke today to Dr. McClain of the Dallas County Medical Examiner's office. Dr. McClain told Bosillo, and he told me that Dr. McClain performed the autopsy on the older child, Devon, who McClain says sustained two incised wounds to the chest. The larger of the wounds, the top of which began above the child's right nipple and which extended 2" in length in a downward direction, had a maximum depth of penetration of 5", exiting the right chest wall on the child's back. The wound penetrated the child's rib cage, breaking the child's ribs.

At my request, Dr. Townsend-Parchman of the Dallas County Medical Examiner's office examined Darlie's injuries on June 6, and she has told me that the wounds would possibly have been self-inflicted.

Based upon the above information which I have received from investigating officers, my own investigation, and Dr. McClain and Dr. Townsend-Parchman, I believe that the wounds inflicted upon Darlie were of a completely different character and severity than those inflicted upon her sons. None of her wounds were deep, penetrating wounds to vital areas of her body such as those received by her sons.

Based on these facts, I believe that someone from inside the house took a knife from the kitchen, cut the garage window screen from outside the house prior to the offense, and then replaced the knife in the kitchen block container. I further believe that Darlie Routier's stories to Rowlett police are internally inconsistent and inconsistent with all of the physical evidence at the scene. I further believe that her repeated statements to the 911 dispatcher about her fingerprints on the knife, her lack of concern and attempts to help her dying son, and her lack of concern for her remaining infant child who was upstairs during the offense and whose condition was apparently unknown to Darlie during the call, are indicative of her guilt and inconsistent with her story that she had awakened after the violent assault on her two older sons and after she had been wounded. I further believe that her story, that she slept through the violent stabbings of her sons only a few feet away from her and through multiple cuts inflicted upon herself, is incredible.

Based upon the above facts, I believe that Darlie Routier committed the capital murder of Damon Routier and Devon Routier in Dallas County, Texas on or about June 6, 1996.

(signed) <u>Jimmy Patterson</u>
Affiant

WHEREFORE, AFFIANT REQUESTS THAT AN ARREST WARRANT BE ISSUED FOR THE ABOVE ACCUSED INDIVIDUAL IN ACCORDANCE WITH THE LAW.

SUBSCRIBED AND SWORN TO BEFORE ME ON THE 18TH DAY OF JUNE, 1996.

(signed) <u>Janice Warden</u>
MAGISTRATE, IN AND FOR DALLAS COUNTY.

****

MAGISTRATE'S   DETERMINATION   OF PROBABLE CAUSE

ON THIS 18TH DAY OF JUNE, 1996, I HEREBY ACKNOWLEDGE THAT I HAVE EXAMINED THE FOREGOING   AFFIDAVIT   AND   HAVE

DETERMINED THAT PROBABLE CAUSE EXISTS
FOR ISSUANCE OF AN ARREST WARRANT FOR
THE INDIVIDUAL ACCUSED THEREIN.
(signed) <u>JANICE WARDEN</u>
MAGISTRATE, IN AND FOR DALLAS COUNTY,
TEXAS

With the arrest of Darlie, another important matter required immediate attention—the care of the third son, Drake Anthony Routier, the eight-month-old infant, brother of the two slain children. Under some other scenario, he might have automatically remained in the care of his father. After all, Darin had not been charged with anything.

But nothing about this case was ordinary, and when police charged the mother with murdering two of her children, the Dallas County Child Protective Services intervened, because murder was viewed also as child abuse. Prior to the killings, there had been no record of abuse within the family, but that made no difference to the state. Complicating matters was the iron fact that Darin believed his wife to be innocent. What if he was able to come up with a million dollars and free the mother? Could Darin be trusted to protect the baby? And would he? The rest of the family, including the grandparents, felt the same way that Darin did. Would Drake be out of harm's way among any of them?

So, until a court could figure it out, the CPS intervened, took temporary custody of the baby, and placed him in foster care, declaring the move to be merely a routine procedure. Drake Routier had, in a matter of weeks, lost his brothers, his mother, his home, and, at least for the time being, his father, too. He was in the care of strangers.

8

THE CASE OF Susan Smith is the macabre standard by which mothers killing their children are measured in this country, not necessarily by law enforcement, but certainly by the public and the media. For when the pleasant young woman with brown eyes was found guilty on July 22, 1995, of murdering her two small children, a fascinated nation felt the verdict was just. The only disagreement among onlookers was whether she should spend the rest of her life in prison or be executed. The court eventually consigned the twenty-three-year-old to a life sentence in the Women's Correctional Institution in Columbia, South Carolina.

On the night of October 27, 1994, Smith released the brake on her automobile, letting it roll into the John D. Long Lake just outside the tiny town of Union, South Carolina. Still strapped into their car seats when the car burbled beneath the water were her two sons, three-year-old Michael and fourteen-month-old Alex. "They were screaming and hollering and crying for their father while the woman who put them in that position was running up the hill with her hands over her ears," prosecutor Tommy Pope, the 16th Circuit solicitor from York County, would damningly claim.

But courtroom dramatics were far away when the car sank and carried Michael and Alex to their deaths. Then Susan Smith concocted a monstrous lie, claiming that a black man jumped into her car at a red light, pointed a gun at her, ordered her out, stole the vehicle, and abducted the kids. The story thrust the Smith tragedy into a media spotlight and, as days went by, people thirsted for information of the missing children.

As police and neighbors searched unsuccessfully for the missing car and kids, the media swarmed into Union, and Susan Smith tearfully obliged their every whim. She repeated her story frequently and the unblinking television cameras broadcast it to the shocked nation. Rumbles of racism percolated. A black man had robbed a white woman and stolen her children! It was a very tense time as readers and viewers anxiously awaited word of what had happened to the two little boys, whose faces were known to all through the smiling pictures released by the family.

Among the few skeptics were some of the local police, who knew the area and its people. Her claim of a carjacking might have had some logic in Los Angeles or New York, but not in Union, a mill town of only ten thousand people, a place where everybody knows everyone else. The cops kept coming back to Susan, questioning disturbing pieces of her story. They said nothing to the media, other than that the fruitless search was continuing. Behind the scenes, in their squad rooms, police suspicions began to focus solely on the mother of the dead children.

She confessed on November 3, after leading the nation on an agonizing nine-day wild-goose chase, and wrote out a confession in her childish script. ''I dropped to the lowest when I allowed my children to go down that ramp into the water without me,'' she said. Her arrest and confession helped calm some of the racial fears, although black leaders would wonder aloud whether the story would have received such headlines if Smith had alleged that the car hijacker had been a white man.

The boys were found drowned, still lashed into their car seats, when the upside-down Mazda Protege was dragged from the muddy lake.

The trial that took place in the huge courtroom in Union County a few months later brought the media swarm back, as more gruesome details of the case emerged. As it progressed, defense attorneys David Bruck and Judy Clarke painted Susan Smith as a victim herself, someone deserving of sympathy despite the awful double-murder of her children. They planted in the minds of the jurors the idea that almost everybody connected with Susan Smith shared responsibility for the tragedy.

Witnesses testified that Susan, as a child, dreamed of being in heaven with her daddy after her father committed suicide. Others said that when she was a teenager, her stepfather, a prominent religious leader with strong Republican Party connections, would sneak into her bedroom and force her to have sex, beginning a sordid relationship. Other witnesses said Susan feared being alone so much that she promiscuously distributed her sexual favors in order to keep men in her life. Her lawyers said the incest and other troubles propelled a mentally ill woman toward a fateful depression that included an obsession with suicide and a desperate need for affection. The case, according to the defense, was not about murder at all, but about "despair and tragedy."

Nonsense, responded the prosecutor, who ridiculed the idea that Susan was suicidal. During the entire agonizing time of the search, she never mentioned wanting to take her own life. The true reason that Smith coldly committed the murders, according to Pope, was that the kids were in the way of her divorcing her husband to marry a wealthy man whose father owned the mill where Susan Smith worked.

The gloomy trial had one final surprising shift, when Circuit Judge William Howard told the jurors they could consider an option of involuntary manslaughter in their deliberations. That could mean the boys died by accident after their mother changed her mind about killing herself and taking them with her. For a judge to even consider a lesser charge than murder in a death-penalty trial was almost unheard of, particularly in a case with such heinous characteristics. The prospect that Susan Smith might face a maximum prison term of five years, or no prison time at all, stunned court watchers.

Pope blistered the jury in his closing remarks with a final comment. "This case screams, just as Michael and Alex screamed, for a verdict of murder. Y'all please give it," he asked. They did. After only two and one-half hours, the jury found the young mother guilty of the two counts of murder.

Two years later, in Rowlett, Texas, police remembered the Susan Smith case vividly while they investigated Darlie Routier's claim of an intruder killing her two sons. There were plenty of similarities, but the cops were thankful for one particular difference. "Thank God she didn't say a black man did it," commented one policeman.

It didn't start with Susan Smith. Twenty-three centuries ago, the Greek playwright Euripides wrote *Medea*, the classic tragedy of a woman who forsook her country and family, and even killed her brother, to be with the man she loved. She escaped to Greece with her lover, Jason, and his Argonauts.

Far from finding the bliss she sought, Medea was cruelly scorned. Jason abandoned her and their two children to marry the beautiful daughter of a king, and the monarch banished Medea and her sons into exile. The king and princess and Jason all made a mistake, for Medea developed a lust for revenge, a burning hatred that knew no bounds.

While deceiving Jason with the pretense of reconciliation, she suggested that he beg the king and his future bride to keep the children with them. She then fashioned a deadly magical gown and a crown of gold for the princess, an outfit that burned the new bride alive when she put it on. When the king attempted to save his daughter, he also died in agony.

A messenger related the news to Medea, who thanked him as a "friend" for bringing such good tidings. To further punish Jason, she planned the ultimate crime, the murder of their sons. In the play, a shocked Greek chorus asks Medea: "But can you have the heart to kill your flesh and blood?" She answers, "Yes, for this is the best way to wound my husband."

Medea brutally stabbed her two boys to death, while the Greek chorus cautioned: "O your heart must have been made of rock or steel, you who can kill with your own hand the fruit of your own womb." Jason, upon learning of the murders, damned her with this oath:

> You hateful thing, you woman most utterly loathed
> By the gods and me and by all the race of mankind.

Even before the ancient Greeks penned tragedies, the deaths of children were spoken of in oral epics relating the strange behavior of the gods. Few topics through history have been so compelling as the murder of children, particularly by their mothers.

But while such deaths have always been with us, what has changed in our lives and societies have been the roles of the child, and of the mother. As Steve Gushee, a religion writer with the *Palm Beach Post*, wrote in a landmark article on the history of child abuse and neglect, "Children have had a special place in our hearts—and our culture—for a relatively brief time, only a little more than 100 years. Childhood itself is a recent and romantic experiment."

In ancient days, when women worked hard in the fields beside their husbands as well as keeping the home, they didn't have time for a truly nurturing motherhood role. Times were harsh, life expectancy was minimal for infants and not much better for adults. Kids were treated as the occupants of the lowest rung of human evolution, and were secondary to the survival of the family and the adults.

It was not unusual for some new babies, particularly females, to be thrown away to die, simply because they were deemed to be a future burden. Shockingly, the practice continues even today in some countries where life is both hard and cheap.

According to Geraldine Youcha, author of *Minding the Children: Child Care in America from Colonial Times to the Present*, all of recorded history recounts instances in which children have been abused, treated as chattel, and killed without remorse. To offset the huge infant mortality rate, women had more children, hoping the strongest could survive. In 1800, the average married woman bore seven children and never expected them all to live.

There was no time for weaklings, nor much emotional investment in the little ones. One professor told Gushee that, "In the mid-19th Century in Philadelphia, a newborn was found in a garbage can every other day. A child in the country was a (working) hand. A child in the city was a mouth."

In olden days, once children survived the first catastrophic years, they were put to work themselves. After reaching the age of seven, which the Roman Catholic Church determined to be the age of reason, they could be assigned to marriage contracts or become a craftsman's apprentice. Single women and widows simply could not support their children and abandoned many of them. Orphanages took some parentless youngsters, but many others had to roam the streets, surviving as best they could. The abuse and murder of children was so routine that records were not even kept.

The United States had already been in existence for about a century before the very first case of child abuse was recorded. Not the first case, just the first *recorded* case. Authorities in New York City were searching a dirty tenement when they discovered a young girl chained to a bed and starving. Still, nothing was done until the city's aggressive and highly competitive newspapers jumped on the dreadful story of little "Mary Ellen." There were no laws on the books to deal with the abuse of a child, and no office existed for such a purpose. But as public pressure grew and yellow press headlines screamed, the city decided the only logical answer was to treat Mary Ellen at least as well as they would treat a dog, for among the laws the city did possess were statutes that protected beasts. So, the Society for the Prevention of Cruelty to Animals pulled Mary Ellen to safety and New York created a comparable Society for the Prevention of Cruelty to Children.

During the Industrial Revolution, child labor was fully exploited, for employers determined the little ones were the cheapest form of labor after outright slavery. Only after the Industrial Revolution shifted society and the economy did roles change. Men held better jobs and women began to stay home and rear the children. It was about this time that the picture started emerging in America of a mother as a nurturing icon and children as something to be cherished. Medical advances helped lower the rates of infanticide and family bonds tightened, until the nation concocted an almost impossibly pastoral image of families—fathers always hardworking and caring, mothers as vats of unconditional love, and children who were always innocent, obedient and perfect.

In the modern era, things have changed dramatically, as the wheel of time has almost turned back to the days when women toiled in the fields at the expense of caring for their children. At a time when medicine has substantially lowered the deaths of newborns, families and mothers are under stress never before encountered, and the result has been that children have become a primary target of violence.

Child advocacy groups estimate that more than 1,200 children are killed by their parents or other close relatives each year in America alone, and in about half the cases, child welfare agencies were aware of previous problems involving the victims.

Every day, three children in the United States die of abuse or neglect, according to the National Committee to Prevent Child Abuse. In 1985, some 810 children died from abuse and neglect, and, only nine years later, in 1994, the number had rocketed up 57 percent, to reach more than 1,270 victims.

Children abused and neglected by their parents account for 3.5 percent of murder victims nationwide, according to the Justice Department. One out of every three children killed by a family member died at the hand of the mother.

In this confused world, many times the deaths involve a love interest of the mother, who believes the child stands in the way of personal happiness. That was suggested to be one element of the Susan Smith case.

Incidents of the brutal murders of children come with revolting regularity. Many books have been written about the high-profile cases, while other murders of children see a brief flash of headlines and then vanish. But they are plentiful. During the same general time that the Routier case unfolded, so did these cases:

- New Brunswick, Canada—Lorelie Turner and her husband were convicted of manslaughter for the death of their three-year-old son.
- New York—Awilda Lopez pleaded guilty to murder for the beating death of her six-year-old daughter, Eliza Izquierdo. Police said she beat and burned the child, whom she called Satan, for months. The case led to an overhaul of the child welfare system, which knew of the continuing abuse and did not stop it.
- Fort Lauderdale, Florida—Pauline Zile tearfully told police that her seven-year-old daughter, Christina, had been kidnapped from the rest room of a flea market. Pauline and her husband, John—Christina's stepfather—eventually were charged with killing the child.
- Dayton, Ohio—The body of four-year-old Samantha Ritchie was found in a water-filled pit. Her mother, Therressa [sic] Jolynn [sic] Ritchie, was charged with murder.
- Front Royal, Virginia—The nude body of Valerie Linrose Smelser, twelve years old and weighing a mere fifty-one pounds, was dumped in a ditch beside the Shenandoah River. The mother, Wanda A. Smelser, and her live-in boyfriend, Norman Hoverter, were charged with first-degree murder. Authorities said Valerie and her four siblings were beaten frequently and locked in a room without food.

Tony Grasha, a psychology professor at the University of Cincinnati, told the *Cincinnati Enquirer*, "Mothers love, care and cherish their children depending on a lot of things: how good mommy feels, how well off mommy is, whether mommy can call on someone, whether the kids are turning out the way mommy wants."

The murderous saga is far from over, and strong arguments can be made that things will only get worse, despite some hope that society is awakening to the ugly fact of how children and infants are bearing the deadly brunt when things go wrong in family life.

"Where are we going? I'd take a good look at the porno on cyberspace to see where we're going," the Rev. Theodore Bush, pastor of the First Presbyterian Church in Delray Beach, Florida, told the *Palm Beach Post*.

One item that made the murders of Darlie Routier's little boys stand out from the other crimes that crowd police blotters around the country was simply that, with the charges brought against her, there was the awful shock that the alleged killer broke some stereotypes. Darlie was no ghetto mom. She was a beautiful white woman in a middle-class family who lived in a wonderful house, had a loving husband, wore designer clothes, and, to outward appearances, loved her kids.

Society has grown so used to reading and hearing of men as criminals that it takes the evil prominence of a Jeffrey Dahmer or a Ted Bundy to break out of the pack of killers and thieves who are arrested every single day in this dangerous land. But when a woman is charged in a sensational double murder, the media pays attention.

That, however, may also be changing. Statistics now show that women commit about 10 to 12 percent of the crimes in the United States. Usually, their victims in homicides are most likely to be someone they know, family members or friends.

"The Victorian notion that females were 'angels of the house' and were not capable of killing has largely gone the way of petticoats and bonnets," observed Liz Warwick of the *Calgary Herald* in Canada.

Canada, a rather placid nation when compared to the crime rate in the United States, provides the interesting point that the U.S. is not alone in seeing women becoming more involved in criminal activity. Warwick reported the Canadian Centre for Justice Statistics showed that women received only 7.6 percent of all of that nation's violent crime charges in 1986. By 1993, only seven years later, the figure had almost doubled, jumping to 13.3 percent.

Whatever the cause of the increasing tendencies of women to be involved in crimes, the murders of children by their mothers still baffle experts. As clinical psychologist Joan Reckseit told the *Cincinnati Enquirer*, "I find [these] very hard to understand even in the context of the psychological and the societal factors." She, among other experts, believe that some mental disorder might be present to trigger such an event by a mother. An inability to properly handle stress, a feeling of helplessness, and a personal history of childhood abuse are other factors that sometimes contribute to a woman exploding into a rage.

Actually, many parents who kill their children usually don't intend to do so. They just get carried away by their rage, according to some experts.

With her double-murder charge, Darlie Routier automatically fell into the rare category of people who might be eligible for the death penalty, upon conviction. In Texas, she might become only the seventh woman on Death Row, compared with 397 men facing the ultimate sentence. That lopsided statistic holds true at the national level. Some 2,960 men are under capital punishment sentences in the United States, while only 49 women occupy Death Row cells.

Actually putting a woman to death for a crime is a rare event, and only one such sentence has been carried out since the federal moratorium on the death penalty was lifted in 1976. She was Margie Velma Barfield, who was executed in November, 1984, in North Carolina on a conviction of murdering her boyfriend. During the same period, 288 men were put to death.

The reason for such a huge difference in the numbers is partly due to all murders not being the same in the eyes of the law. A murder that is particularly violent and accompanies another element of crime, such as kidnapping or cruelty, usually drops into the death-penalty arena. The argument that the person will present a continuing menace to society by living is also used. Women do not usually fall into such categories, because their murders usually involve passion and emotion, which means it is not as likely to have been carefully planned, or, in legal terminology, "premeditated." In addition, women are more likely to have had a clean criminal record prior to a "crime of passion" murder and jurors will often see them weep with remorse on the witness stand. Both items weigh heavily in consideration of a death sentence.

9

ON JUNE 16, the Sunday before Darlie Routier was arrested, the huge *Dallas Morning News* had carried not a word about the case. The investigation was continuing, but other matters crowded crime for the headlines.

The local section contained stories about crowds who were using the new light rail service of the Dallas Area Rapid Transit system, 200 Chinese senior citizens obtaining citizenship, and African-Americans from Plano to Oak Cliff participating in the Juneteenth celebration to mark the day Texas slaves received word of their freedom. Columnist Jerome Weeks commented that, "Increasingly, it's murder out there," but he was writing about books on crime fiction. Meanwhile, the true-to-life, peculiar case in Rowlett wasn't mentioned in the paper as the news spotlight moved away. The horrible crime had been committed and, at last reports, the police were still looking for the stranger who broke into the Routier home. The voluble talk-show hosts had long ago moved their radio audiences to more interesting items, such as the authorities in Arlington ordering John Dosher to stop giving piano lessons in his home because he was violating a city ordinance.

But on Tuesday, June 18, the temporary lull in news

coverage ended the moment the handcuffs were put on Darlie. A dozen days had elapsed since the killings. Now this was news that reached far beyond the outskirts of Dallas. The clean-scrubbed good looks of the victims and the alleged killer made it a photographic treasure house for the news media.

The following day, Dan Rather and the *CBS Evening News* carried a brief report on the arrest of Darlie Routier, as did the *Today* morning show on NBC, but the first thorough nationwide television coverage came over a cable station. The CNBC network, headquartered just outside of New York, decided the Texas case bore enough shocking resemblance to the infamous Susan Smith episode to warrant a full story.

That link was made immediately by the CNBC host, who introduced the segment with a mention of the Smith tragedy, then added that "apparently something similar has happened again, this time in a small town in Texas."

Correspondent Rick Davis set the scene in Rowlett, which he described as "a small town down the road from Dallas." Attention in the village, he said, was on a single upscale house in a neighborhood where "sorrow has turned to shock" over the arrest of Darlie Routier in the brutal murders of two of her three sons. "Her story is a lie," he said of the police conclusions, adding that while her arrest stunned the community, it also brought relief from worry about a mad killer on the streets.

The problem with the story for a visual medium such as television was a lack of sources who would discuss it. On the official level, only the beleaguered Sergeant Poos could comment, and the CNBC show proved no exception to that rule. The Rowlett police otherwise avoided the cameras and reporters in order not to say anything in public that might haunt the eventual trial. Only Poos would   talk,   and   while   his   demeanor   was friendly and open, he weighed every word before uttering it.

"Initially, we had a community on the verge of panic, thinking there was a psychopathic killer just walking down the alleyways. We've had very little violent crime, and this was a shock to the community," he confirmed for CNBC. Later in the interview, he said the cops "had visions of neighbors shooting neighbors accidentally because of something going bump in the night. We were trying to keep a handle on that."

The difficulty with calming such fears among residents had been the possibility of tipping off Darlie Routier about their growing suspicions, for they had not been ready in those early days to confront her. In other words, they couldn't simply come out right after the murders and say that the mother, not some demon stranger, was likely to be the one charged. To do so might have let the neighbors sleep better, but could have destroyed the case they were building against Darlie. It was "a very awkward situation," Poos said.

The correspondent interviewed a couple of neighbors. A father with two young sons about the age of the Routier boys said that, with the arrest of Darlie, "I feel better, but I still have one eye looking out the back of my head." And a woman neighbor added, "It's nice to know there's not a crazy person out here, although there really was one." Ominously, the television correspondent agreed that even in "a place where neighbor knows neighbor, you never know everything about your neighbors."

CNBC returned to questioning Poos, who was fast putting the proper spin on a story without really divulging anything. He was asked how soon the police became suspicious of Darlie Routier, and tiptoed around the answer, which brushed over the volatile issue of when she was given her Miranda warnings against self-incrimination.

"This was a very awkward case to handle," Poos replied. "From the very moment that the first officer and paramedics arrived on the scene, things did not match up. The story that Darlie Routier was telling the officers, that an intruder came in and did this, was simply not being substantiated by the physical evidence at the scene that the officers were seeing at the very beginning of the case."

He was asked if the community thought the birthday party at the cemetery was odd. "Very definitely. That was pretty shocking to us all when we saw that. It was one more piece of the puzzle that didn't make sense. That helped propel us toward the final outcome of this case."

When pushed to expand on the investigation, Poos edged into generalities. "A crime scene can talk to you," he said. "When you walk into a location and start looking around, there are things that, without wanting to sound metaphysical, they speak to you. You see these things. Physical evidence is left behind, furniture is moved. All of that should substantiate what the witness is telling you. That was not the case here. Her story was of someone breaking into the home, committing a terrible violent act and then fleeing the house, and yet the physical evidence at the crime scene was telling a totally different story."

None of his comments were new, but the correspondent asked for an example of the mismatched story and physical evidence. Poos handled that with ease. "Blood wasn't found where it should have been found if it happened the way she said. She was not behaving, according to officer statements, like a woman who has just lost her two children, or had been viciously attacked, or had her two children killed in front of her, would be acting."

She didn't want to get near the bodies? "That is correct. One of the officers made a comment about trying to render first aid or trying to stop the bleeding, and she refused to even touch the children.''

Was one of the kids still alive when police arrived? ''Paramedics thought there may be life signs, and they certainly don't take a chance in a situation like that, so she and that child were transported to the hospital.''

Finally, the interviewer brushed too close to the evidence, asking about the knife found in the kitchen, reportedly used to cut through the screen. Poos dodged the issue. ''That's what I understand,'' he said. ''I've been staying away from the exact details.'' He refused to comment further about the crime scene.

Poos acknowledged ''there have been so many rumors flying around here. At one point, one was circulating that one of the children was disemboweled, and that was not the case. We've had to suppress a lot of things, not suppress, trying to put down rumor. It was bad enough as it was without those kind of things being added to it.''

CNBC then played the strange message that Darin had left on his telephone answering machine on June 7, the day after the murders, but two weeks before Darlie's arrest. Around the nation, people heard his choked voice: ''This is Darin. Something terrible has happened. Darlie is okay. She's in ICU right now. We just wanted to let all of our friends and family know that Darlie is okay, but Devon and Damon were stabbed to death.''

Poos said the husband was no longer a suspect because of the consistency of his story, which he had told police over and over. To quiet another popular rumor, Poos admitted, ''He was a suspect, everyone was a suspect early on in the case because we didn't know what we had. We knew we had problems and things weren't matching up. We suspected everyone and we never closed the door on that up until we made the actual arrest.''

Asked if Darlie ever returned to the house after getting out of the hospital, Poos stumbled for the only time in the interview, venturing a guess on something he did not know for a fact. "No, I don't believe they went back into the house at all." The family didn't have much choice other than staying away, because police had only recently cleared the crime scene. "We held it for quite a while, because we wanted to be sure we got everything out that we needed out of there. Once you release a crime scene, you can't go back. You get one shot and you've got to do it right." It was one of the few times Poos was in error. Not only did the Routiers briefly return to their home, but authorities did have to go back, a new warrant in hand, to pick up more evidence.

The cable network then switched to Becky Sebastian, editor of the *Rowlett Times*, to gauge community reaction. Sebastian, a longtime newshound who knew Rowlett as well as anyone, said that the brutality of the crime shook the small city because such things might be expected to happen in a big place, like Dallas, but not in her hometown. She described the awkward behavior of some people who were "relieving their emotions" by driving by the home on Eagle Drive, shouting obscenities into the night.

The interviewer asked if members of the media had thought a family member might be involved in the killings, and Sebastian confirmed that "there was some suspicion from the beginning" that perhaps the father, Darin, might be somehow implicated. But mostly, the area media had accepted Darlie's story. Reporters, as well as neighborhood residents, thought that perhaps someone who knew the house, had seen valuables lying about, had "targeted it and come back."

Questioned about the reactions of the Routiers' friends and neighbors, Sebastian, not bound by the same strictures that required Poos to be very careful with his words, was able to report some new information. She agreed with the police about the shock that slammed the neighborhood. "One said, 'We never have even dreamed it up until the arrest.' " But then Sebastian described her meeting with a close friend of Darlie's, who said that when the couple had come home briefly, she had met with them. When she gave Darin a hug, "she could feel the horror and the hurt," but when she hugged Darlie, "the emotions were not there." The friend described Darlie walking through the home and appearing "more concerned with how the house looked than she was about actually returning to the scene where her children had died."

CNBC wrapped its coverage of the case with an interview in New York with author Maria Eftimiades, who wrote a best-selling book about the Susan Smith case and was able to compare and contrast the two events. One thing was clear, she said. Just as law enforcement didn't believe Darlie, the South Carolina cops had not believed Susan. Things didn't match up in either case, she said. Indeed they did not.

MOTHER'S ARREST IN KILLINGS
HAS TEXAS TOWN IN DISBELIEF

None other than the prestigious *New York Times* also deemed the story worthwhile, thus giving it a stamp of legitimacy. In its Sunday edition of June 23, 1996, the newspaper of record carried a four-column story on page 14 of its national edition, which circulates across the United States. It had a picture of Darlie, and a heartbreaking new photo of the slain brothers, Damon and Devon, wearing little white sports coats and dark bow ties, leaning toward each other, their foreheads touching.

The same day, a much smaller paper, the *Garland News*, a biweekly publication in the town adjacent to Rowlett, headlined on its front page:

CONTRADICTION
ROUTIER STORY, EVIDENCE DON'T MATCH

The accompanying news story was a straightforward account of the arrest and the police information contained in the warrant, but of equal interest in the Garland newspaper was its lead editorial.

CITY AN INNOCENT
VICTIM OF TRAGEDY

Rushing to the barricades to defend civic pride, the editorial warned that the tragedy had brought "national media" to Eagle Drive and that "far-reaching implications" were in store for eastern Dallas County and Texas. Rowlett, it stated, might soon be lumped with other infamous town names such as "Waco, Killeen, and Union, City, S.C."

Then it painted the recent history of Rowlett, which "is not a community of third-generation families and lifelong friendships." The editorial said that, instead of the neighborly togetherness of yesteryear, we use our cars now to go our separate ways after work and use the telephone to bridge the geographical gap to friends. "The suburbs have become a portrait of the upwardly mobile," it declared. "We have little allegiance to a neighborhood."

The editorial explained that modern kids have a similar struggle with relationships, then warned that "all of Rowlett will be branded by the Eagle Drive tragedy. People want to know, and remember, the situations surrounding a macabre event. The 'where' is as central to the curiosity as any element.

"The negative exposure is inevitable for a Rowlett which finds itself an innocent victim—a city which simply found itself in the wrong place at the wrong time."

* * *

It was not the distant media centers that grabbed the story, however. After the initial burst of coverage, news editors and news directors decided that the Texas case deserved coverage, but not the full-blown treatment given to the South Carolina case, which had set the precedent. "Susan Smith did it first, and better," said one caustic veteran.

By Tuesday, June 25, it was the Dallas and Rowlett-area media that were doing the open commentaries.

Dallas Morning News columnist Marlyn Schwartz asked, "How well do we really know our neighbors?" She wrote that friends are always shocked when someone with whom they have shared holidays, car pools, and barbecues is accused of a crime. That would be true among the neighbors along Eagle Drive in Rowlett when Darlie was charged, Schwartz declared.

"Many refuse to believe it's true. Still others are looking at everyone around them in disbelief. This accused killer is someone they could have sworn they knew well. If they couldn't trust her, whom could they trust? And even more important, how well do we really know anyone?" the writer asked.

Not well, she reasoned. Because of the transient nature of our society, "many of our closest friends are people we've known for just five or six years," having never met their parents and people from their past.

On the same page, staff writer Leslie Barker talked with psychologists to obtain advice for readers on "After Rowlett, what do you say to the kids?" One psychologist suggested parents tell their youngsters that, "Any mother who would do this would be very disturbed, and normal mommies aren't like this. Mommies can get angry, but they aren't going to kill."

Another had a different, but equally frightening slant. He proposed telling kids that the mommy in question,

Darlie, "was really sick," instead of saying that she was really mad. "Don't just say, 'A mommy got mad and killed her kids, and I won't kill you.' "

Over at the *Lakeshore Times*, Greg Lynch and Becky Sebastian were getting tired of picking up the telephone and talking to nutcases. One caller insisted that the secret to the slaying lay in the date the murders were committed, June 6, 1996. For, he explained, that was the dreaded 6-6-6, the number of Satan. Not only that, the caller insisted, but everybody in the house had a first name that began with the capital letter *D*—Darlie, Darin, Devon, Damon, and Drake. Was it more than a coincidence, the caller wondered aloud, that the capital *D* was also the first letter in the name of the Devil?

The next dose of national attention, in a much bigger arena than cable, came on July 3, 1996, as millions of Americans gathered in front of their television sets on the evening before Independence Day and heard Stone Phillips, the host for *Dateline NBC*, introduce the first story of the night. "There are crimes that shock us and crimes that break our hearts," intoned Phillips. "This is the story of a murder that's done both. It happened in a small town in Texas. Two little boys were killed in their home. Police went searching for a stranger who, their mother said, had come in the night. Then, a startling announcement from police: Their prime suspect was no stranger to the boys."

The TV newsmagazine's correspondent Len Cannon took over. The opening scene was the powerful view of Darlie squirting Silly String and singing beside the balloon-covered double grave. It made no mention of the memorial service that preceded the party.

"It was an unusual sight. A birthday party in a cemetery," Cannon said. "Just eight days after little Devon and Damon Routier were brutally murdered, family and friends gathered at their graves to celebrate what would have been Devon's seventh birthday.''

The closeup of Darlie, blonde hair swept to one side, the angry red scar on her throat plainly visible above the open collar. She speaks: ''If you knew Devon and Damon, you would know they are up in Heaven and they're up there having the biggest birthday party that we could ever imagine.'' Her voice is pleasant and joyful on the summer day, and the national audience could begin to wonder about the demeanor of a woman who lost her two children only a week and a day earlier. No grief shows on her face. There are no tears as she comments: ''And they wouldn't want us to be down here bein' sad, even though our hearts are breaking.'' For those unfamiliar with the case, the scene was peculiar, to say the least.

''It was a vicious crime in a quiet Dallas suburb,'' Cannon said. He described how Darlie said she had been asleep with the boys downstairs, her husband asleep upstairs, when a lethal intruder broke into the house.

A matter-of-fact Darlie said, ''All I was thinking about was trying to save the babies. I mean Darin and I tried to save the babies. . . .'' Finally the voice breaks, her only show of emotion in the show. ''But it was too late, my babies were gone.'' Sudden tears in her averted eyes.

The scene cuts to a ringing telephone in the police station and a dispatcher re-creates for *Dateline NBC* the events of 2:31 A.M. on June 6. ''Rowlett 911. What is your emergency?'' As a siren screams in the background, the correspondent describes how ''Darlie Routier was screaming, 'They stabbed me and my children.' ''

Sergeant Dean Poos explains that when a policeman ''entered the house, he saw Darlie Routier standing with a towel wrapped around her neck, with some blood on it. Darin Routier, the father, was attempting to administer some form of aid to one of the children lying on the floor.''

Darin Routier is shown in a white shirt, suit and tie, comfortably seated, calmly discussing the bloody events as if talking about a business deal gone sour. The dark beard is perfectly trimmed. No emotion shows in the eyes behind the wire-rim glasses. Pictures of the slain boys line a cabinet behind him.

''She's yelling—Darin, Darin, Darin, Darin, Darin—I mean, just traumatically. The very first thing I see while I'm running in there is I see them laying on the floor, just completely, you know, just laying lifeless. I mean completely lifeless. And he's got these huge gashes on his chest and I'm like, Oh my God!''

The reporter notes Darin gave CPR to Devon for a few minutes. Darin continues: ''And then I realized, when I checked his pulse, that I wasn't getting any air inside of his body. That's when I checked his pulse . . . and I knew that he was gone.''

The correspondent has Poos describe Darlie's various versions of what happened and how Darlie had ''chased the man out of the house.'' The murder weapon, a butcher knife taken from the kitchen. A cop found a window in the garage that had a screen cut. Police scoured the neighborhood but found nothing.

The scene shifts to the graveside party eight days after the attack. There is a new shot of Darlie talking about the good jobs being done by the cops. ''You know, the support and the hard work that these detectives and policemen are putting into this is incredible,'' she states.

Cannon discusses how the Routiers had given police complete access to their home and their lives, turning over photos, videos, and personal possessions.

Twelve days after the murders, he said, the Routiers were again at police headquarters, each being questioned for about six hours. "Then, late that night, authorities made a stunning announcement."

Poos is shown reading at the news conference. "At approximately 10:20 P.M. this evening, investigators from the Rowlett Police Department arrested Darlie Routier. Mrs. Routier was charged with two counts of Capital Murder stemming from the deaths of her sons, Damon, age 5, and Devon, age 6."

The reason for the arrest, according to the correspondent, was that police felt her story "didn't add up," such as with the 911 emergency call, when Darlie talked about how she had picked up the knife and may have smudged any of the intruder's fingerprints. "This set off some warning bells in our minds," Poos said. "This woman, who had just seen her two children stabbed by an intruder, would have her thought processes so together as to be worrying about fingerprints.

"When the responding officer asked her to render aid to one of the children, she seemed to have been taken aback by it. She wouldn't touch the children. She wouldn't get near them."

The correspondent and policeman discussed how Darlie's stories changed as time passed. "[At first, she said] She woke up with the stranger standing over her, assaulting her," Poos said. "Later, Mrs. Routier made a comment that Damon walked up to her on the couch and woke her up, which totally conflicted with original stories and comments she had told us."

There was blood all over the crime scene, but the only bloody footprints that were found were Darlie's. Blood had been washed away at the kitchen sink. Police found a second knife that they believed was used to cut the garage screen, then was replaced in the kitchen. Nothing was taken from the home, no sign of struggle. "There was no physical evidence to corroborate anyone else being in that home,'' Poos said. That led the police to believe she inflicted her own wounds.

The correspondent asked Darin what he thought when his wife was arrested. ''I thought they were joking. I thought they were kidding,'' he replied. Cannon said Darin and Darlie had been high-school sweethearts and had known each other for eleven years. ''She was eighteen, he was twenty when they got married.'' The picture shown is a glamour shot of Darlie and Darin in formal wear, her blond hair swirled high, the generous figure emphasized by a slit skirt and low-cut top.

''She became a full-time mom,'' he said, then showed Darlie's mother and sister, who also staunchly defended her. ''She was very close to them. She loved them with all her heart,'' said Darlie Kee, seated on a sofa with one of her other daughters, Dana.

''There's no way she would have ever, ever done that to those two little boys. Those boys were her world. They meant everything to her,'' insisted Dana.

The reporter said the family believed the police were guilty of a rush to judgment and were ''prejudiced'' by the searing example of Susan Smith.

The correspondent then brought in Dr. Kenneth Decal, a psychiatry professor at Southwestern Medical Center in Dallas, to explain some of the reasons that more than 600 children are murdered by their mothers every year.

''More often than not, it is a rational act. A cold-blooded one, but a very distorted and disturbed one that gets filtered through a very severe mental illness that changes one's thinking, one's way of looking at the world,'' the professor said.

That led the correspondent into some relatively new ground. He asked Darlie Kee whether her daughter had been upset and depressed. ''No,'' she said. ''I know she wasn't unhappy.'' Several other questions of that sort elicited only more negative answers.

"But according to a social worker who interviewed her in jail, Darlie Routier was depressed and suicidal following the birth of her third son. That she felt she couldn't keep up with three children. And that her husband once found her writing a suicide note," he reported.

With that point emphasized, the mother changed her story somewhat. Perhaps there were moments when Darlie wasn't perfectly happy and serene. "I know she did go through a period when she said that she felt like she was having post-part depression after having the baby. But I guarantee you that she was not going to commit suicide, and she would never, ever harm those children," insisted Darlie Kee.

And her allegedly conflicting stories? Her mother answered, caustically: "If you were stabbed in the throat and almost killed, and then lose two little boys, how much sense would you make? Wouldn't you be in some sort of shock?"

The camera is back on Sergeant Poos, who admits there are no witnesses and no confession in the case, but says authorities are certain they have the murderer in custody. "You don't charge somebody with Capital Murder unless you're absolutely sure."

Darin is shown a final time, equally sure in just the opposite direction. "I have no doubt, not a doubt for a second, that someone came in, killed my children and slashed my wife and got out before I could do anything about it."

Back in New York, Stone Phillips wrapped up the story with the note that Texas authorities have taken little Drake Routier into protective custody because they were "concerned the child's life could be in danger if Darlie Routier gets bail." The end comes with his comment that "she has pleaded innocent to charges of Capital Murder."

The show did not ignite the country in outrage, as the

earlier massive media coverage did for Susan Smith. The televised thumbnail sketch of the case was at best the usual surface treatment of a complex issue, but it at least took the Routier story into millions of living rooms where it had never been heard of before.

Just as the local media, the Associated Press, and *The New York Times* had done, *Dateline NBC* had offered a sober and factual look at the matter. Then, inevitably, along came the *National Enquirer*, and the story's collapse into tabloid fodder. On July 9, six days after the *Dateline NBC* piece, the *Enquirer*, which boasts the largest circulation of any paper in America, appeared in grocery store checkout racks with screaming front-page blood-red, yellow, and black headlines:

NEW KILLER MOM
WHY SHE SNAPPED
THE UNTOLD STORY

The scandal sheet had several color photos of Darlie, both smiling with Darin and weeping in her mug shot, and pictures of Devon and Damon, and spread their "special report" over two pages.

" 'PERFECT MOM' KILLS HER KIDS" shouted a huge headline on a strip of scarlet across the top of the report, adding in tiny type, "... COPS CHARGE." The tabloid headline had all but convicted Darlie Routier, although her trial was so far in the future that a date had not even been announced. The promised untold story was a general rehash of things that had already been printed elsewhere, plus some comments from one neighbor.

The publication meant the tragedy of Eagle Drive had completed the first lap around the media track. Local press and television stations had it first, then the top national newspaper, a worldwide wire service, a cable network, then a commercial network television magazine, and finally the grocery store tabloid.

The story, however, did not have staying power and failed to hold the national spotlight. *People* magazine was missing from the fold of usual media suspects and Darin said that no motion-picture production studios or television producers had contacted him. A month after the murders, with participants under a court's gag order and no new information available, the media turned away from Darlie Routier.

So, despite the burst of coverage, despite the pictures, despite the few interviews, a major question had gone unanswered. Just who were these people? By now, the Routier family, relatives, and close friends, stung by callous treatment from the media and the damning accusations of police, had joined together in an understandably bitter, us-against-them attitude.

Darin and Darlie were mysteries.

10

IT WAS EASY for Darlie and Darin to remember each
other's birthdays, for they were born almost exactly two
years apart, Darin on the first day of 1968 and Darlie on
January 4, 1970. They were close from the very start,
before they even knew each other.

The Llano Estacado anchors the southern point of the
Great Plains that form America's farm belt, and in that
windswept vastness that spreads across the bottom of the
Texas panhandle sits Lubbock, a city of about 130,000
people, clear across the state from Dallas. It was a cow
town from its founding in 1891, until a land rush of the
1920s transformed it into the metropolis of the South
Plains.

As Sarilda Routier recalls it, she was only fourteen
years old and in the ninth grade at Lubbock's Cooper
High School, when her cousin, who was not much older,
wanted to drive over to New Mexico to see an airman
she was dating at Clovis Air Force Base. She told Sarilda
that a date had been lined up for her, if she would only
do this one great favor, please, and Sarilda agreed. The
cousin then called her boyfriend and said he had to round
up somebody, quick. The girl she was bringing was a

high school senior, she said, and on the trip over from
Lubbock, she drilled the young Sarilda on the courses
and things a senior would be expected to know.

Sarilda's date on that trip in 1964 turned out to be a
quiet, retiring young man named Leonard Routier. He
was a machinist for the Air Force and, on leaving the
service, returned to Lubbock and set up his own shop.
Three years after that first meeting, when Sarilda really
was a senior in high school, the two young people were
married, throwing the school principal into a tizzy. A
married woman was among the teenagers! That just
wouldn't do! Sarilda was banned from physical education
classes, for fear that she might contaminate the other
girls, and the principal gave her an order: If you get pregnant, tell me immediately, even before you tell your husband! That's silly, she responded, and ignored him. She
was from tough pioneer stock and inherited her name
from a pair of ancestral sisters named Sarilda and Arenda,
both of whom died of scarlet fever in the Old West.

Darin was born on New Year's Day, 1968, not too
many months after his mother's graduation. What the
school principal didn't know wouldn't hurt him. Another
boy, Deon, came along in 1970, and a girl, whom she
named Arenda to keep history alive, was born in 1975,
the year after Sarilda and Leonard moved from Lubbock
to a new subdivision called Lakeside Heights, which was
built amid the cotton fields beside a lake that actually
was the size of a pond. Darin transferred into the third
grade at Cooper, where he would remain through high
school.

Like his father, Darin was cut from quiet cloth, a boy
who didn't like confrontation, even though he possessed
physical strength. His little brother, the two-years-
younger-but-feistier Deon, picked on him when they
were little boys, and Darin would be the one who backed
down. Then one day, at the age of thirteen, Darin

changed, and when Deon pushed, Darin pushed back, finally standing up to his little brother, who quickly realized that the free ride of so many years was over. Respect replaced fists in their arguments, but Darin continued to control his temper.

His mother recalled one day when he was thirteen and she was driving Darin and his best friend somewhere when the boys started playing a juvenile game called Slug Bug, in which the first kid to yell out when they spotted a Volkswagen Beetle got to hit the other boy. The friend bopped Darin, again and again, while Sarilda watched and grew frustrated. Darin wasn't even trying. "Hit him back," she commanded. Instead, Darin balled up his fist and hit the car door, breaking a bone in his hand. When his mother asked why he would do such a thing, Darin explained, "If I hit him, I would have hurt him." Darin would rather take the beating than hurt anyone.

He was raised in an almost idyllic, church-going home. "We had a Brady Bunch family, but by comparison, the Bradys were dysfunctional," recalled Deon. The kids only remembered their parents having one big fight, and that was over Leonard not being in the right frame of mind when Sarilda demanded that he use the vacuum cleaner and clean a room. Angered at his unexpected surliness, she said if he would not be a happy helper, then he shouldn't help at all. To underline the point, she pulled the vacuum plug from the wall. Leonard replugged it. Sarilda cut the plug off with a knife and left the house, sitting up with a woman friend for hours to complain about her husband. She finally went home at 1:30 A.M., only to find the lights on. Rather than go inside, she sat in the car until she almost froze. Finally, she knocked on the door, ready to apologize, and it was opened by her chagrined husband, still busily cleaning the house. That, in the Routier home, qualified as a big fight.

Darin's life began to change when he entered Cooper High and his determination to succeed led him into some interesting situations. With his good size, topping six feet, he played and would earn letters in track, basketball, and football at Cooper, where being tough was a requirement because the eleven-man football team only had twelve members. Darin played everything from lineman to fullback to defensive back, ruining his knees in the process and teaching him a lesson about trust. Doctors operated to repair both knees, but gave him painkillers for only one leg. He never forgot the agony he endured at the hands of so-called medical experts.

But his success on the athletic fields had another benefit, one that was almost worth the knee problems. Because he was a good-looking, successful jock, Darin was pleasantly surprised to discover that pretty girls liked him.

At the same time, he realized that he was going to need an automobile if he was to squire young ladies around the teen spots of the Llano Estacado. Needing a car meant he needed money, which meant he needed a job. At the age of fourteen, he applied for work at a nearby restaurant, the Western Sizzler, but was turned down because of his age. He went back a few days later to the same place, lied about his age and said he was sixteen, and was hired to wash dishes. Darin was the first kid in his class to have his own checkbook, and his destiny was set in the world of commerce. By the time he graduated from high school in 1986, he was working full-time in the food-service business and had moved out of the family nest to live with some friends in a house owned by his grandparents. Although still a kid, he was eager to be on his own.

The year of 1970 was an eventful one that demonstrated the distance between the generation of World War II and the dawning of a new day. The Beatles, the most popular musical group in history, had already had their run and disbanded that year. The United States and the Soviet Union were joined in the space race by satellites launched from Japan and China. The traditional and mushy *Love Story* by Erich Segal was published, but failed to balance the scale of changing public opinion when weighed against such voices as the debut of the satirical cartoon strip *Doonesbury*, and the motion picture *M*A*S*H* with Donald Sutherland and Eliott Gould changed the way Americans looked at war.

The war in Vietnam still dominated the lives of Americans. National Guardsmen opened fire on a thousand protesters at Kent State, killing four of them, and the peace talks were finally getting underway in Paris. American troops were still on the ground in Vietnam, and among them was a young member of a Naval Construction Battalion, the famed CBs, called SeaBees. Larry Peck was a long way from his home in Altoona, Pennsylvania, and welcomed mail call as much as he welcomed a cold beer on a sultry Vietnamese day. Four days after the start of the year, Peck got the word he had been awaiting: His beautiful blonde wife of only a year, Darlie Paulette, had given birth to a baby girl. He was a father!

There was no doubt what the child's name would be. His bride was the third woman in her family to bear that unique name, starting with her great-grandmother, Darlie Goodman. Darlie Paulette's own mother was named Martha Darlie. The new little girl was named Darlie Lynn, and she was immortalized when her SeaBee dad jumped onto a bulldozer, cranked it up, and carved her name in wide swaths of letters on the rugged face of Marble Mountain, outside of Da Nang.

Larry Peck could play thirteen musical instruments, everything from violin to banjo to trumpet, and brought his daughter up with a love for music, but it took more than banjo music to hold a family together in the rambunctious 1970s. He and Darlie divorced after seven years, during which time they briefly lived in Lubbock, and she left Pennsylvania for a new life with a new husband, Dennis Stahl, whom she married in 1978. They lived in a succession of Texas towns and moved to Lubbock in 1978, where she gave birth to another daughter, Dana. Two years later, a third daughter, Danelle, was born. Darlie Lynn, however, remained in Pennsylvania with her father and an extended family of relatives, including her mother's two sisters and one brother. At the age of thirteen, Darlie Lynn Peck moved back to Texas to be with her mom and start school. It was 1984, and she entered Monterrey High in Lubbock, later switching to a vocational-technical school, Dunbar, so she could work while going to school.

Darin held a responsible position at the Western Sizzler in Lubbock, having worked his way up the corporate steps from dishwasher to stock-room boy to head cook and now was the assistant manager. He liked the job okay, but the money wasn't all that great. Hell, even the waitresses, who got tips for their service, made more money than he did. One of those waitresses, Darlie Stahl, who had been working there since 1983, thought her young boss was mature for his age, handsome, and wholesome. She had an idea, and both at home and at work, she began dropping hints that Darin ought to meet her daughter, fresh out from Pennsylvania. Darin said he already had a steady girlfriend, a beautiful Texas Tech coed, who, at twenty-one, was older than his seventeen years. Why would he want to meet some kid teenybopper? Wait, Darlie said. Just wait until you see her.

It happened on Mother's Day of 1985. Through the doors of the Western Sizzler sashayed young Darlie Lynn Peck, a tiny blonde bombshell of a girl with a dazzling smile and a figure hot enough to wilt the lettuce on the salad bar. "Well-developed for her age," people would say, no matter how old she was. Other teenaged girls could only look at that blond hair, those large breasts bouncing beneath a T-shirt, and that great butt filling out tight Daisy Duke cutoffs and ask, "When's that going to happen to me?" Her mother-in-law, Sarilda Routier, would one day observe that "Darlie has such a cute body that she oughta just walk around naked all the time." Men constantly ogled, turning to watch her walk away from them.

At that first meeting, the first moment, Darin was instantly smitten and forgot the Texas Tech girl on the spot. "He lit up and just stared and stared," recalled Darlie's mother. "The sparks were flying." Darin and Darlie went out on their first date that same night. "He was a handsome guy and had a lot of gorgeous girlfriends," his brother, Deon, remembered. "But he was in awe of Darlie. He'd always say, 'As pretty as she is, how can she like me?'"

A few months after introducing the two kids, Mama Darlie felt it was high time the two of them had a serious talk about his intentions toward her daughter. She hauled Darin into the restaurant office, and the young man surprised her. "You want to know if I'm sleeping with your daughter," he said. "The answer is yes." At home, she confronted Darlie, who wavered before admitting the truth. But once Mama Darlie knew, there was nothing she could do. "I didn't like it." That was about all she could say.

But they were just so damned *young*! Darin was only seventeen and Darlie was just fifteen, but age just didn't matter to them. Deon's wife, Dana, who briefly went to school with Darlie, said the new couple became an instant item and "were just silly in love."

*   *   *

Darin was truly in love, both with his new girlfriend and the promising world of business. He just knew he and Darlie would be all right once he got a financial footing, and that the path to success did not lead through the kitchen of some restaurant. In a stroke of *"Where the heck am I going with my career?"* Darin, on a whim, filled out a postcard advertisement from an electronics school in Dallas. Out of the blue, a head-hunter called and wanted to interview him, and the visitor sat down with the ambitious young man and his mother in the sun room of the Lubbock house.

The next thing he knew, he was gone from Lubbock, headed for Dallas and Video Technology Institute, which would teach him the basics of electronics. Surprisingly, it turned out to be a comprehensive educational process, about half classroom theory and half practical laboratory work. His high school education, with a single trigonometry course, had not prepared him for the mathematics involved, but he buckled down to learn as he watched a number of his fellow students fall by the wayside because of the tough subject matter. But while he studied six hours a day outside of the classroom, his personal life was stumbling. Far from home and for the first time alone, he missed his tightly knit family and, in particular, he missed Darlie, who was still in Lubbock. Her mother remembers Darlie as being a responsible girl, seemingly eager to prove that she was capable of being an adult. At sixteen, she was working in a McDonald's and talked her mother into letting her have a party at the house while Mama Darlie went on a trip to Las Vegas. It was a test and a question of trust. Young Darlie plastered party invitations on cars around the school, ordered and paid for the spread, and even hired a bouncer to keep the peace and a baby-sitter to watch after her little sisters. When her mother returned, everything was in its place. Darlie had passed the test.

Darin was living almost hand-to-mouth and was too proud to ask for financial help, so he worked part-time jobs that barely paid minimum wage. He lost weight, eating on a dollar a day, and having noodles for dinner for four straight months. Eventually, however, the plan came together. He graduated from VTI in October 1987, only one of a dozen people to finish the grueling technical course that had begun with a class of 172. Now his darling Darlie, seventeen, moved down from Lubbock to be with him. The families did not like this, but recognized the inevitable. They simply would not be separated and the long-distance relationship was a problem, because Darlie did not know how to drive and depended on friends for the long round trip to Dallas. She finally got her driver's permit at the age of eighteen.

Life was not easy at first as they lived in a $237-a-month apartment. "If we left food out, the roaches would jump on it," Darin recalled. Spiders the size of golf balls prowled the torn wallpaper. But now out of school and with a skill to back up his determination, Darin landed a job in his new field. He went to work for an electronics firm named CuPlex, and on a ski trip to Purgatory, Colorado, seated side-by-side on a lift heading up to a snowy summit, Darin asked Darlie to marry him. It was a really stupid question, for no one had the slightest doubt that she would.

The Great Wedding Dress Hunt began. Darlie had her heart set on one she spotted in a bridal magazine, but it seemed out of the question. A designer original, it had a price tag of $1,650. But Darlie knew how to shop and she tracked that dress like a hound dog after a rabbit, eventually finding it displayed in a shop having a close-out sale. It was now only $850—a bargain, but still far too much for her budget. More stalking. The dress showed up in a wedding shop, the price trimmed to $425. Now she was within striking distance. The Christmas holidays came and went and it was prime time for sales in department stores, Darlie's favorite hunting time, and she scoured the advertisements. There it was! THE DRESS! She excitedly grabbed her future mother-in-law to drive her over to the store in time to take advantage of the four-hours-only sale, worrying every mile that the clock was ticking and someone else would steal her dream. She got there and found the fabulous St. Laurent gown waiting for her, the price cut to a little over $200. Victory was sweet.

The ceremony was performed in the sun room of the Routier home in Lubbock, on August 27, 1988, with the bride radiant in a beautiful white wedding dress. Only a few friends were invited. The best man was the kid who Darin had refused to hurt in the Slug Bug incident, now grown up to be a drummer in a rock-and-roll band. The maid of honor was Barbara Jovell, a friend who also worked with Darin at CuPlex. Jovell would later share another very important moment in Darlie's life, when, with undisguised envy and contempt, she took the witness stand against her former friend in the murder trial.

11

SHORTLY AFTER THE wedding and a honeymoon in Jamaica, Sarilda's new daughter-in-law brought an injured baby rabbit into the house in Lubbock. Darlie was terribly upset and determined to save the animal, so she telephoned a veterinarian, who asked the length of the rabbit's hair as a way to determine its approximate age. Darlie described the injury and said the hair was only about an eighth of an inch long. Sorry, the vet replied, that rabbit is going to die. Don't waste your time trying to save it, came the advice. Darlie slammed down the telephone in frustration. She felt the vet was wrong. She could do it! Sarilda watched in amazement as Darlie flung herself into trying to save the bunny, buying special milk and feeding the rabbit with an eyedropper, tucking it into bed with her at night and staying awake, talking to the wounded animal. When it died, Sarilda watched in awe as Darlie cried and cried, completely heartbroken. *What a gentle soul this girl has*, her mother-in-law thought.

According to Deon, his brother Darin was born to be an entrepreneur. Even as he worked in the restaurant business, there was no doubt that Darin would one day be his own boss. While Deon went to Texas Tech and became an electrical engineer, Darin preferred the world of work to the study of a classroom. VTI had been hard enough with the books, and he was anxious to get started earning real money.

The first attempt failed, although he prepared well. After working at CuPlex, Inc., for about a year, he proposed to the men who ran the company, which manufactured printed circuit boards for computers and electronic equipment, that they buy transistors from him at a lower price than they were paying their current supplier. Given permission to go ahead with his plan, he went back to Lubbock with a briefcase filled with business plans, financial projections, and hard data to back up his request for a $7,000 loan to buy the machine that would make his business work. The banker listened politely and gave Darin the money, but brought him back to the real world by explaining the loan was granted, not because of his dazzling preparation, but because his mother and father were favored customers with perfect credit at the bank. Darin bought the machine, which didn't work properly, and quickly folded his first attempt at private enterprise. However, he never missed a payment on the loan and paid it back in full to establish his own credit rating.

He never lost his enthusiasm to run his own business. ''I can do this'' seemed to be his personal motto and he was always looking around CuPlex for a niche where he could make a difference, something that would springboard him and Darlie into their own business. Darlie also worked at CuPlex for about eight months, learning to press the image on printed circuit boards, and outside of the company, she and her husband were full partners, believing in his dreams of success. The next time, he would rely on the two of them, rather than bet on some dumb machine.

Darin and Darlie also had a higher priority. They wanted a family, and before they had children, they wanted a home of their own. In 1989, they got both, when he was twenty-three and she was only twenty-one. They wanted a suburb, not a city, somewhere to raise kids. CuPlex was located in Garland, right outside of Dallas, and adjacent to Garland was a nice little town where it looked like they might swing a deal on a nice house. They began to look at Rowlett as their new home.

Rowlett has been identified by one historian as "the only town in Texas with two faces." The first railroad through the area, built in 1886, ran parallel to Main Street, which was on the south side of the tracks. Buildings were constructed along that thoroughfare to face north, toward the railroad and its passengers. Then, Texas State Highway 1 (also known as the Bankhead Highway) was built farther to the south of Main, and the buildings added "second" faces to have frontage along the new, paved highway that served the growing numbers of automobiles. It would one day stretch all the way from Washington, D.C., to San Diego, California.

Today, Rowlett has settled into another phase of having two faces. One is the community itself, and the other is the suburban entity of its giant neighbors, or what the local media refer to as "the Metroplex." That is the urban sprawl created when Dallas and Ft. Worth grew together and gobbled up surrounding communities as bedroom facilities for the tens of thousands of Texans who run the two cities.

Originally, the area didn't even have a name, since it was little more than a few shacks amid vast stretches of prairie, dense thickets, and forests that teemed with wild game. Early roads were just winding dirt trails. An early settler who used his railway profits to buy up land in the area drove a stake to denote the location of a future town. It was known as the Pleasant Valley community when the Missouri, Kansas, and Texas Railroad, known as the

K.T., or "Katy," pushed tracks through. The village took its first official name, Morristown, from Austin Morris, who became the first postmaster in 1889. As development along the rail line proceeded, another stop also was called Morris, so this Morristown changed its name to avoid confusion. Henceforth it would be known as Rowlett, to bear the name of an early Texas settler and surveyor named Daniel Owen Rowlett, the leader of a band of immigrants that migrated to Texas from Kentucky after he was given a large land grant for his service in the Texas Revolution. Through his property ran a large creek that was a major tributary to the Trinity River, and although he never actually lived near the water source, it was also given his name.

Stores and businesses mushroomed around the new settlement and railroad, which connected the tiny farm community to the commerce and facilities of Dallas, only twenty-five bone-jarring miles away by railway coach. By the turn of the century about ten short years later, Rowlett could boast two doctors, a cotton gin, three general stores, a barbershop, a blacksmith, two churches, the rail depot, and the post office. Soon, a bank, telephone exchange, a hardware store, and a newspaper came, and the town, with a population of 300 souls, was solidified.

Water and concrete eventually gave Rowlett its destiny. In 1921, the Bankhead Highway came through, bringing prosperity, and the citizens finally decided in 1952 to incorporate and officially create the city of Rowlett. Soon after that, in the 1960s, Interstate 30 was finished, but bypassed Rowlett, meaning the merchants and residents could no longer count on business from the heavy traffic down the Bankhead Highway. Instead of being a knife in the heart, as the interstate system was for many small communities across the country, I-30 allowed Rowlett to prosper quietly in the shadow of the wild growth of Dallas.

That was because Rowlett soon had something the growing "Metroplex" area would need for its very survival. In 1971, when Rowlett's population was only about 2,400 residents, the City of Dallas and Dallas Water Utilities completed a giant reservoir right on Rowlett's doorstep. Suddenly, the little community in the middle of dusty Texas had direct access to a lake fourteen miles long and covering 22,745 acres, with much of its most attractive shoreline within the Rowlett city limits. Residents found they could work in Dallas during the week and take the family to the beach on holidays. Instead of being left behind, the city sprang to an entirely new level of prosperity, and in the first decade of the existence of Lake Ray Hubbard, the population of tiny Rowlett tripled.

The 1994 population had zoomed to 30,250 residents, mostly young and upwardly mobile families, who wanted a good place to raise families while being able to make a living. The median age is only 29.8 years and the average buying power for a Rowlett family is a high $64,140 annually.

Dallas, of course, had all of the problems of any huge city. The Dallas Police Department would report 217 murders in 1996, a dramatic improvement from the 276 the previous year. However, the "clearance" rate was only 71 percent, meaning that about one murderer in four was not caught.

The percentage of murderers apprehended, however, looks good when viewed through another group of statistics. The Dallas police said only 12 percent of the 17,960 burglaries in the city were solved, and about 10 percent of the 17,143 cases of auto theft. There were 740 sexual assaults, with 56 percent cleared; 6,122 robberies, with a 24 percent solution rate, and 9,201 aggravated assaults, cleared at a 58 percent pace. Overall, there were 100,401 crimes significant enough to be reported in Dal-

las in 1996, and less than 25 percent were solved. It was
no great wonder that people sought safety in the suburbs.

No matter what happened in Dallas, excitement usually
was minimal around Rowlett. Records show that ''a boy
named Rice was shot and scalped along Rowlett's
Creek'' in 1845, fire wiped out two of the larger downtown buildings in 1910, and an escaped circus lion was
shot to death beneath a railroad bridge on Joe Burkard's
farm in 1928. Before the murders of the Routier boys,
some Rowlett policemen had only worked one other recent homicide, a body of someone killed elsewhere and
dumped within the city limits. Dallas was used to crime;
Rowlett wasn't.

Texas was among the states worst hit by the economic
hard times of the 1980s, and when financial pirates nationwide used the easing of government regulations to
raid the savings and loan industry, many elements of the
economy suffered, including real estate. As a result, one
of the busiest parts of government was the Department
of Housing and Urban Development, which had to pick
up defaulted loans. Houses were for sale everywhere.
One of those was a bungalow at 4016 Bond Street in the
Westwood Estates section of Rowlett. It was on a corner
of a comfortable neighborhood, small but with potential.
Fixer-uppers, they were called.

Using their personal money rule of never paying retail,
Darin and Darlie obtained a HUD-guaranteed loan for
$10 and bought the little brick house with a $68,923
mortgage. And just in time. Two days after they moved
in, Darlie gave birth to their first child, Devon, on June
14, 1989.

Instead of a tiny newlywed apartment, they now had
a home, a child, and Darlie's cat of almost a decade,
Smoke. There was a fireplace in the living room, a dining
room that Darin and his father wallpapered, a small den
for an office, an efficient kitchen, a nice main bedroom,

and a spare bedroom. At an age when most of their peers were still partying, Darin and Darlie became homeowners.

The Bond Street home became not only their home, but their headquarters, as Darin began another enterprise, one that he parlayed into success. He would work during the day at CuPlex, where he was a valued employee, and in the evening, launch his own business. He had carefully watched the production lines at CuPlex and seized on an idea to become a subcontractor of transistors especially modified for that company's needs. The parts were cheap enough individually, but the upgrade needed to make them usable jacked up the prices. Darin figured he could do it cheaper. With a bag full of transistors and a spool of wire, he and his wife spent their evenings cutting the wire into proper lengths, stripping off the rubber covering, crimping the ends, doing a quick twist-tie and putting the assembled product into a box. On a good night, watching television, they could turn out a thousand, and the following day he would take them into CuPlex and sell them for cash. "We couldn't make them fast enough," he said.

The house became the business. A neon sign in the little office glowed with the company name, Testnec, which was pronounced with a little French flip to it. It was their word and they could pronounce it any way they wanted. Darlie, the young mother and housewife and transistor builder, never said "Hello" when answering the home telephone. Instead, a caller would be greeted with a chirpy *"Test-nique."* Their products would be sealed and neatly labeled, and Darlie would send out invoices that a larger business would have envied. The customers never actually saw this business called Testnec or whatever, and what the customer didn't know didn't hurt them. What the customer did know was that they were now buying these transistors for 25 cents each instead of

35 cents. What they didn't know was that Darin and Darlie were building the things for a couple of pennies apiece. Soon, Darin was just working at CuPlex for the benefits the bigger company could offer. In reality, he was making 80 percent of his money with 20 percent of his time. Word of his efficiency spread and he began brokering parts to other companies, several of which tried to hire him.

And they were making good money, indeed, for a young couple; money which allowed them to begin accumulating material goods of good quality, for both Darin and Darlie preferred high-ticket items. "Why pay $300 for a desk when you really want the $600 desk?" asked Darin. "Eventually, you will get the bigger desk and have to sell the cheaper one for $75 at a garage sale. It's better to save a little longer and get what you want, the quality things that will last longer." The philosophy, combined with Darlie's dogged determination to shop every thrift store and pawnshop in the Dallas area, where once-worn clothes and jewelry ended up on bargain shelves, took them to a higher level of clothing, furniture, trinkets, and toys. "At some auctions, people just would stop bidding when they saw Darlie was interested in something," said one family member. She loved garage sales, and on the day after Christmas, Darlie and Sarilda would be out of the door at dawn, hitting the sales to start buying gifts for the next year. She grabbed a $700 fur coat at a going-out-of-business sale in Pennsylvania for $160.

Darin didn't want just some ordinary car, so he shopped until he found a used Jaguar, a 1986 sedan. It had an engine with a dozen powerful cylinders, all leather seats, and no plastic. He paid cash on the spot for it. The speedometer could reach 160 miles per hour, and one evening on an empty and silent stretch of long Texas highway, he mashed the accelerator and the Jag leaped past the speed limit, and soon hit 90 mph, then over the century mark . . . to 110! . . . *120 with room for more. Lord, what a rush!* Then he remembered he was a family man, dropped back down to a reasonable speed, and went home, happy with his purchase. It was a classy car, and that sumbitch could move!

The top-of-the-line purchasing plan also involved their family. Little Devon was decked out in Guess?, Tommy Hilfiger, and Gap clothes, all of which would be cleaned and packed away when he outgrew them and passed on to their other children. ''Better to do that than buy cheap stuff and have it wear out so you have to buy it all over again,'' said Darin, adding with a smile that Darlie had to be kept on a strict budget, because ''she can save me right into the hole with her 70 percent off bargains.'' Her shopping partner was often her mother-in-law, and Sarilda was pleased as punch that her son had married Darlie. ''Darlie allows Darin to love me and me to love Darin,'' she once said. ''There is no jealousy between us.''

Darlie was a flashy gal. Her girlish beauty matured and she held her figure, loving to dress up, have her hair done, and be squired about by her tall, handsome husband. Gold and jewels adorned her fingers and her neck and her ears. Some neighbors would recall times on Bond Street when Darlie might show up at a garage sale wearing only a shocking-pink thong bikini that brought traffic to a stop, the same skimpy outfit she might be seen wearing while mowing the lawn. A later occupant of the house would wonder about the hot-pink walls of the main bath, and the cream-ceilinged master bedroom, where large diamond mirrors adorned black walls.

The business prospered, and Darin finally was secure enough to quit CuPlex after about four years of working for them, and move out on his own, taking the business out of the living room and into its own building in Rowlett, not far from the police station. At least it should be secure, he said. He brought along one employee, Barbara Jovell, "Basia," the friend from CuPlex who had been maid of honor at the wedding. He and Basia did the electronics work in the back, while Darlie kept the books up front.

Their second son, Damon, was born on February 19, 1991, and the young couple was overjoyed, except for one problem. The births had taken an unexpected physical toll on Darlie. Muscle tone fled from her large breasts, and they sagged almost to her waist. That, to Darin and Darlie, was simply unacceptable, and they looked into medical options. Doctors said a routine lift of the breasts would mean almost rolling them up to where they used to be, and that would mean a loss of sensitivity to her nipples. That, too, was unacceptable. The alternative, therefore, according to the physician, was to give her implants, which would make her substantial breasts even larger! They agreed, and the operation was performed. Darlie wasn't quite through with her body yet. She eventually got a small tattoo of a flower on her right front hip, where it couldn't be seen, and had her navel pierced for a ring. Everyone in the family was aware of the changes, and none had anything bad to say about her self-beautification project. She was such a pretty girl, why not? "It was all part of the boob job," Sarilda would recall. Heck, Darin wanted his wife's breasts to be as big as possible.

Two years after Damon was born, the couple needed more space. Darin was only twenty-five years old, but had a solid financial basis and no longer needed HUD's help to get a mortgage. He and Darlie wanted a brand-new house, somewhere in a nice neighborhood, a safe place with access to good schools, a good area where the boys could grow up. The Bond Street place had seen better days, and they were never really satisfied with it after a big flood left behind three feet of water and forced them to live in a motel for a while. Out on the edge of Rowlett, the Paris Construction Company was building the Dalrock Heights area. In 1993, the Routiers sold the house on Bond Street, borrowed $122,300 on May 17, and took title to a beautiful home on a sweeping corner. The address was 5801 Eagle Drive.

12

IT WAS A grand time to be in the computer game. Anyone who understood electronics had a step up on the general population. As the economy recovered with a high-tech roar, Testnec was in the right place at the right time. The business which began with an ambitious teenager answering a matchbook advertisement was growing rapidly, with the owner able to pay himself a nice salary. For 1995, Darin reported to the IRS a gross income of some $264,000 for the business, and paid himself about $100,000.

Life was good.

Darin took two vacations a year, one with his pretty bride on their anniversary and a second one with the kids. The young couple got to see islands in the Caribbean and resorts in Mexico. Having never lost his taste for sports and fully under the spell of the Dallas Cowboys, he began collecting expensive memorabilia, everything from an autographed Muhammad Ali boxing glove to a jersey signed by former Cowboy quarterback Roger Staubach. Darlie turned the new house into a showcase, complete with an ornate fountain smack in the middle of the front lawn and a gazebo and spa in the back. A brick front rose two stories, and a curved staircase just inside the big door led upstairs. The drapes were velvet, the crystal by Waterford, the formal dining room with its rosewood furniture dominated by a crystal chandelier, and their bedroom owned by a king-sized four-poster bed. Leather and fur hung in her walk-in closet beside cashmere sweaters and designer dresses. For the boys, individual bedrooms and a game room filled with electronic gadgets, Nintendo for them and a karaoke singalong set with blaster speakers for Darlie's beautiful soprano voice.

In fact, maybe it was too good. They were just so damned *young* to have so much stuff, some people complained. They had to be living beyond their means. The critics didn't know most of the stuff was used, sniffed out by pawn-prowler Darlie. The bills were all paid.

The business was doing just fine, thanks to a nimble, state-of-the-art, high-speed, computerized machine that could test up to 30,000 points at a time on circuit boards. Customers enjoyed doing business with the sincere young man, who started roping in clients from as far away as Asia. Clearly, he had a business head on his shoulders. And they had even more ideas for making money.

Darlie wanted to raise Persian cats, got a stock of five of the expensive animals and had Darin hammer together some cages. She loved cats, and was broken-hearted over the death of old Smoke at the age of eighteen, when he met an untimely end during a washday. Somehow, he hid in the dryer at the wrong time. She loved him so much that she gathered literature on a first-class pet cemetery burial and headstone. Rounding out the family was a little white Pomeranian dog named Domain.

Darin was working a more practical scheme. A 30-foot cabin cruiser, with plush seats, a television set, a roomy interior, and a lot of potential was on the market. He bought the vessel for $24,000 and envisioned bringing it up to pristine condition. In fact, he'd already began running ads in the local paper, selling romantic night voyages for anniversary couples out on the lake. According to his calculations, it eventually would pay for itself. It was called the *Collette,* but they planned to change the name to *Dalene*, the same name they planned to give their daughter, if they ever had one.

Critics sniffed again. Did you hear the racy tale of Darlie renting a hotel room in Dallas and taking a gang of her girlfriends to a male strip joint? It was a Mother's Day party for Mama Darlie, but *really!* At least, it was gossiped, she didn't kiss the dancer. The way she sashayed around in those Daisy Duke cutoff shorts. Every man in the shopping center would stare, and she knew it. The girl was not without detractors.

Like the distant cousin, a cute teenager who came out to live with them a while, only to develop a crush on Darin. The girl wrote a love note to him, but tore it up and dropped it into a trash can, where Darlie happened to find it while cleaning house, taped it back together, read it, and hit the roof. She read the riot act to the kid and sent her packing back home. Darin, who never saw the note or flirted with the girl, pleaded innocent.

Parenting two energetic, small boys can be a chore. Devon was absolutely fearless and loved to do a backflip dive into the big hot tub. He was a charmer, with a gift of gab that would persuade a twelve-year-old friend to do whatever Devon wanted. Slight and pigeon-chested, he was still the leader. Devon tried his best to coax his father into buying him a multiblade Swiss Army knife, but Darin knew his son too well. A knife would be an invitation to danger. No way, he said. Maybe when you're older.

In Devon's shadow was the shy little brother, Damon, who had a speech problem, and wouldn't even venture upstairs at night without the lights on and an adult holding his hand. Although he had his own bedroom, he preferred to sleep in the red-framed bunk bed in his brother's room, with all the happy Disney characters romping on the wallpaper. Damon did not like to be alone. That did not mean Damon was content to be victimized by his brother. Yes, there was the incident where Devon tied a rope around Damon and pushed him down the stairs, but Damon was infuriated, got up, and knocked his big brother around a bit until Devon backed down. It was almost a replay of the relationship between Darin and his little brother when they were kids.

They were sharp, too. Not allowed to track puddles of water through the house to get to the kitchen from the hot tub, the boys figured out how to jimmy a garage screen with a knife, climb in near the refrigerator, and grab a Popsicle on a summer day.

Other kids would come over and spend hours upstairs in the game room, bestowing on it the name of "The Nintendo House." A clubhouse was planned for the backyard, and bikes were ridden throughout the neighborhood, where the brothers might seek out a swim at a neighbor's pool in the hot summertime.

Darlie got pregnant for the third time, but suffered a miscarriage. A few months later, in 1995, she again was pregnant and she and Darin both wanted a little girl this time. Dalene would balance out the two rambunctious boys. That was not to be, for on October 28, they became parents of a third son, and named him Drake.

Devon had already turned six and was in the first grade at nearby Keeley Elementary, where he was given a "Wrangler Award" for good citizenship. Darlie threw herself into the schooling process, becoming a "room mother" to help the teacher. At Halloween and Easter, she helped with decorations, then, unable to leash her shopping impulse, went out the very next day to buy cut-price decorations for the same holidays next year.

Damon was four and still at home. Darlie hired people

to help her around the house, and no longer spent a lot of time at the office. Instead, she and Darin shifted a lot of their personal paperwork out of the office and back to the house, planning to get a big file cabinet to hold it. They were meticulous and conservative, and the paperwork was considerable. Each time they went on vacation, they would update their wills and leave specific instructions on who would care for the boys, how their possessions would be distributed, and how the money would be distributed. They were generous, too, quietly buying Christmas presents for the kids of some friends who had fallen on hard times.

Sarilda had a major beef with Darin and Darlie. The Routiers were a church-going family and the young couple had dropped out of organized religion, except for some sporadic visits now and then. Sarilda emphasized that the issue was bigger than just them, because they were the parents of three children, and parents have obligations. Devon and Damon, she said, were asking some touchy questions about Jesus and the Devil, about Heaven and Hell. "If you don't take them to Sunday school, I'll come down and do it myself," she warned. No matter how much love is involved, there is a limit to in-law involvement, and Darin promised that maybe they would start going to Sunday school.

Later, Sarilda would sadly recall one such religious conversation between her son and her grandsons after the death of the family cat, Smoke. Devon asked, Where do you go when you die? Does it hurt? Darin went into a long, gentle explanation. Death is not like a visit, he said, because you can't come back. "Well," Devon replied, thinking about that. "I don't want to go." Damon, cocking his head to one side, wasn't so sure. He had loved that cat. And he had loved his great-granddaddy, who also had died. So maybe death probably wouldn't be so

Devon and Damon Routier pose for a 1995 Easter photo. *(AP/Wide World Photos)*

Darin and Darlie Routier. *(Courtesy Darin Routier)*

June 19, 1996. Darlie Routier is arrested for murder. *(Rowlett Police Department)*

Darlie Routier with her court-appointed attorney, Doug Parks. *(AP/Wide World Photos)*

Mama Darlie Kee. *(Don Davis)*

The Routier house in Rowlett, Texas. *(Don Davis)*

Darin Routier holds up a picture of his youngest son, Drake, for Darlie to see from her cell window. *(AP/Wide World Photos)*

Darlie Routier's attorney, Doug Mulder. *(Don Davis)*

Dallas County Prosecutor. *(Don Davis)*

Prosecutor Greg Davis.
(Don Davis)

Reporter Joe Munoz at Kerrville Courthouse. *(Don Davis)*

Damon, Darlie, Drake and Devon Routier. *(Courtesy of Darin Routier)*

bad, if he could be with them again. "I do. I think I want to go," he told the astonished adults.

Darlie, too, had entertained some thoughts of death. She had emerged from the birth of Drake with a bad case of postpartum blues, and the beautiful girl realized she was becoming a woman. The years loomed large and her menstrual cycle was in chaos. She moodily confided to her private journal that she had come close to taking her own life, but the one day in May that she felt most likely ready to do something to herself, she had called Darin to tell him how she was feeling overwhelmed. Darin had come home immediately and stopped her from thinking that way, kissing away the depression, showering her with love. Once her period resumed, she felt almost back to normal, and intent on losing the twenty pounds she had put on with the Drake pregnancy. As summertime neared, she was only five pounds away from her normal 125, getting back her 23-inch waist, and could start thinking again of the bikini and the boat, and that trip she was planning to Cancún with a woman friend.

There were other things to look forward to, also. In two years, she and Darin would celebrate their tenth wedding anniversary, which was being amplified by plans of her younger sister, Dana, who wanted to be married at the same time. Darlie had found a bridal shop over in Sherman where beautiful wedding dresses that cost $700 were on sale for $200 each. She bought two, one for herself and one for Dana. She would sing at the ceremony, and she bought little pillows that Devon and Damon would use as ring bearers. The boys were excited, talking about throwing rice at Mommy and Daddy, and squirting them with Silly String.

There was a summer trip planned back to Pennsylvania coming up in a week, and Darin's high school reunion over in Lubbock. Since he didn't want to charge any more on his VISA card, Darin put the $2,000 worth of airline tickets to Pennsylvania on American Express, extending his credit a bit too far and having to float part of that cost. American Express, which requires a payment in full every month, sent him nasty notes, which he tossed in the trash. Darlie normally kept the books, and since she was spending more time at home with the kids, Darin was having to wear the accountant's hat as well as that of CEO. Cash was short for the moment in his personal account, but he had $7,000 in the business account, and some $20,000 due in accounts receivable. He planned to pay Amex off in the next month.

To him, Tuesday, June 5, 1996, seemed like any other day, with the main problem being that the Jaguar had broken down, and the mechanic guessed the problem could be solved by either a $3 rubber hose or an $800 transmission job. Wouldn't know until he got into it. It reminded Darin of the old joke about people who owned Jaguars: "I am so rich that I will pay 60K for a car that is in the shop 280 days per year." Of course, he hadn't paid anywhere near that price for his Jag, but breakdowns were part of the package. To him, the problem wasn't the classy English workmanship, but the General Motors parts.

He had worked until the afternoon, with Basia and Darlie's kid sister, Dana, helping in the electronics shop. Basia was grumpy, as usual, complaining that more and newer equipment was needed when what she really meant was that she wanted a raise. Ten dollars an hour wasn't enough, she claimed, although Darin knew that was the most she had ever been paid. Darin felt Basia thought her technical skill equaled his and, therefore, she should be paid the same as he, not remembering that he owned the company and she only worked there. The fact that Darlie and he wore gold rings the size of nuggets apparently bothered her, as did their spending on the boat, the big house, the fancy clothes, when Basia apparently felt that money should be going back into the business!

Another point of friction was that Darlie and Darin had agreed to hire Basia's mother to do some housekeeping for them at Eagle Drive and that just wasn't working out. The woman, a Polish immigrant, disapproved of how Darlie dressed, spoke, acted, and, in particular, of how she cared for the baby. Halena Czaban had only moved to Dallas two months earlier, to be close to her daughter. She had been a registered nurse in Poland, a factory worker for fifteen years in America, and now was doing housework and washing other people's clothes. She had started working for Darlie on Tuesday, and didn't want to go back for a second day, but did. The two women had already begun to bicker.

Of particular interest was that, on both days, Halena Czaban saw a suspicious black sports car cruising near the house. Once it was in the alley, with some unknown man staring at the open garage. The next day, when Basia came by to pick her up after work at Testnec, the mystery car had pulled up about the same time, then sped away. She had seen it before, Helena told her daughter, not only in the alley, but back in April, just after she arrived in Dallas and was invited over to dinner with the Routiers. It seemed like the same car, she said.

With the Jag in the shop, and the Nissan Pathfinder left for Darlie's use on June 5, Basia had given a ride home to both Darin and Dana, dropping them off and picking up her mother for the drive back to her apartment in adjacent Garland. They arrived on Eagle Drive at 5:15 P.M., and Basia went inside and exclaimed, "Hey, everything looks nice and clean." Freshly done clothes lay on a counter, ready to be taken upstairs. She had a beer and noticed that both Darlie and her mother were acting moody, so they left quickly. As Basia drove away, she waved good-bye to Darin and Dana, but had to grab the steering wheel quickly when a dark car with tinted windows zoomed past.

A short time later, the Routier family and Dana had a dinner of chicken noodle soup and Darlie's homemade bread, then Darin played with the boys in the carpeted "Roamin' Room," as the downstairs family area was called, until about 9:30 P.M., when he took Dana back to her place in the Duck Creek Apartments, some fifteen minutes there and back. They joked about the ride. He was having to chauffeur her around because she didn't have a vehicle of her own. Tough luck, teased Darin. Mama Darlie had asked him to see about a $5,000 bank loan for Dana to buy a truck. She was too young to get the loan herself. It didn't break his heart that the loan was turned down, for he was too conservative to like the idea of having his name on somebody else's loan application.

When he got back home, Darlie was already in her long-sleeved Victoria's Secret nightshirt and panties, lying on the couch downstairs, watching television, the baby asleep on her stomach. Devon was already asleep, too, and Damon was curled up, about to nod off. Darin stretched out beside her, reaching up for a hand. They talked about the transportation problem, and Darlie thought it was too much like her high school days, when she had to depend on other people for wheels. If Darin took the Pathfinder to work, she would be idled, and she wanted to go buy that filing cabinet and take little Drake by the photo studio, which was running a special on taking pictures of little kids in front of a screen that made it look like they had angel wings.

And they discussed the cabin cruiser, having discovered the hard way there was truth in an old saying that a boat is a hole in the water into which you pour money.

They had decided to get rid of it. Darin was an electronics entrepreneur, not captain of the *Love Boat*.

"Let's go upstairs," he suggested. She declined, saying she was too tired and the baby sometimes kept her awake. If she could just stay down here tonight.

Darin brought her a pillow and a blanket, then picked up the baby and kissed his wife good night. The baby on his shoulder, he got a bottle of milk from the kitchen, then went up the long staircase. He tuned in his big new television set in the game room and watched the basketball playoffs while feeding Drake. He put the baby in the crib in the master bedroom, climbed into the four-poster alone and went to sleep.

A few hours later, in the darkest part of the night, all hell broke loose.

13

DARLIE SPENT HER first night in the Lew Sterrett
Justice Center naked, crying, and trying to sleep on a
mattress attached to the floor of a tiny, bare cell. Guards
watched to be sure she didn't commit suicide, even after
taking away her clothes to prevent her from making a
noose. She was only a few miles from Rowlett, but she
might as well have been a million miles away from her
beautiful home awash with possessions, a place that bespoke success, the place of a family that had been destroyed. Police had spent four solid hours that night
trying to convince Darin of her guilt, telling him about
some of the evidence, like the undisturbed mulch in the
flower bed outside the garage window that the assailant
supposedly went through. Darin was flabbergasted. What
mulch? There's no flower bed under that window! He
was solidly in her corner, as solid as the bricks on the
front of their house. Well, they said, we found these papers that show Darlie was looking for a tombstone.
Darin wanted to scream, *That was for her cat!* She
didn't try to help the wounded children, they said. Yes
she did, he countered. I saw her. I was there, you
weren't! "All Darlie and I are guilty of is waking up,"
he told them. Within a few days, Darin was telling

people, including reporters, that he would sell everything he owned to clear his wife. "They have no physical evidence that she actually did this. She has been
totally victimized."

And now came Mama Darlie, the lioness protecting
her young after realizing she wasn't going to have a heart
attack, as she first thought. The pain ripping through her
was only heartbreak. There was one thing she had to
know for herself, however. On her first visit to the jail,
she looked her daughter straight in the eyes and asked
the awful question, because if what the cops claimed was
true, her child needed some serious mental help.
"Mama," came Darlie's reply, soft and sincere and direct, "I didn't kill my babies. A man came in." That was
enough. Mama Darlie believed her and, like Darin, would
never waver. If the police hoped to get some information
from inside the family other than what they had already
gathered during their extensive interviews before the arrest, they could forget it.

The main item on the agenda for law enforcement authorities was to keep Darlie behind bars. That meant a
series of legal steps, each of which had to be taken carefully to lay the groundwork for the eventual trial.

She was no longer referred to just by her name, but
also by a couple of numbers. Darlie Routier was inmate
number 010470, and went into the system as case number
F-9639972. The *F* stood for Felony. The case officially
was sent from the Rowlett police to the Dallas County
District Attorney on Friday, June 21, the same day that
Darlie had a visitor in her small cell. Jamie Johnson of
the Child Protective Services came by to conduct an interview that, in theory, would have a lot to do with the
future of Darlie's youngest boy, Drake. The child had
been scooped up into protective custody after the murders
until decisions could be made in a calmer climate.

It was not an unbiased meeting, for Johnson would later testify that she had made up her mind before setting foot in the jail that Darlie posed too much of a danger to the infant to be allowed near him.

The two-hour interview with Johnson roamed far afield. And Darlie made another in a series of errors because she could not bottle up her feelings and her ideas. First, she had met frequently with police investigators. Now Darlie talked, openly and freely, with Johnson, and said things that would haunt her during future court hearings. As a mother, she was trying to do what was best for Drake. As a prisoner, she was handing a big bag of potential evidence and clues to the prosecutors. Any lawyer in the land would have told her to keep her mouth shut.

In only a few months, the celebrated murder case involving six-year-old beauty princess JonBenét Ramsey in Boulder, Colorado, would take place, and the value of a family member swiftly hiring an attorney could clearly demonstrate how a police investigation can be legally hamstrung for months on end. At Darlie's trial one attorney would comment, "If she had gotten lawyered up right at first, she probably would not be sitting in this courtroom today."

By the time Jamie Johnson departed to write up her notes, Darlie had discussed how she had been so depressed that she had considered suicide, how she had suffered depression after the birth of Drake, how the couple was under financial pressure, and how stressful it was trying to care for three little boys. She also discussed the contents of her private journal, which police had found, and confirmed she had written her thoughts of suicide.

This wasn't a picture of mental stability for a mother. The CPS worker decided to recommend that Darlie not be allowed anywhere near Drake.

*   *   *

Several of the top defense lawyers in Dallas would be approached about representing Darlie Routier. The night she was arrested, her husband Darin met with one of the best legal minds in the Texas area, Peter Lesser. A native of the Washington Heights section of New York, the iconoclastic Texas émigré once worked as a television reporter in Dallas before he began building a successful practice as a defense attorney. A friend had arranged the get-together so the bewildered Darin could get a general idea of the legal landscape that he and his bride were about to travel, and Lesser laid out the road map. Darin didn't like what he heard, but acknowledged that Pete Lesser knew a hell of a lot more about criminal law than he did. According to Lesser's grim scenario, the case would stretch out over the next six or seven months and, in the meantime, Darlie would be declared ineligible for bond. She was going to have to be told upfront, Lesser said, that she would be behind bars until the trial, no matter what might be said concerning bail, already set at an astronomical and unreachable $1 million. Darin took that to mean the idea of bond was just a formality. A double-felony charge for murdering her boys meant Darlie had no chance whatever from the moment of her arrest of being able to spend nights anywhere but in a cell. None.

But Lesser was intrigued by the case and willing to cut his price in order to represent the young mother. You get $100,000 and I can do it, Darin said he was told. Unfortunately, at that moment, Darin had to admit the accounts receivable and the business checkbook seemed pretty empty. A hundred grand!

If Darin could scrape together $100,000, he would have to choose between hiring a top lawyer or using it to post the required 10 percent of the $1 million bail figure that might get Darlie out of jail. Right now, however, since he didn't have the cash, he didn't have the choice either.

Other lawyers smiled when they heard about that cut-rate price. They knew Lesser could charge a hell of a lot more for this case, and was offering a reduced fee. Some guessed that it would cost $150,000 or more to defend Darlie, and that was just for a really good lawyer. But not the guy at the top of the tree, the crème de la crème, the fastest gun, the man atop the pyramid, the lawyer who could charge almost $250,000 to defend a Capital Murder case. That was Doug Mulder.

The possibility of obtaining a sufficient amount of cash through a book deal or a motion picture or television contract eventually had to be examined. Some nineteen people interested in doing books would approach Darin as the weeks passed, but none had money to lay on the table. The book idea, for now, was discarded. That did not mean that Hollywood was totally uninterested, and after the news of Darlie's arrest, a few independent producers made inquiries. They were willing to sign up the family on a contract, but also did not send any checks.

A few days after the arrest, one insider in Los Angeles, Tom Colbert of Industry R & D, an agency that sells ideas to networks and other media, said there had been no calls to his office by legitimate producers. "This case is such a downer," said Colbert. "It's just such a downer. Nobody went after Susan Smith either." To the big dogs in the entertainment industry, Darlie Routier was a "second banana" in the category of interesting women criminals, Colbert said. Hollywood likes happy endings.

Indeed, during the postarrest phase of the case, Darlie was being painted as a villain and a ruthless killer, hardly the sympathetic female role so beloved by television movies-of-the-week. Producers might be able to do something with an embittered middle-class woman who killed her husband after he exchanged her for a younger trophy wife, à la Betty Roderick in San Diego, whose shooting spree inspired two movies. However, trying to build a screenplay around a young woman accused of butchering her own children was too much of a challenge, even for television ''docudramas,'' which play fast and loose with the facts.

Darin, in a copyrighted interview with the *Dallas Morning News*, had promised to sell everything, but would that even be enough? ''My whole life is for sale: my business, my home, my personal belongings. It will take everything I own to prove her innocence,'' he declared, already starting to trade his valuables for cash. Some friends took antiques on almost a lease basis, promising to let Darlie and Darin reclaim them when the trial was over. A buddy bought the Jag with the pledge that it was only temporary. Darin could buy it back for the same price anytime he wanted. But the money wasn't there yet. Not even close.

In the legal arena of the largest city in Texas, Darlie and Darin couldn't afford the price of a top, independent defense attorney. Therefore, her fate was put into the hands of lawyers appointed by the court—public defenders.

Actually, she got a pretty good draw when her case was assigned to Wayne Huff and Doug Parks, two veterans who knew how the system worked. Public defenders, since they are paid by the state, just as are the district attorney's lawyers, also have access to state-paid investigators, paralegals, and such. Just because someone works for the public doesn't mean their clients are without resources.

Heading into what is known as an examination trial, in which a judge would determine whether probable cause existed, the new lawyers already had a problem. The police had seized the media initiative and were busy blackening the name of the suspect.

14

ON THE SAME day that Darin's interview was published by the *Morning News*, official sources broke their silence long enough to put Darlie's diary into play. Police said it would be used as evidence, and contained both some suicidal thoughts and an apology in advance for something she was planning to do. Importantly, the police in Rowlett were hinting that the seeds of a motive were contained in that little book, but they remained vague about exactly what that might bc.

As a square prison mug shot of a disheveled Darlie was distributed to the media, Rowlett Police Lieutenant Grant Jack, the head of the department's criminal investigations division, said that despite the lack of witnesses and no confession, the authorities had a good case. "We don't have any major piece of evidence or any one big piece—it's a combination of all the evidence that tells the story."

The theory that Jimmy Patterson had outlined in the arrest affidavit would become the mantra of the prosecution, because no matter how they looked at it, they had a shaky motive and no confession. Their chips were being bet on the collection of blood and forensic evidence, items that, when interpreted by experts, would show that the murders did not take place the way Darlie had described. They would use the old Sherlock Holmes theory that when you eliminate all other possibilities, whatever remains, no matter how unlikely, must be the truth. They would prove not so much who did it, but that no one other than Darlie could have done it.

After weeks of saying nothing, the police were suddenly ready to talk, as if to boast that they had solved the deadly riddle. In fact, defense lawyer Wayne Huff grew irritated at the sudden avalanche of police comment and snapped at reporters, "If you want some leaks, get them from the Rowlett Police Department."

On June 26, on the fringe of downtown Dallas, Judge Phil Barker presided over the evidentiary hearing, to listen to lawyers from the Dallas County District Attorney's stable argue that probable cause existed for Darlie Routier to be held for trial. Elsewhere in the courthouse that day, a county grand jury would listen to similar information to determine whether to issue indictments against the woman from Rowlett.

Still, Darlie wasn't the biggest news story of the day. Terrorists blew up an apartment building in Saudi Arabia, killing nineteen American servicemen. The U.S. Supreme Court ordered the Virginia Military Institute to admit women. But in Dallas, Texas, the media spotlight was on Darlie.

When she stepped into the courtroom, the subject of all of this attention looked like anything but a notorious fiend who'd used a butcher knife to take the lives of two of her children. Darlie had been led through private corridors from the jail for her court appearance and just shuffled in, every bit of glamour she had ever possessed wrung out of her. Her hair had been hastily pulled back in a ponytail, and looked more like a sheaf of baked straw

than the usual perfectly coifed blonde. Her generous figure was invisible beneath the large, faded white prison
coverall with DALLAS COUNTY JAIL stamped on the back
in blocky black letters. There was a trace of lipstick, and
the normally sparkling eyes were wide and questioning.
The most remarkable aspect of her appearance was at the
open collar of the bulky coverall, where the long, jagged
scar was visible across her throat, a downward slash that
began at her right collarbone. Far from healed, a ridge
of injured pink flesh surrounded a dark line of congealed
blood. Instead of someone to be feared, Darlie Routier
looked pale and lost, and an audible gasp could be heard
from the spectator section, where Darin and a tearful
Mama Darlie sat near the front row, holding hands for
support. Darin waved to his wife, who silently mouthed
the words "I love you" back to him. They had not had
a chance to meet earlier that morning.

This hearing would be a test run for a part of the prosecution's case against Darlie Routier. The District Attorney needed to expose enough evidence to get her held
for trial, but did not want to show too many cards at this
stage of the proceedings. Later, the defense would be
given access to all evidence, but in the opening gambits,
the prosecution wanted to keep as much as possible under
wraps. Already, some 400 pieces of evidence were said
to have been gathered by authorities. None would be presented today.

It was Wednesday, only three days since *The New York
Times* had carried its big story on the Rowlett tragedy,
and finally police were talking openly, if guardedly,
about their case against Darlie.

Today, Lieutenant Jack and Detective Patterson would
summarize the evidence. As Jack was led through a maze
of questions by the prosecutors, it became clear that, almost from the start, investigators had a great deal of trouble reconciling Darlie's version of the events with the

evidence found at the house on Eagle Drive.

The pattern of answers was set early and repeated often. Assistant District Attorney Greg Davis would ask the policemen how a specific section of Darlie's story compared to physical evidence. "Inconsistent," Jack would reply. Another question. "Inconsistent." Another question. "Inconsistent." He was clear and certain.

The detectives testified that Darlie, in her call to police, claimed to have picked up the knife in the utility room, but there was no blood evidence that indicated somebody had dropped or thrown down a knife there that had blood on it. In fact, the police said, only Darlie's fingerprints were found when the knife with the sharp five-and-one-half-inch blade was tested. She claimed to have chased the intruder from the house, but the only bloody footprints that were found led from the kitchen sink back toward the room where the bodies were discovered, the opposite direction from her alleged pursuit of the killer. And, of course, they said, there was the matter of the deep and mutilating wounds inflicted upon the boys when compared to what they described as superficial slashing wounds to the mother. The cops spoke of her odd reactions. How she had worried about mussing up any fingerprints on the knife. How she did not help render aid to her dying children.

At the defense table, Darlie looked down at her lap and shook her head, as if in disbelief at their conclusions. Or she would drill the testifying detectives with a hard stare. At times she sat as still as stone, with no reaction whatever, or she might be slightly emotional, biting her lip.

Carefully, the prosecution was trying to build a circumstantial case that might override a couple of severe shortcomings, and apparently succeeded. At a break in the proceedings, a *Dallas Morning News* reporter overheard Judge Barker tell the Rowlett policemen, "You guys did a good job on this, looks like.'' But court watchers were aware that, up to this point, only the police had been heard from.

In the last half of the hearing, the court-appointed defense team of Doug Parks and Wayne Huff had a chance to attack the police theory. Central to their argument and questioning would be the vital points that there were no eyewitnesses to the crime and that there was no apparent reason for Darlie to slay her children. Using as a guide the general theory that murder usually results from ''motive, means, and opportunity,'' the case might not be as strong as it looked at first.

True, Darlie had access to the knife that was believed to have been used in the killing, and so possessed the means of committing the crime. True, she was alone with the children, and so had the opportunity. But where, the defense team pressed, was the motive?

It was up to Detective Patterson to gulp and answer: ''I'm not sure what the motive is right now.'' It was a huge admission.

The defense was only getting warmed up. They went through the police version of events step by step. And although this was only a preview of the coming trial, Huff and Parks repeatedly shot holes in the official story, creating what some future juror might view as reasonable doubt. To the spectators on June 26, the police case did not appear as seamless as originally thought.

Darlie's lawyers wanted to know if she sounded ''hysterical'' when she called 911 for emergency help. Patterson responded, ''She made it sound like she was crying on the tape.'' Since no one outside of officialdom had yet heard the tape, his answer was somewhat short of conclusive. She made it sound like she was crying? How could he tell if she was merely acting? Huff raised an eyebrow, but let that point slide for now, but it was obviously something to be examined in depth at a later date.

They moved on to another puzzling point, how Darlie chased the intruder out through the garage, but the door was found closed and dust was undisturbed on the windowsill. The lawyer had Lieutenant Jack confirm that the window in question was only "a few inches off the floor." He asked if, at that height, "someone could step over the window without disturbing the dust at all." Yes, replied Lieutenant Jack, they could.

On the point of not helping the mortally wounded kids, the lawyers maintained that Darlie removed a towel from a kitchen drawer and placed it on the back of one of the boys.

Her wounds were different than those inflicted on the boys, the defense attorney said, but could that have happened in her struggle with the killer? Jack confirmed that might be the reason, but maintained it was a false idea because there was no intruder that night, and therefore no fight.

Examining the inconsistent answers she gave police, Huff maintained she was in shock and was groggy from the painkillers she had been given because of her wounds when Patterson interviewed her. Jack admitted the cops knew she was taking "something for the pain" while giving her early statements after the surgery, but she wasn't under the influence of the drug "to the point she didn't understand what we were talking about."

Huff wanted to know more about when the police started to zero in on Darlie Routier in the double murder. "When did you conclude that Mrs. Routier was your main suspect?" he asked. A wrong answer could be devastating to the prosecution case, but Patterson dodged, "I don't know. Five or six days after the incident." The defense would plan to attack that idea, for if the cops were convinced so early in the case that her story wasn't matching the facts, an argument might be made that her constitutional Miranda rights were violated by continued intensive police questioning in the absence of formal charges.

Huff noted that even without the presence of a lawyer at her side in those early interrogatory sessions with police, Darlie steadfastly maintained her innocence. The whole thing was merely police trickery, he said. Not only did the lawmen not have a motive, they also had to acknowledge Darlie's insistence that she was not the culprit, and that the deed was done by the mysterious intruder dressed in black.

The hearing lasted a little over an hour, and Judge Barker determined that there was probable cause to hold Darlie for trial. He ruled the bail would remain at $1 million, pending a future hearing. Darlie was led from the courtroom, heading back to her private cell in the nearby jail. Before leaving, she managed to once again turn to Darin and silently mouth the words "I love you."

Family members and friends were uplifted by the defense questioning, saying it showed serious weaknesses in the state's circumstantial case. The first opportunity the defense had to strike back had been a success. "The things we felt were wrong all along were brought out today," one relative told the *Dallas Morning News*. "The guy is still out there somewhere."

There had been little doubt in advance of the judge's decision, but what few cards had been shown in this serious game demonstrated that the case was not as firm as the prosecution would like.

There was great concern in the office of the District Attorney, where prosecutors now realized their case would have to be tuned to a higher degree before it went to trial. After watching the shaky performances of Grant Jack and Jimmy Patterson, considerable thought would have to be given about whether the lead investigators should even be witnesses at the trial. How would jurors react if a skilled defense attorney had a chance to slice and dice the two main men in the investigation? Instead of presenting strength and certainty, they had repeatedly stumbled under relatively benign questioning, and those words were now on the record. Patterson had opened a big door with his reply of today that he wasn't sure about a motive. And Grant Jack would have to repeat his thoughts that Darlie's wounds may have been caused in a struggle and that police knew she was on drugs when she was questioned at the hospital. Those bobbles and more. But how might jurors react if the cops whose conclusions had led directly to Darlie's arrest *were not* put on the stand? Would prosecutors be viewed as being unsure of their case? Maybe this wasn't going to be as easy as the prosecutors had hoped.

Darin and Mama Darlie almost had to fight their way through the media mob gathered in the courthouse corridor. He never slowed his stride and was defiant in his response to the events of the day. "She is definitely innocent," Darin declared. "I just know it. It's just real simple. We know it. We love her!"

15

THERE WAS NEVER really any doubt that Darlie Routier would be indicted, for the grand jury system is a peculiar anachronism of American law, a hearing in which the prosecutors hold all the cards. The only thing "grand" about it is its size, from a dozen to twenty-three people. The word is of French origin and the opposite of the "petit," or "small," jury of only twelve people who actually hear a trial.

The major factor in a grand jury session is its total secrecy. Officially, it convenes in private to evaluate accusations against people charged with crimes and determines whether the evidence warrants a bill of indictment. The defendant rarely gets a fair shake. Prosecutors normally use the presentation to gauge the strength of their case and the grand jury witnesses are usually called to repeat their story when the trial begins. However, at that moment in the process, the evidence and witnesses have a definite slant for the state. The defendant is not heard from, nor is the defense lawyer allowed into the session, and everything that is presented is done so in secret. An alternative form of reaching the same decision is through a preliminary hearing, which is held in open court. But a prosecutor in a preliminary hearing risks allowing the defense to get a good look at the state's game plan.

The grand jury system is rooted deeply in our culture, dating back to the Norman Conquest of England in the eleventh century, growing over the years to protect people against malicious charges by the Crown. It took root in Article 5 of the Bill of Rights in the United States Constitution as one of the guarantees against the violation of due process in criminal proceedings. Despite the honorable history, the grand jury system has come under much criticism in recent years for being too one-sided. A good district attorney can usually get a grand jury to indict almost anybody, on almost any charge, and have the defendant bound over for trial.

So, despite hearing no confession and listening to no witnesses to the murders in Rowlett, the Dallas County Grand Jury of the 194th Judicial District Court obediently followed prosecutors' suggestions, and early on Friday afternoon, June 28, returned a pair of true bills of indictment against Darlie Routier. The first charged her with capital murder in the death of a child under the age of six. The legal jargon did nothing to minimize the horror, saying that she "unlawfully then and there intentionally and knowingly caused the death of DAMON CHRISTIAN ROUTIER, an individual, hereinafter called deceased, by stabbing said DAMON CHRISTIAN ROUTIER with a knife, and the deceased was at the time of the offense under six years of age."

The second indictment was multiple capital murders. It charged she "unlawfully then and there intentionally and knowingly caused the death of an individual, to-wit: DEVON RUSH ROUTIER, by stabbing said DEVON RUSH ROUTIER with a knife, and during the same criminal transaction said defendant did then and there intentionally and knowingly cause the death of another individual, to-wit: DAMON CHRISTIAN ROUTIER, by stabbing said DAMON CHRISTIAN ROUTIER with a knife,

"And further, said defendant did unlawfully then and there intentionally and knowingly cause the death of an individual, to-wit DEVON RUSH ROUTIER, by stabbing said DEVON RUSH ROUTIER with a knife, and during a different criminal transaction but pursuant to the same scheme and course of conduct said defendant did then and there intentionally and knowingly cause the death of another individual, to-wit: DAMON CHRISTIAN ROUTIER, by stabbing said DAMON CHRISTIAN ROUTIER with a knife."

Under Texas law, the seriousness of the charges warranted placing Darlie in jeopardy of the death penalty, but authorities held off officially making such a decision until all of the evidence was compiled. However, Norm Kinne, the Dallas County District Attorney, said that the death penalty probably would be sought.

Both bills were signed by John Vance, the County Criminal District Attorney, and Ray W. Paul Sr., the foreman of the grand jury which had been in session ever since January. The matter had been before them for a week, since June 21, immediately after her arrest.

"We have a strong case," Kinne said. "The grand jury didn't waste its time returning the indictments."

Asked by a reporter about the vague and circumstantial elements of the case, Kinne replied, "Many times circumstantial evidence is far stronger than eyewitness testimony." Scientific evidence, he said, could be very firm and "not subject to error."

Darlie remained in jail, suffering with the other prisoners as a summertime heat wave mercilessly baked the huge brick facility behind the Dallas County Court House. She spent much of her idle time writing long letters to friends and relatives, her thoughts free even if her body was confined. For some reason, she began to speculate on the case itself, and wrote to some that she even knew the person who had killed Devon and Damon. She was totally unaware that every word she wrote was read first not by the addressee, but by jail personnel. Copies were made of her more interesting comments and passed along to the District Attorney.

The case now needed a judge, someone who could stay with it through the remainder of the preliminaries and on through the entire trial, and it ended up on the desk of sixty-five-year-old Judge Mark Tolle, a tall, lean man who was due to retire from the bench at the end of the year, after a career that began with a degree from Notre Dame, followed by admittance to the bar in 1955. When he stepped down, he would become what is known as a "visiting judge," who could handle special assignments. Tolle was therefore in the unique position of being able to follow the confusing Routier case almost anywhere, and there was a distinct smell in the air that this trial would not be held in Dallas.

The first thing the judge wanted to do was get a handle on the publicity before headlines and broadcasts drove the whole thing into the same sinkhole of sensation that had turned the O.J. Simpson trial into a televised legal circus. There would be no TV cameras in his courtroom. The link with the Susan Smith double murder was too much for the media to ignore, and already the story had demonstrated an astonishing ability to mushroom. Not only the local media, but *The New York Times* and the *National Enquirer* both had run stories, and it continued bubbling onto national television. The audience was massive and could easily include potential jurors. In news parlance, that showed the Routier story had "legs" and demanded coverage. Tolle didn't know that the story was fading fast on the scope of the out-of-town media.

In reading the material that was being published, lis-

tening and watching various broadcasts, one could determine the reports were merely variations on a theme. The
police and the prosecutors, after their initial burst of
pride, were adding few new facts to what had been
known almost from the start.

Tolle decided to put a cork in the information bottle.
Without sources, the media would be hard-pressed to
continue spinning the story of Darlie Routier. On June
28, only three weeks after the murders and the same day
that Darlie was indicted by the grand jury, Tolle imposed
a comprehensive "gag order" on the case. The exhaustive dictate, six pages long, cited the extensive pretrial
publicity, and claimed the expansion of such knowledge
might prevent Darlie from receiving a fair trial.

The judge ruled that Darlie, any lawyer on the case,
the cops, all witnesses and "prospective" witnesses were
henceforth barred from talking to the media. Including
all "prospective" witnesses in the order was a sweeping
move that made everybody think twice before talking to
reporters. What did "prospective" mean? Anybody—
neighbors, friends, passersby—who had ever had any
dealing whatsoever with the Routier family was now on
warning. To show he meant business and to put some
teeth in his ruling, Tolle said violators could be fined up
to $500 and put in jail for up to six months. The order
immediately dampened the already slackening media
coverage.

One person who was happy to see the case go into public
limbo was Sergeant Poos, who had been the public information officer during the tense weeks leading up to
the arrest. He now handed over all public disclosure to
the District Attorney's office, which planned to say little.
After a while, his telephone stopped ringing.

The press naturally opposed the gag order, with many
journalists feeling that the judge overreacted. "It wasn't

like the D.A.'s office was faxing us secret documents,'' said one reporter. ''There had been no significant amount of leaks.''

The impact was immediate, and, after one hearing, Darin dodged reporters' questions with a terse, ''I didn't get no Get Out of Jail Free card.''

Before the case was done, however, the gag order and its severe penalties would be sharply tested and found to be hardly worth the paper on which it was written.

As Darlie languished behind bars, with the story failing to stir the nation as had the Susan Smith episode, the media turned away from the Routier saga and toward more current stories. The family decided to take a page from the police and prosecutors' actions and give the story a spin of their own.

In late July, Darlie Kee, the defendant's mother, learned she was being sought by a court officer who wanted to serve her a subpoena to keep quiet. Kee had been very active, even writing the governor and the attorney general to urge them to get involved in forcing police to hunt for the ''real'' killer, whom she contended was still walking around free. Before the legal papers could be served, Mama Darlie made a dramatic attempt to get her comments to the media, and in doing so, opened a direct challenge to Tolle's gag order.

She telephoned the *Fort Worth Star-Telegram* and other newspapers, and arranged several radio and television interviews, to declare that her daughter was innocent. The crowning moment, however, was a ninety-minute appearance with Darin on the Rick Roberts talk show on KRLD radio. Interviews with newspaper reporters were dry and objective, devoid of the passion that Kee and Darin were able to bring to the live radio audience, and the Dallas listening audience was captivated.

For an hour and a half, they presented their alternative version of the situation, declaring repeatedly that Darlie was innocent of any wrongdoing. Kee challenged the police statement that the wounds received by her daughter were superficial, attacked the results of lab tests, and claimed the Rowlett police had lied about facts to trick Darlie into giving them a written statement. Local news reports, Kee said, had been biased and sensational. Ironically, she praised the gag order issued by Tolle and said she wished he had done it sooner. It was a devastating broadside against the prosecution. Perfect radio material, because the prosecution team did not have to be given equal time.

That did not mean the other side wasn't aware of the show. "We were just sitting back here listening to the radio and thinking, 'My God, what are these people doing?'" observed a startled Sergeant Dean Poos, back at the Rowlett Police Department.

Chief Randall Posey issued a statement of his own. "Although I am outraged that the Routiers would so directly violate Judge Tolle's court order, the Rowlett Police Department will continue to obey the spirit and effect of the gag order," he said. "As we have said from the beginning, the Rowlett Police Department will not discuss the details of this case with anyone. We feel confident in our case and that the evidence will come out in the proper place, which is in court." Of course, by making that comment, he also may have violated the gag order by claiming that police believed their case was solid.

Assistant District Attorney Greg Davis filed papers to haul Darin and Darlie Kee before Judge Tolle for a hearing on the way they ignored the gag rule. Tolle was on vacation at the time, so nothing was done on the spur of the moment. It was just as well that there was a delay, because now it was a policeman's turn to break the order, and the judge could deal with both transgressions at the same time. On September 11, Assistant Chief Deputy Bob Knowles of the Dallas County Sheriff's Office told the *Dallas Morning News* that Darlie "seems to be getting alone fine" in jail and had shown little grief about her situation. That comment about her perceived reactions was a spin for the prosecution.

Knowles was ordered to appear before Tolle on the same day that Darin and Darlie Kee were to face the music, and the judge was in a quandary. He couldn't lash Darin and Darlie without giving equal punishment to Deputy Knowles, and possibly criticize Chief Posey also. So on September 21, he just gave everybody a verbal slap on their wrists and told them not to do it again. Don't slip up again, he warned them. Everyone agreed.

Darin later grinned when he discussed the impact of both the gag order and the judge's warning. "Any information I want to get out, I get out," he said.

That was only for show. In fact, Darin had been walking a thin line, wavering between keeping things together and just deciding to let it all go right to hell. He broke dishes, he walked the floor and cried, he went out to a firing range and shot up paper targets, which, in his imagination, had very specific faces. Some afternoons, he would make up some sandwiches and a jug of coffee, and drive past the house on Eagle Drive. It was little more than a shell now, heavily damaged by the police investigation. He planned to just let the bank take it over. Darin knew he could never live in that place again, not without Darlie. Then he would park at the Diamond Shamrock service station on Dalrock Road, near the entrance to his old neighborhood, switch off the engine, slide down in the seat, and pull out a set of binoculars. Then he would watch the area for hours on end, hoping

to see that mysterious black car that had been reported
around his house the days before his children were killed.
The police hadn't been able to find the mystery car.
Maybe he could.

16

RAISING MONEY WAS a priority for Darin Routier and his extended family. He still had the everyday routine costs of a mortgage, groceries, and utilities, but now he was also trying to round up the cash to bail Darlie out of jail, where she had a million-dollar price tag placed on her freedom. He had stated earlier: "My whole life is for sale. My business, my home, my personal belongings. It will take everything I own to prove her innocence." No matter what he did, he would not be able to come up with a million dollars. In the District Attorney's Office, a bit of worry gnawed at the prosecutors. Darin was known as a resourceful young man. *What if he could pull the money together?* They decided to do nothing at the moment other than make sure the million-dollar barrier was not lowered.

The defense lawyers had an idea. Only a week after the evidentiary hearing, court was in session again to hear arguments for a reduction in bail. In exchange for a chance to lower the bond, Darin had to endure the embarrassment of making his finances public. In doing so, cracks appeared in the facade of the tightly knit Routier household. The big house, the Jaguar, the yacht, the prospering electronics company, the fancy clothes were precariously balanced on a steep slope of debt. That was okay while Darin had money flowing in from customers, enough to keep the bills paid, but now events had overtaken him and the creditors were calling for cash.

Darlie's lawyers filed papers claiming that the million-dollar bail was excessive and should be reduced to only $100,000. At that figure, the defendant would only have to post 10 percent—just $10,000—with the court in order to be set free pending trial. A million might be out of the question, but $10,000 was a realistic figure. If the judge would agree.

Darin went to court armed with all of his financial records, papers that detailed the delicate structure of his outward success. His debt load was substantial. Darin estimated it at close to $200,000!

He told the court he earned a taxable income of $54,000 in 1995, up from $35,000 the year before, and about half of what had been commonly thought he made. The money sounded like a reasonable figure to support a modest suburban lifestyle for a year, but the tastes of Darlie and Darin were not modest, and as a result, the outflow of money was approaching flood proportion. Police were speculating that arguments of financial difficulties may have had a role in the crime, that money may have been part of the motive.

The debt included two mortgages on the house on Eagle Drive, totaling about $130,000. Darin estimated that if he could sell the place, he would take a loss, since the market value was only about $100,000.

They were in hock to the IRS for about $10,000 in overdue back taxes. Credit cards added another $12,000 to the debt. He owed $24,000 on the boat.

When asked about his company, Darin responded that Testnec Electronics grossed about $260,000 the previous year and had been on approximately the same pace for the current year, until the murder of his sons. After that, he had been unable to work, and the income was impacted. "I haven't been able to make any money," he said.

He promised Judge Tolle that if Darlie could be turned loose on bail, he would watch her like a hawk, and there was no reason to fear that she would run away to avoid her trial. "I believe in Darlie. She has never lied to me." It made no difference. Tolle said the bail would remain at one million dollars and Darlie would remain in jail.

That 10 percent figure the family had been betting on was now back at $100,000. It still loomed as an impossible plateau, a financial Mount Everest that couldn't possibly be climbed. Mama Darlie went home, emotionally crushed, and broke down crying, throwing pillows and screaming, "I want to be with Devon and Damon! Where they are is better than this!"

Overlapping the bail reduction hearing was another one in the same building on the status of little Drake Routier. The question was whether the child, who had been in foster care since his mother was arrested, should be returned to the care of his father. Darin and Darlie had seen the child twice, under close supervision, since June 19.

The pattern was set even before the hearing began, with the Child Protective Services filing an affidavit stating that Darin had placed himself in a precarious position. "He has said he intends to stay with and support his wife," it read. "It is believed he would be unable to protect his last surviving son, Drake Routier, and that, therefore, Drake would be in considerable danger of physical abuse or death if he were allowed to remain in his father's care."

With the official attitude of keeping the child out of harm's way, no matter what, there was little chance that Darin would be rocking his remaining boy, Drake, to sleep anytime soon. This hearing was more to determine who, besides the natural parents, would be looking after the child.

Of particular interest was the CPS concern that perhaps the boy had already suffered some abuse. Court papers raised the question of a recent black eye the baby suffered, a mild injury Darin said was sustained when Drake accidentally fell and struck his head on a coffee table.

The most damning testimony in the custody battle came from Jamie Johnson of CPS, who had interviewed the neighbors, friends, and family members, including Darlie. Johnson revealed details of her jailhouse talk with the defendant.

"She was under stress," said the caseworker. "She said that she was still recovering from a depression she suffered after the birth of Drake. She was slightly depressed and stressed with taking care of three boys." Darlie had told Johnson that the dual pressures of money problems and raising three small children had driven her at one point to consider taking an overdose of pills.

One day, Darin had come home unexpectedly and found her writing a suicide note, said the caseworker. "Darlie had called him at work . . . and sounded very depressed. She was talking about how much there was to do at the house and she couldn't keep up. He said, ' I'll see you later ' and she said something that made him worry. Like, 'Well, yeah, maybe you'll see me later,' and he came home."

Detective Jimmy Patterson, whose uncertain testimony at the preliminary hearing had worried prosecutors, went on the stand again, and testified about entries in the diary which also contained suicidal thoughts. He spoke particularly about one in which Darlie expressed what the policeman said was a need to be forgiven for something she was going to do. Darlie, at the defense table, shook her head in disbelief and mouthed a silent word at the detective: Liar.

The most awkward part of the hearing was the appearance on the witness stand of Darlie. She faced an impossible choice. She and her lawyers had learned a lesson through her open discussion with the CPS caseworker. Once said, words could not be retracted. It was long past time for Darlie to shut up.

Therefore, she could not answer many of the questions that might have influenced what would happen with Drake. To speak might open more evidentiary doors for the investigators. Her attorneys protested that she should not have to testify at all, but the court demanded that she take the stand.

Before being questioned, she carefully unfolded a piece of paper that had been given her by her lawyers, and read in a small voice: "I invoke my constitutional right against self-incrimination."

"Do you love your son?" A blistering, no-win question.

Darlie, her eyes tearing, gulped and looked at the paper. "I invoke my constitutional right against self-incrimination." A dozen times, she would plead that Fifth Amendment right to silence.

CPS was adamant in how it viewed the husband's intractable position. "Darin Routier must be able to recognize that his wife could be responsible for murdering her sons and that, therefore, she will not be able to care for or see their surviving child," said a report submitted by caseworker Johnson. "To be a responsible parent, he must choose his son's protection over his wife's defense."

It was a decision that someone with the wisdom of King Solomon would have had trouble making, and Darin, who was close to an emotional meltdown over the crushing events of the past month, could not find a way through the bureaucratic maze. Defending his wife meant losing his son. To keep custody of Drake meant he had to abandon his belief in Darlie's innocence, and he would not do that.

Finally, a deal was struck between the CPS; Drake's own court-assigned lawyer, David Cole; Lubbock attorney Banetta Johnson, who represented the paternal grandparents; and the court. Drake was placed in the temporary custody of his paternal grandparents, although Sarilda and Leonard Routier both believed Darlie to be innocent. They would supervise their son's visits to see his own little boy, and Darlie was barred from contact. The Child Protective Services office in Lubbock would oversee the placement, and a trained and certified child advocate would keep close watch on Drake's situation.

Sarilda told Judge Shannon she would abide by the strict guidelines, but not necessarily because she was ordered to do so by the court. "I have already lost two grandbabies, and I have no intention of losing another one," she said.

On July 4, Independence Day, little Drake Routier was taken to Lubbock, in the care of his grandparents.

17

HUFF AND PARKS decided to make a dramatic move, perhaps the most important of the entire case, and in the middle of July filed a motion to change the site of Darlie's trial. Dallas County had been so saturated by publicity that a fair hearing of the charges against her "is rendered either impossible or highly unlikely." Tolle scheduled a hearing in September, at which time he would weigh the arguments.

Prosecutors, too, filed a motion about the same time, seeking to add the death penalty to the case against Darlie Routier. Even in Texas, calling for a death sentence is difficult except in certain types of cases that are specifically spelled out, such as the death of a police officer or firefighter, a murder committed during a felony, or multiple murders. The legislature, however, had only recently tagged another clause to that list: the death penalty could be sought when the victim is a child under the age of six. The prosecutors were planning to split the charges against Darlie and go after her first on the capital murder charge involving five-year-old Damon. If they lost, they could always retry Darlie for the death of Devon. Tolle added that motion to the growing list of motions that he would decide in September.

*   *   *

Before that major preliminary hearing, however, the prosecutors went back into court in August for a special hearing. The defense had filed for another bail reduction, and the prosecution was worried about reports that Darin had been successful gathering funds, particularly after he told a reporter that he had a cashier's check for $100,000 in his pocket. Now that the District Attorney had announced the death penalty would be sought, the state had the necessary tool that could keep Darlie behind bars until her trial began in several more months. In a two-day hearing, they fought for a motion to do away with bail for her entirely!

Greg Davis, however, had to put some more evidentiary cards on the table to convince the court to keep Darlie in jail, no matter what. His major point was playing the tape of the graveyard gathering, and he said, "What you've got is an individual who has shown no remorse. That video is a grotesque scene in which, five days after she butchered her children, she was able to laugh and joke with the news media." That was an important point, for he had used only the truncated and edited news version of the Joe Munoz tape, and not the fuller version that police had recorded with their hidden camera, the one which also showed the somber blessing that preceded the party.

Jimmy Patterson was again on the stand, because of his role as lead investigator, and rattled off the list of topics on which police felt Darlie had been inconsistent. Patterson gave a better account of himself this time, but defense lawyer Wayne Huff pushed the detective to explain that her statements to him in the hospital had been made shortly after her surgery, when she was under the influence of drugs.

The prosecutor did open up more of their case, however, when Davis put Charles Linch on the stand. Linch, a trace evidence analyst from the Southwestern Institute of Forensic Science, known as SWIFS, introduced some of the forensic material that had been gathered, which included traces of fiberglass and rubber on the blade of a knife police found in a kitchen rack, material that could have come from the screen allegedly sliced by the man Darlie claimed attacked her. Linch also said the blood evidence at the scene did not square with the mother's version of events, including evidence of blood being wiped from the kitchen counter and blood being washed down the sink.

Still struggling awkwardly to come up with a possible motive, Davis floated a few balloons. He confronted Darin Routier as a witness, probing the idea that he and Darlie fought on the night of the murders. Darin disputed that coldly, saying that a conversation is not an argument. The prosecutor suggested perhaps there might have been an affair with Darlie's kid sister, Dana, and Darin refuted that, also. A third part of the fishing expedition searching for a motive came with Davis indicating that perhaps Darlie's wounds did not include her breasts because she did not want to mar the implants of the 1992 operation.

The defense team played the 911 emergency tape and Darlie's voice rang loudly in the courtroom, her hysteria evident. Both she and Darin sobbed into their fists as the cries of panic reverberated from the machine. The defense did not present any witnesses of their own.

The decision once again went against Darlie when the court ruled in favor of the prosecution. Bail was no longer an option.

That left Darin with about $100,000 and a decision.

The Routiers had become somewhat disenchanted with the performance of the public defenders, who seemed to lose every round. A pedestrian job, they felt, wasn't going to be good enough to save Darlie, particularly now that her life would be at stake in the coming trial. They dispatched a close friend on an errand around the Dallas County Court House, and he asked twenty-five police-men, lawyers, and judges, "Who would you hire to de-fend you if you were in Darlie Routier's shoes." The answer was unanimous—"I'd hire Doug Mulder."

From that moment, Wayne Huff and Doug Parks were on borrowed time. "Save your money," Huff advised the family. "You don't need him." For the time being, Mulder came aboard as a consultant to Mama Darlie, not as the attorney of record for Darlie Routier. While the family was deciding whether to hire the private attorney, the public defenders had one last major piece of business before the court—the change-of-venue request.

The mystery of whether the trial would be held in Dallas was solved on Thursday, September 12. By nine o'clock in the morning, a crowd that had grown to know each other by sight assembled once again in the gray marble corridor of the right wing on the sixth floor of the Dallas courts building. Some wandered to the far end and stared out the wide window that overlooks a blacktop lot where a Justice Center patron could park all day for two dollars. To the right was the massive buff building that was the jail, Darlie's home since she was arrested. In the near distance, unheard cars hurried along the I-35E freeway, and, beyond that, fields of green settled into a bland and flat horizon.

Things were more than chilly between the media and the Routier family, which felt the press was no longer being fair. Tolle's six-page gag order was tacked to the courtroom door, and it not only forbade cameras and re-cording equipment, it prevented reporters from conduct-ing interviews in the hallway. That created a no-man's land that kept reporters and cameras on one side of the glass doorway at the end of the hall, and Darin Routier, his family and supporters on the other side, just outside the court.

Only when the preliminary hearing was about to start did the two throngs mix, but they weren't on speaking terms as they all filed into the small courtroom in which Tolle presided from his tall bench in one corner, flanked by clerks, marshals, and the flags of the United States and Texas. Fluorescent lights bathed the room in bright gray light, making the pale wood trim and benches shine with a false glow.

The case had become increasingly complicated in the past few weeks, but Tolle had already made his rulings on the mountain of motions submitted by the opposing parties. A man who acted quickly and firmly, he intended for the day's proceedings not to take up a lot of time. Darlie came into the court almost unseen among the taller lawyers and marshals. She glanced around, saw Darin fifteen feet away, and gave a wan smile. The paleness of jail was fully upon her, and the white jumpsuit now clashed with the cap of darkening brown roots of her normally blonde hair.

Tolle, who liked a tight ship, opened court right on time. First, the bilingual judge announced in fluent Spanish as well as English that other scheduled cases would be dealt with only after the Routier matter. Then he read in a near monotone the list of decisions he had made on the various motions. He did not explain each in detail, for there were so many, leaving that work to the lawyers who had filed them. The judge just read them out by number—Roman numerals I through XIV and ordinary figures 1 through 37-E—and disclosed whether he granted or denied them. Most of it was boilerplate legal action, such as the defense asking that the Texas death penalty statute be overturned, and the decisions came about as expected.

The centerpiece was the change-of-venue request, and

Tolle announced that he would grant that motion, but held back formally announcing the place. He left it for the time being as "any county in Texas" other than Dallas.

After having made his decision, the judge had been working hard to find an empty courtroom somewhere in Texas that he could borrow for a month or so. Apparently the criminal and civil calendars were extraordinarily busy throughout the second largest state in the union, and the hunt was narrowed to three counties—Kerr, Bexar, and Harris. Scheduling problems weighed against Bexar and Harris.

Already media representatives, lawyers, and the Routier clan had begun to call around, looking for potential lodging in Kerrville, and the court clerk in the small town west of San Antonio acknowledged that plans were being laid for rounding up a jury. Still, it remained unofficial and Tolle gave away nothing.

Prosecutors did not choose to argue against his ruling. Why should they? The case had just landed in one of the most politically and socially conservative areas in all of Texas. The last three capital murder crimes tried in Kerr County had all ended with solid convictions and death penalties. Greg Davis slept well that night.

18

FINALLY, WITH SOME cash available, Darin no longer
had to depend upon the taxpayers to furnish a legal team
to defend his wife. To penetrate the web of evidence
being built to ensnare her, Routier wanted a Texas-sized
champion, a legal gunslinger who could light up a courtroom simply by walking through the door. When he
found his man, there was no hesitation writing out the
retainer check. In October 1996, Doug Mulder accepted
the case and things started to change immediately. "He
knows she is innocent, and he knows he can prove it,"
family members said.

Mention Mulder's name in Dallas legal circles and you
get smiles, either of embarrassment or envy. There's no
middle ground where this big-time lawyer with the gray-
ing hair is concerned. Other attorneys either love him or
hate him, but none deny his effectiveness. He loved handling the Big Case, and since he had tackled enough of
them to become very rich, even by Dallas standards, he
could afford, now and then, to do one that was of interest
to him. The challenge of extricating Darlie Routier from
a trap of seemingly insurmountable, although circumstantial, evidence brought his star into her orbit—that and

the headlines the case was getting. If nothing else, Doug Mulder would receive an immense amount of free publicity, for although the trial was now going to be in far-away Kerrville, the Dallas media would provide saturation coverage. A win would be another notch in the belt. A loss wouldn't hurt.

An Iowa boy, Mulder was still in law school at Southern Methodist University when he wrote a letter to the District Attorney of Dallas County in 1964, asking for a job. Of course, Mulder wasn't the only law student looking to land a job in the prestigious office of District Attorney Henry Wade, and the D.A. certainly wasn't impressed with the applicant's transcript, which showed grades that were only slightly above average. A personal interview changed his mind and Wade hired the young man to join a staff that was large but still overworked.

Doug Mulder, who had never tried a case in his life, started work for the man who convicted Jack Ruby of shooting Lee Harvey Oswald, the assassin of President Kennedy. He had yet to write his first appeals brief, but was in the office that made history as the defendant in the landmark *Roe* v. *Wade* abortion case. The "Wade" in that matter was Henry Wade. Mulder might only be a lowly prosecutor in the misdemeanor court division, but just the fact that he was working for Wade gave him early status.

Like an actor landing a first theater role in summer stock, he knew from the moment he set foot before a judge that the courtroom was to be his real home. Unfortunately, Mulder lost his first case, then won his next two trials and went on to establish the best record of convictions Dallas County had ever seen. By the time he was thirty years old, Mulder was Wade's chief assistant and running the office.

Defense lawyers hated to meet up with Mulder as the prosecutor in one of their cases, because he was always

precisely prepared, surgical in cross-examination and
downright seductive with a jury. Fellow prosecutors likewise grew to dislike the way the hard-headed young man
ran the District Attorney's Office. To many in both
groups, he was known, behind his back, as "Mad Dog."

So Mulder didn't receive much sympathy when a big
case finally detonated in his face. As usual, he had won
a murder conviction, this time against Randall Dale Adams, accused of the shooting death of a Dallas police
officer in 1976. The jury sentenced Adams to the electric
chair. The result meant that Mulder, who had let another
prosecutor pick the jury this time, had won all twenty-
four of the death-penalty cases he had tried.

Three years later, the Supreme Court of the United
States said the jury selection process in the Adams case
was flawed, and, in a rare instance, overturned the death
penalty. The governor of Texas then reduced Adams's
sentence to life in prison, which would dodge the neces-
sity of a new murder trial.

A movie producer researching a project later exposed
potential errors in the prosecution of the case, and the
Texas Court of Criminal Appeals, a dozen years after the
first trial, reversed the guilty verdict. Adams was not tried
again. The court of appeals also cited Mulder's work in
the case, claiming evidence was suppressed and witnesses
were allowed to perjure themselves. Mulder has denied
the claims and even today maintains he could try that
case again and Adams would still be found guilty. But
the Adams case stained Mulder's formidable reputation.

Sixteen years in the stable of the district attorney was
enough as far as Doug Mulder was concerned, and when
Henry Wade retired, Mulder jumped at the chance to
switch sides of the courtroom in 1980, when a man accused of murder said he would pay Mulder $100,000 to
defend him. Mulder was only making $65,000 a year at
the time, but cultivating expensive tastes, and he decided

to take the money and the case, which never went to trial, despite his fat paycheck.

Flamboyant lawyers are almost synonymous with Texas, and a new one, Mulder, was stepping forward. In the coming years, his prowess as a defense lawyer would grow rapidly, and people accused of capital crimes would count themselves lucky to obtain Mulder as their lawyer. He seemed to find magic in the dirt of felonies. Just because someone may have signed a confession, or had an anvil of evidence hanging over his or her head, didn't mean they would go to prison—not if Doug Mulder was at the defense table. People opened their checkbooks wide to gain his services.

He made the jump to superstar Texas lawyer with the case of Walker Railey, a Methodist minister accused of trying to murder his wife to cover up an affair with the daughter of his former bishop. The wife had been assaulted so brutally that she fell into a coma from which she emerged with permanent brain damage. With Mulder as his legal advisor, the first grand jury to hear the case didn't even indict Railey. A second one did, and the case went to trial. Mulder won and Railey was acquitted. Some jurors would later say they believed the preacher was guilty, but were convinced by Mulder that the prosecutors had not proven their case.

There were two cases that were relevant to the one he was about to undertake with Darlie Routier, one good and one bad.

Mulder didn't win them all. Only two years earlier, Mulder was the defense lawyer for Joy Davis Aylor, who was convicted on a charge of paying someone to kill her husband's girlfriend. With that conviction, Aylor became the sixth woman on death row in Texas. Oddly, Mulder was not in the courtroom when the verdict was read. He said he was working elsewhere when the verdict was returned and aides failed to get him in time.

The other case took place in 1982, when Mulder was hired to defend two men accused of a triple murder near the town of Brady. This was to be a big win for Mulder, and the Routier team could take some comfort from it. For one thing, the trial was held in Kerr County, and a Kerrville jury reached the verdict that set the accused men free. An even more significant point was that Mulder, in Dallas, had a cocounsel in that case, a low-key Hill Country lawyer named Richard Mosty.

When Mulder took the Darlie Routier case, which was set to be tried in Kerrville, he immediately hired Mosty to work with him again. Mosty had practiced law in the area for more than two decades, and served on both sides of the courtroom, both as defense attorney and as Kerr County prosecutor. As a result, his name was widely known in the area, and his reputation respected.

The two men were a study in contrasts, Mulder the flamboyant, dominating character, while Mosty, forty-six, could almost smother a jury with an aw-shucks friendliness while skewering a hostile witness. Both worked extraordinarily long hours and, as former prosecutors themselves, knew how to attack a state case to maximum effect. They would lead a team that would include several other lawyers and investigators. Darlie Routier's chances of beating the charges took a big step forward with Mulder and Mosty in her corner.

Assistant District Attorney Greg Davis, leading the defense, is no punching bag for ambitious defense lawyers. Just as Mulder before him, Davis had worked his way into being the best trial lawyer in the stable of the Dallas County District Attorney's Office, and had sent his share of capital murder defendants to death row to await their execution through lethal injection. In fact, on the wall of Davis's office is a drawing of a hypodermic syringe.

He is the epitome of the responsible lawyer, soft-spoken and efficient, although somewhat aloof and distant. But there is no doubt that he is effective. For Greg Davis, a tall, forty-five-year-old lawyer, the Routier case would be the capstone of his career thus far.

Davis' preparation was as meticulous as ever, perhaps even more so because he knew the Routier defense would be tough. He kept photos of Devon and Damon posted around his office to remind him constantly of why he and his staff were compiling those big black notebooks, the diagrams and charts, the boxes of evidence, even building a life-sized model of the window through which Darlie claimed the intruder escaped.

A chief prosecutor for two years, Davis had a knack for finding the weak point of a defendant's case, as demonstrated when he shot down a false confession by one man in order to link Juan Rodriguez Chavez to the killings of twelve people. Chavez is now on death row.

The situation with Darlie Routier would depend upon Davis' ability to explain to the jury complicated technical testimony about blood spatters and DNA without either losing their interest or talking down to them. His directness and clean-cut demeanor would go far in Kerrville, along with his ability to point repeatedly at Darlie and tell the jury members that the little blonde woman sitting over there, looking so weak and innocent, was a cold-blooded killer of her own children.

For professional court watchers, it was a dream match. Had the trial been held in Dallas, the audience probably would have been made up of lawyers drawn to watch this contest, not so much to see what happened to Darlie, but to watch Mulder and Davis.

But it wasn't being held in Dallas. It was in Kerrville, and Davis didn't like that at all.

19

KERRVILLE, IN THE quaint hill country of west Texas, is less than seventy miles west of San Antonio, sandwiched between Interstate 10 and a shoulder of the Guadalupe River. However, it is about an entire planet away from Dallas, and its beginnings could not be more humble. Joshua Brown, an industrious fellow, established a small business there in the 1840s, using hand tools to hack shingles from the tangles of squat cedar trees that thrive in the area. He donated four acres of land for a town square, and that became the heart of the new town named to honor Major James Kerr, one of Brown's friends who had helped Texas win independence from Mexico. Whether Kerr ever visited Kerrville is not known.

One of the first industries to arrive was the United States Army, which established nearby Camp Verde, imported men and some strange beasts from Egypt, then set about determining if it should use the camels to traverse the deserts of the West. The experiment ended abruptly with the start of the Civil War. A more traditional animal came along after the war when ranchers brought giant herds of cattle down Water Street en route to the Chisholm Trail and markets further north. But it would be neither camels nor longhorns that put Kerrville on the road to success.

As realtors are fond of saying, location is everything. In the 1920s, word spread that the tiny town on the Guadalupe was the ''healthiest spot in the nation,'' and a stampede of visitors was on. Perched at 1,654 feet above sea level in rolling scrub hills, Kerrville is high enough to shed the most scorching temperatures that plague the Texas summer, but low enough so that a normal winter is on the moderate side. The average annual rainfall of 31.5 inches keeps it relatively green, and the average temperature swings from 47 degrees in January to 81 in July.

Visitors thronged to the area and, as the Chamber of Commerce now proudly states, ''the campers of yesteryear became the residents of today.'' It also became a retirement haven, which spawned its major industry, health care. There are three major hospitals and a sprawl of supporting medical companies in Kerrville, as well as 74 churches for a population of 18,187, which represents about half the total number of people in Kerr County. The Texas Heritage Music Festival is an annual event, stemming from Kerrville's most famous resident, country music's Jimmie Rodgers, who once lived at 617 West Main. The ''Blue Yodeler'' is enshrined in the halls of fame of country, blues, and rock and roll. Beautiful sprawling ranches are hidden beyond the city limits, owned by people with money and fame who are able to set aside their regular jobs in Dallas and Houston and San Antonio and fly their private planes into Kerrville, where they doff their city clothes, put on boots and jeans, and transform themselves.

In 1996, some 1,046,744 visitors pumped $106,558,179 worth of economic activity into the area. For 1997, the first major influx of visitors would come not for January's World Mohair Extravaganza, nor for the Texas Sheepdog Demonstrations, but for the double-murder trial of Darlie Routier.

Despite his earlier victory in Kerrville, Doug Mulder wanted no part of the place for his newest client. The wisdom of changing the venue from Dallas had backfired, and there was little doubt that a conservative, church-going, all-white hill country jury would be a harder sell in a case involving the death of children than would a racially mixed jury from a metropolitan area, before whom the defense lawyers could attack the way police did their jobs. A cowboy's wife with rock-hard Republican political beliefs would not be as sympathetic a juror as a low-income Hispanic mother with five kids who had problems with law enforcement.

As soon as he officially replaced the public defenders, Mulder asked Judge Tolle to move the trial back to Dallas, where it had started. He said the reasons for asking Tolle to change the venue in the first place—mainly the press coverage—had not turned out to be as bad as first thought. Indeed, the lawyer insisted, the media had presented balanced reports of the case, favoring neither side. And, Mulder argued, returning the trial to Dallas would mean that everybody involved wouldn't be put to the trouble of having to travel all the way down to Kerrville, thus saving the taxpayers of Dallas County an estimated half-million dollars. "It can be tried here, and it should be tried here. I see no reason to waste the taxpayers' money when we can get a fair trial here," Mulder declared, adding that Darlie herself now wanted to be tried in Dallas.

The judge could barely conceal his disdain. This flew directly in the face of the staunch arguments that had been made by the previous defense team only a month earlier. No, Tolle decided without hesitation. Motion denied. The trial would stay in Kerrville.

The tactic failed, but put the court on notice that Mulder was not going to be as passive in his defense as the public defenders. More than one observer said Tolle was going to have to run a strong court to keep Mulder from taking over.

Jury selection began late in October of 1996, four-and-one-half months after the deaths of the Routier children. About one hundred and eighty citizens, all residents of Kerr County, were to be winnowed down to the needed twelve plus alternates. They were ordinary folk, spurring one Routier relative to tell a reporter, "They all look like nice people. That's what we're looking for, just good home folks who can think and who know injustice when they see it."

Each prospective juror first had to fill out a questionnaire of thirteen pages, which were examined in detail as the lawyers searched for clues to personalities and feelings. For the prosecution, the jury selection work is vital, particularly in a death penalty case. The state would need total agreement on a guilty verdict, while the defense only needed to have a single juror hold out in order to get a mistrial. A juror who somehow gets on the panel but does not believe in the death penalty could jeopardize the entire case.

It was a lengthy process, consuming weeks of court time, and Tolle was very conscious of the calendar. By the time the jury selection was done, the case was well into November, which meant it would be useless to start such a trial with the long Thanksgiving, Christmas, and New Year holidays just over the horizon. So the jurors were chosen, then told to go home and wait. After being picked to hear one of the most publicized cases in Texas, they were being instructed to spend the next two months not thinking about it.

The jury was, in theory, unreadable, but one person

who helps lawyers analyze such groups felt it was an open book. He summarized that the Kerrville jury mirrored the area's very conservative moral beliefs. "You have seven guys wearing cowboy boots and they hate son-killers. Then you have five women, who hate baby-killers. She's done!" was his observation. Under such a scenario, the defense team was going to have to prove Darlie was innocent instead of having the state prove beyond a reasonable doubt that she was guilty.

Darlie would be tried for the murders of her boys in January 1997. Meanwhile, the judge gave permission for a hairdresser to attend to the prisoner in jail, because the once-blonde Darlie now had two-tone hair that had grown out during her incarceration, with a wide dark stripe in the middle and lighter at the ends. Her new lawyers insisted that if a jury saw her in that condition, it would remind them that she had been in prison. Mousy hair would be as prejudicial in the jurors' eyes as hauling her into court in handcuffs. The defense wanted her to look like a Sunday School teacher. Fine, ruled the exasperated judge, she can have a hairdresser. That was just one of Mulder's subtle touches, and he also took over the dressing of Darin. Gone were the gold nugget rings, replaced by a single gold wedding band. Gone was the neat beard, for this was still a place where long hair on men wasn't really accepted. Small things, but important. Throughout the trial, the opposing sides would work on the jury's commonsense, God-given abilities, with the prosecutors attacking the mere appearance of things and the defense portraying a humble mom framed by bumbling police.

The week the jury of seven women and five men was chosen, the national television show *Day & Date* broadcast a skewed version of the Routier saga, clearly tilted toward the angle that the imprisoned Darlie was innocent. In recent years, it has become popular among savvy sup-

porters of people charged with crimes to use such info-
tainment shows to push their point of view. After all,
these shows are about entertainment, not news.

It was all Texas that day on *Day & Date*, with perky
hostess Dana King sitting in front of the famed South
Fork ranch house and telling how today, the show would
talk about the resurrection of the popular *Dallas* television show, fourteen-year-old singer LeAnn Rimes, who
was becoming nationally popular, and an entrepreneur
who gave limousine tours along the route that President
Kennedy was killed. They would also report about the
controversial murder case involving Darlie Routier, and
the segment led the technopop show.

It began with the usual pictures of the house, the boys,
and Darin and Darlie, with a man's deep voice reciting
the usual elements of the case. It became obvious the *Day
& Date* cameras had been allowed inside the house to
photograph the interior as the voice-over reported the
events up to the burial. There was a brief shot of the
cemetery, but then the scene shifted to police headquarters and Sergeant Poos once again making the official
statement from way back in June.

For anyone familiar with the case, the show was a
shocker. Television is a visual medium, and the Routier
case contained one of the most jolting pieces of videotape
ever to hit the airwaves. Texas viewers knew what had
happened at the cemetery, where Darlie appeared to be
having a terrific time celebrating the birthday of one of
her dead boys, merrily shooting Silly String and giggling.
But *Day & Date* did not use that extraordinary footage!

Instead, the show jumped to interviews with friends
and relatives, all of whom said Darlie was innocent and
could not have possibly committed the heinous crime.
"Why, why, why would you arrest this young woman
who did nothing except wake up and find her children
murdered and her throat slashed?" asked Sandi Aiken,

Darlie's aunt. Neighbor Terry Neal echoed that, saying Darlie loved the boys so much she wouldn't even spank them. Darlie's mother-in-law, Sarilda Routier, said it plainly: "All I know is Darlie didn't do it."

To balance that, all the show had was Poos making his original arrest statement, that the stories told by Darlie and the evidence at the scene didn't match. Indeed, Poos' comments were lost when Sandi Aiken read a letter from Darlie in jail, telling how she dreams about the boys, "talking to them and loving them."

"I know what I saw and I don't know why they would want to blame a mother for something like this. The whole world could have been falling down around me at my feet and I would not have touched a hair on their precious heads," Aiken read from one of the letters written in Darlie's bold, neat hand on lined notebook paper.

The show continued in that vein, with Darin condemning the work of overzealous police and Sandi Aiken saying that "none of this has been fair." The reporter said a private investigator hired by the Routier family had turned up important evidence on Darlie's behalf, such as blood spots outside the house and the discovery of unidentified fingerprints on the window through which Darlie said the killer escaped. It was good shock television, but lousy journalism.

Observers close to the case were left wondering what had happened to Tolle's gag order; why the explosive graveyard scene was not in the *Day & Date* report; and whether the show, seen widely, might taint the jurors who had only recently been selected. Nothing happened, and the peculiar television show passed as a blip on the publicity screen.

Darlie was moved to Kerrville from Dallas on the first weekend of the new year of 1997. At the county jail she was strip-searched, given a pail of water and a mop, and ordered to scrub the floor of her new cell. The family gathered in a small condo to save money, reporters on expense accounts found accommodations in the better motels and hotels, the government types congregated at the Holiday Inn, people on their own nickel sought reasonable lodging closer to the interstate highway, and several couples with nothing better to do hauled in mobile homes to camp out for the duration.

Events were troubled in several ways. A bit of calm and sunshine the weekend prior to the trial was giving way quickly to an Arctic cold front sweeping in from the northwest, promising snow and sleet. This would not be one of Kerrville's famed temperate winters. Adding to the sour mood in town was the Dallas Cowboys football team, which spent its Sunday being routed by an upstart expansion team, the Carolina Panthers, and its weekdays embroiled in lawsuits against players.

Kerrville's first courthouse had been made of logs, and renovations have been almost continuous over the past century and a half. Even while the trial was in progress, workmen would be busy renovating a wing on the ground floor. The place has a quaint and spare look, a Texas *Bastille* combining old brick and new block, all done the color of dirt. Television production trucks were stationed in the narrow driveway, their satellite dishes pointed heavenward, ready to speed any news of Darlie Routier to a waiting world. Christmas lights still sprinkled the branches of bare trees and would glow at night during the first week.

The line formed early on Monday as a pair of friendly deputies in cowboy hats, boots, and gunbelts let people go through a metal detector, one at a time, checking for contraband. They weren't looking for guns as much as they wanted to insure that Judge Tolle's order against cameras and tape recorders was honored. Single file through the arched warning device, then up a short flight of stairs to a small, sunwashed square anteroom. The clerk's office was on one side and a few private offices set aside for the court were on the other. A single window allowed light inside the entranceway, and opposite that, double doors with panes of frosted glass opened to the courtroom. High ceiling, portraits of long-ago judges on the walls, rows of fold-down wooden theater chairs guaranteed to break a spine with long use. A low bar with a gate separated the audience from the business area of the court, where tables held the notebooks and tablets of the prosecution and defense teams. The jury box was on the distant side of the narrow room and the judge would command the performance from a high bench at the far end, flanked by flags. Faded fluorescent lighting did little to assist the little bit of sunlight that filtered in through worn venetian blinds that were kept closed. A shelf of lawbooks covered the rear wall and the floor was protected by a threadbare gray carpet that had felt many a bootprint. The heating system didn't work.

Greg Davis was ready to lead the prosecution, backed by Toby Shook and Sherri Wallace. To their right, the defense table would have Darlie surrounded by men in coats and ties, a formidable array of legal talent, with the redoubtable Doug Mulder heading a unit that included Richard Mosty, appeals specialist John Hagler, Preston Douglass, and Curtis Glover. Investigators from both sides added to the crowd before the bar.

It was time to start.

20

MONDAY, JANUARY 6, 1997, was not a good day to start a trial, or do almost anything else. Even Darin's little dog, Domain, had a rough start when a black poodle chased it during its morning walk. The weather in south-central Texas had turned foul, and the overnight temperature didn't rise above the freezing mark, with the forecast predicting a 100 percent chance of rain or sleet. The courtroom itself would play a role in the unfolding trial, for jurors sitting before three big windows of single-thickness glass would need sweaters and heavy socks to get through the day. The courthouse furnace groaned and clanked as it tried to pump heat into the old building, and the noise echoed ominously in the room where Darlie Routier was on trial for her life.

She sat at the defense table, surrounded by her attorneys. Her blonde hair had grown down to her shoulders, but lay lank and without body. She wore a muted red-patterned dress with a fluffy white collar, with a peach scarf tied at her neck to hide the big scar. She was so pale that all of the color in her face seemed to have drained into her blue eyes.

Darin was not in the courthouse, staying away at the instruction of Mulder, but a full family team gathered in a little foyer just outside the courtroom door. Mama Darlie and Sarilda Routier examined everyone who walked in and out.

Judge Tolle got down to business promptly at nine o'clock, hearing some preliminary motions in which the defense complained they had no log or contact sheet that would show the sequence in which police photographs had been taken. The prosecution said they had no such thing. Tolle finally told them to quiet down.

"Gentlemen, cease your bickering," he said, a remark that he would use, in varied forms, many times in coming days as the lawyers continually attacked each other.

The preliminaries done, the judge was ready to bring in the jury, except there was a problem. One of the jurors was missing, and the trial was delayed for a while until the person was found, sitting in the audience. Instead of being sequestered, the juror had watched the opening round that the panel was not supposed to see. All seven women and five men of the jury were reunited, and the trial began at 9:55 A.M., with the opening statement of Greg Davis for the prosecution.

For sixteen minutes, he painted Darlie Routier as a terrible person, "a self-centered woman, a materialistic woman cold enough, in fact, to murder her own children." She had, he said, enjoyed the steady money being earned by her husband, buying designer clothes and leather furniture and a cabin cruiser. But hard times came to the family business in 1996, and Darlie got a bad case of the blues when "the money train was beginning to peter out." Simultaneously, she was depressed after having her third son, felt her natural beauty was eroding, and found she was "no longer the blonde center of attention." The two older boys, Devon and Damon, required more care as they were growing, and she saw "her freedom and buying sprees go away." The money crunch became so bad, Davis claimed, that the young couple had no savings, no retirement plan, had been turned down for a $5,000 loan, and were down to $2,000 in the bank.

On the night of the murders, she intentionally sent Darin up to bed with the baby alone so she could be with the boys downstairs. A short time later, she killed both of her sons with an eight-inch serrated-blade chef's knife, then staged a crime scene. A knife used to slice through the window screen was found by police in a kitchen knife-holder, he said. Greg Davis asked the jury to return a verdict that Darlie was "guilty of the capital murder" of her five-year-old son, Damon.

Richard Mosty did not hurry to start his presentation of the defense's opening statement. The jury knew he was a hometown Kerrville boy, and he intended to play on that relationship, so he meandered softly to the center of the courtroom, a threat to no one at all, and certainly not to the jurors. He was on home turf and instantly personalized the case by referring to the defendant as "Darlie" as he launched his well-practiced thirty-six-minute appeal.

He said the police had put too much emphasis on the early, mixed-up comments of a traumatized mother who had seen "her children being killed in front of her." Instead of being overwhelmed by motherhood, the defense would demonstrate that she "devoted everything to these kids."

Then he attacked the prosecution's prime weakness: the motive. "The state suggests that, in the blink of an eye, this lady changes from a doting mother to a psychotic killer." The evidence would include a bloody sock found some distance from the house, Mosty said, and the state would have the jurors believe that Darlie ran out of the house while her husband was asleep and her babies were dying and planted it 75 yards from the house to be found by police.

"By six o'clock [on the morning of the murders], the Rowlett Police Department had decided Darlie was guilty," he stated. "They never blinked, they never looked back. They focused the crosshairs on Darlie and never took them off of her. That was it."

That would leave many things unexplained, primarily the evidence that strangers and a black car had been seen cruising the area, and an item that remained "a mystery to this day."

Mosty said that since June the police investigation had fallen apart. Things that were claimed earlier had been changed to fit a better picture, he said. Blood evidence "means nothing" because it was improperly interpreted, and the reports of mulch not being disturbed outside the escape window was ridiculous because there was no mulch there. "The state's theory has evolved and changed over and over," he said. "I don't think the evidence here will ever tell you what really happened."

And just because the police dropped the evidence ball did not mean the jury had to rescue them. "Your job is not to solve the crime," Mosty said. The defense attorney concluded that the police, with tunnel vision, drew a flawed ring around Darlie, who was nothing more than an unjustly accused person, a caring parent and "an American mother, just like any other mother" who loved her children. Mosty told the jurors, "The true murderer is still on the streets."

The first two witnesses to be called were Joanie McClain and Janice Townsend-Parchman, the doctors who performed the autopsies on the slain children. McClain immediately struck the jury with the reality of the murders, describing how the body of Devon had been received in a plastic body bag, wearing only Power Ranger briefs. He weighed only 46 pounds and measured 46 inches in height, or 3 feet 10 inches. There were four "sharp-force" injuries to the chest, wounds that punctured vital arteries and caused the little lungs to fill with blood, and smaller cuts on a leg and an arm. In her opinion the child could have lived only a few minutes after sustaining such deep wounds to the chest.

The description of the autopsy on Damon Routier was just as graphic. The boy was 43 inches in length, slightly shorter than his older brother, and weighed 40 pounds. He had six huge stab wounds that also penetrated lungs and other vital organs but had not sliced open the arteries. As a result, his blood just oozed into the lungs until they were full, and death would have followed within minutes.

Grisly autopsy photographs were passed to the jurors, and when Darlie caught a glimpse, she grimaced and averted her eyes.

The testimony of Townsend-Parchman, however, quickly turned from the rather routine task of reporting on an autopsy to her examination, at the request of Detective Patterson, of the wounds that Darlie had sustained. Instead of a slow opening, the trial had gone right to the center of the case, homing in on the question of whether the young mother had herself inflicted the stab wounds she had sustained, as the prosecutors claimed.

The medical expert, a stern-looking woman with her dark hair pulled tightly to the rear and braided into a long pigtail that hung down the back of her flower-patterned dress, had a no-nonsense approach. After describing the request from the police and the cuts, as she saw them, that day on Darlie, she was asked to approach the defendant. Both women were small, actually about the same size, but the tension between them was almost electric.

Darlie stood and pulled aside the white ruffled collar on her red dress, and the jury paid rapt attention as they got their first clear view of the red scar that went across the bottom of her throat. The physician pointed to the healed rip, described it as "very superficial" and pointed out the blade did not strike vital organs, or go very deep. She said she examined Darlie for ten minutes. This was a powerful piece of testimony, for Townsend-Parchman directly said the neck wound wasn't serious and that it was "possible" that Darlie did it to herself. A doctor would know, wouldn't she?

That is the purpose of cross-examination. What one lawyer may set out as incontrovertible fact, an opposing attorney may show in an entirely different light. Before the defense was done with Dr. Townsend-Parchman she had waffled to say she made no notes about her encounter with Darlie, admitted that the wounds "could be construed" as being defensive in nature, that one slicing blow actually went all the way to the bone of the defendant's arm, that someone else also "possibly" could have been responsible for the cuts, and that most of the so-called hesitation wounds she had seen, wounds reluctantly inflicted by people on themselves, were not as deep as the wounds sustained by Darlie Routier. In effect, the physician could say little more than Darlie had indeed suffered cuts. Anything more than that was pure supposition on her part.

The third and final witness of the day was William Gorsuch, a rotund and bearded neighbor of the Routiers, who lived nearby on Eagle Drive. Gorsuch, a telecommunications engineer from Marigold, Mississippi, described how his own son played with Devon and Damon. The parents, however, were not close friends. On the night of June 5, he went into work at about 8 P.M., and noticed that as he drove away, his boy was playing over at the Routiers' place and that Darin was mowing the front yard.

William Gorsuch is a careful man. Before he left work at 1:25 A.M. the following morning, he telephoned his wife to let her know he was on the way home. They own a handgun, he explained. "and she knows how to use it." Once home, he parked in front of the house at about ten minutes before two, got out, and looked up at the stars for a few minutes, then went inside, taking care that nobody was going to follow him inside his home. He saw no one outside, no strange cars. "I'm a good size, but some people . . . " he offered as to his extraordinary precautions. After relocking his front door, he turned on the home security alarm system that he had installed himself, checked all the windows, had a drink, and went upstairs to sleep on his waterbed. He and his wife did not like air conditioning, and slept with the window open to catch whatever breeze would blow up Eagle Drive.

Gorsuch awoke when he heard a single distant scream, and was almost back to sleep when he heard Darin run outside, yelling: "Someone has stabbed my children and my wife." A police car arrived, then another. He and his wife watched from the open window, and then he grabbed his pistol, went downstairs, turned off the alarm, and stood on the porch as more official vehicles and men in uniforms arrived. It finally dawned on Gorsuch that maybe standing there holding a gun at his side wasn't too wise with so many policemen running around, so he went back inside and put it into a file cabinet. Judge Tolle nodded in agreement when the witness made that observation.

Gorsuch added little to the unfolding case, other than being able to say that he saw no strangers in the streets or alleys when he got home in the middle of the night. Of course, with his emphasis on guns, alarm systems, warning telephone calls, and meticulously checking the locks, he left a clear impression that he did not feel he lived in a safe neighborhood.

On the evening of the first day of trial, the members of Darlie's family gathered in the lounge at the Inn of the Hills, an upscale lodging facility. They were worried, but also somewhat confident now that the trial was finally underway. It was generally agreed that Mosty had done a fine job with the presentation, the first three witnesses had not hurt their case, and that Greg Davis was Satan.

Darin, who had not been to the courthouse, was briefed on the day's testimony, and confirmed that his sons used to play at the Gorsuch home, which they called "the Halloween House" because of a black-and-orange decor. "They'd say that Mommy needed to go over and decorate" the place, he said.

Outside, the weather was worsening, and Darin was feeling the gloom. Not only was he missing his imprisoned wife, but the state's contention that he was broke was finally coming true because he had sold everything he owned to pay for her defense. Standing beside a green pool table, he crossed his arms and summed up his financial status. "I'm down to $32."

The parade of uniforms began the second day of trial, which would be cut short because of the vicious weather battering the Texas hill country. Roads were covered with ice and the wind needled exposed skin. Only two witnesses would be heard, David Waddell and Matt Walling, both of whom had changed jobs in the previous eight months. Waddell had left the Rowlett police force and Walling had been promoted to lieutenant there. But it was their actions on June 6 that were the reason they, and other members of the Rowlett Police Department, were currently living with the prosecution's other witnesses at the Holiday Inn down the street from the courthouse.

Waddell, now an officer in Plano, presented a rather nervous appearance on the stand, despite his short haircut and trim uniform. His actions had become known in the case because he was the first officer on the scene, and what he had experienced was part of the groundwork for the earlier hearings, but now he had to go through it all all again.

He explained for the prosecutors how he had been in the middle of an overnight shift when the emergency call flared on his radio and he sped to 5801 Eagle Drive. He was a veteran of Special Response Team training, but suddenly found himself alone in a shattered household, with two small children lying wounded on the floor, an obviously wounded woman screaming to the police dispatcher on a telephone, and a confused husband trying to answer questions. When he asked "who had done it," Darlie just pointed toward the open rear door and said someone was still in the garage.

Waddell then told Darin to help, and the father was on his knees, trying to perform CPR on Devon, but told the policeman air was blowing out of the chest every time he pumped. The officer testified he instructed Darlie to fetch some towels and put them on the other child's back, but she ignored him.

As Doug Mulder paced along the far wall of the courtroom, drawing all eyes while doing nothing, the policeman said he assumed the attacker was still in the garage and went to look into the dark space, while Darlie's yells echoed in his ears. She had managed by then to tell him that the attacker wore a dark shirt and baseball cap, but didn't know whether he was white or black. She said she fought with him between the family room and the kitchen as he ran away.

Waddell said he returned to the kitchen area after deciding not to go into the dark garage alone, and took a protective position, with his weapon drawn, until help could arrive. One of the boys, lying on his stomach with his eyes open, was gasping "like he was trying to breathe."

Eventually, his sergeant, Walling, arrived and they searched the garage and found nothing. They moved cautiously around broken glass and blood on the kitchen floor. He stayed with the family while Walling went outside to continue his search, and told Darlie to sit down by the glass door. The next moment, two paramedics appeared and began emergency treatment. Waddell went to check the upstairs area and found the third boy, an infant, standing up in his crib, looking over the railing. When he came back down Darlie had moved to the front porch with the paramedic, and when the ambulances took away the wounded victims, Waddell was assigned to stand guard at the front door, which he did until relieved at 3 A.M.

Doug Mulder smoothly began the cross-examination, friendly and polite, saying he had just "a couple of things" to talk to the officer about. The attorney was specfic, almost niggling, about exact times, at one point even making sure they were both in agreement that there were sixty seconds in a minute. The answers were then written by the attorney on a big paper pad propped upon an easel. He was building a timeline, in which minutes and seconds would count.

Then Mulder unlocked a tactical gate that would resurface throughout the trial, asking Walling about how he was prepared as a witness. The policeman explained that the Dallas County District Attorney's Office had brought him into a courtroom and questioned him on a witness stand some three weeks ago. "We went over my testimony," he admitted, and other police witnesses also took their turns on the stand.

The defense lawyer switched back to the house and mocked the officer's actions for not being more aggressive. "I'd think you'd take your gun out and hotfoot it in there," he said. The policeman replied that if something happened to him, there would be no one left to protect the family.

How about doing more than just protecting? Mulder

asked. You said Darlie didn't help the boys, but couldn't you have given first aid? "Not under the circumstances," Waddell responded, and Mulder swiped at the cop's courage again. "You didn't want to stick your nose into the garage," he charged, and didn't want to "go back and help everybody." The officer responded that he had used his radio to call for help. Mulder's questions grew sharper.

"You did nothing to help that child."

"No."

"Were you nervous?"

"Yes."

"Were you scared?"

"Yes."

Mulder had the policeman admit that no matter how Darlie reacted after he was on the scene, he had no knowledge of what she did before he arrived.

At lunchtime on the second day, Mama Darlie and her daughter Dana were scheduled to fly to New York to appear on the Maury Povich show, but bad weather canceled the flight. After court resumed, the defense introduced the 911 emergency tape as evidence, played in "real time" and giving the jury a taste of that horrible night on Eagle Drive. Darlie's recorded wailing and keening cries filled the courtroom, and a male juror wiped his eyes as she screamed, "My babies are dying!"

Matthew Walling was the fifth witness and came on just after the tape was played. A veteran of ten years on the Rowlett force, he recently had been promoted. His presentation would be a by-the-book *Dragnet*-type emotionless recitation. Just the facts.

He arrived right behind the first ambulance, no more than five minutes after the emergency call, found Patrolman Waddell inside with Darin and Darlie behind the policeman. His testimony traced how he performed the first comprehensive search of the house and grounds, and he described the difficulty encountered when he opened the heavy gate in the backyard.

It was when he recalled talking to Darlie while she was being tended by a paramedic that a telling fact emerged. He said she told him that she had awakened on the couch to find someone standing over her, which he noted was somewhat different from what she had told Dave Waddell, that she had fought with the intruder in the kitchen area.

As Walling assigned arriving patrolmen to different duties, he also escorted neighbor Karen Neal upstairs to retrieve both the baby, Drake, and the barking little dog, Domain. Just as he touched on doing a walk-through of the crime scene with three other law enforcement representatives about dawn, Judge Tolle decided it was time to call it a day. The weather was worsening by the hour in Kerrville and he wanted to give jurors an early opportunity to get home. The prosecution was done with Walling, and Doug Mulder could start the next day with his cross-examination.

After two days, the prosecution had proved little more than the fact that Darlie Routier lived on Eagle Drive and something terrible had happened in the early morning hours of June 6. But it was still very, very early in a trial such as this. Too early for a juror to see any sort of pattern.

21

THE ICY CONDITIONS were unrelenting and radio stations broadcast long lists of schools and businesses that would be closed for the day. Almost everyone involved in the Darlie Routier capital murder trial, however, made it to court on time. Even Mama Darlie managed to catch a quick ride to the courthouse when the steering gave out on her car. But one juror had been listening to the radio and thought the announcer said that governmental offices would be shut down due to the weather, and assumed that meant court would not be in session. The juror stayed home. It took another hour before Tolle could correct the situation. Goofs by jurors who couldn't figure out where they were supposed to be had delayed the trial on two of its three days.

Matt Walling returned to the stand for Doug Mulder's cross-examination, and again the defense lawyer used the big paper pad to list the exact times that the police did specific things. Mulder took his time while writing, "Walling did not see the vacuum cleaner when first went through kitchen." The easel dominated the middle of the court and drew the eyes of the jurors, who could sense that Mulder must be going to such great lengths for some reason. Was there something hidden in those times? At the prosecution table, Greg Davis was wondering the same thing and was growing tired of the giant stage prop.

The questioning of Walling actually yielded very little new information, but Mulder niggled at inconsistencies with barbed little comments. "Nobody has a perfect memory," he noted when Walling testified that he never saw blood on Darlie's hands, while in an earlier deposition, he had said she had it on her hands and arms. Slight, but enough to damage his credibility somewhat by indicating that his story had changed. The lawyer expanded that into a discussion about how the police "forgot" things, referring to Walling's "first story." The policeman admitted that by the time he wrote his report he had been awake more than twenty-four hours. He was telling the jury that perhaps his memory wasn't as sharp as the creases in his uniform.

When Mulder finished, Greg Davis had a few points in response, and Walling testified that an automatic security light came on when he entered the Routier's backyard and stayed on for eighteen minutes. That inferred that, had anyone fled through the yard, the light would have been on by the time police arrived. It also indicated that if Darlie had planted the sock found in the lane, she would have had to stab the children, go out the front door, and around the side of the house in plain view without being seen, possibly even by alert neighbor William Gorsuch, drop the sock, return home and stab herself before calling police. Neither scenario seemed likely.

Sergeant Dean Poos, who had spent so much time as the police spokesman in the early stages of the case, was on the witness stand only ten minutes, just long enough to describe the process by which the emergency call from Darlie had been recorded at police headquarters. Then came Barry Gene Dickey, the president of Graffiti Productions, Inc., a recording expert whose company had the equipment necessary to filter the extraneous noise from the almost-incoherent tape and digitally transfer the clean copy to a laser disc for playback in the courtroom. The result was a high-tech demonstration that changed Darlie's weeping and stammering and screaming into a deciphered text that could be both read and heard by the jury.

On the big screen of an RCA television set, lines of words scrolled past, translating the indecipherable into English. And even without the terrible screams, the cold words alone were frightening, with Darlie out of breath and panting like a dog. It was agony, with or without the sound effects, even when Darlie uttered peculiar comments like "He ran out . . . They ran out in the garage." Several times, she used the plural words "they" and "them" while at other times she would use the singular "he."

The prosecution decided to let the tape recording speak for itself, but Richard Mosty had some sharp questions in cross-examination. Since the entire call had not been transcribed, the defense attorney wanted to know who decided what would be cleaned up for the tape and what would be excluded. Mosty contended that the sounds that were washed away and the jumbled consolidation of the seven parts of the tape that were filtered and re-recorded could leave the jury with an inaccurate understanding of that vital conversation. Dickey, the engineer, said the content had been decided by "a collaboration" between himself and Greg Davis, but added that Davis did not order him to leave out certain things on the new recording that had so far cost Dallas County $10,000 in production costs.

In a pure Texas moment, the down-home demeanor of Mosty and the equally Southern-speaking Dickey had a discussion of whether Darlie was referring to one or more people by the use of the term "Y'all," as in "Y'all go look out in the garage." Mosty noted that "some people mess up in their syntax, their English, don't they?" Dickey responded that he understood the term perfectly because he grew up in Grand Prairie.

The laser-disc presentation sparked a flurry of defense objections. Tolle ruled against them and when his decision was contested, the judge snapped that the defense lawyers could "take it up on appeal." With that, the jury was led from the room and Mosty heatedly asked for a mistrial, claiming the judge's unexpected remark indicated to the jurors that Darlie would be convicted. The judge refused the mistrial, but when the jury returned, Tolle ordered them to disregard his statement, a suggestion that was akin to trying to put an escaped horse back into the barn.

Prosecutor Greg Davis then began the introduction of a long line of health care workers from the Baylor hospital, in the hope of painting Darlie Routier as a most peculiar patient.

Dr. Alex Santos, the trauma surgeon who had operated upon her, was first on the list, and he gave a general overview of the emergency room procedures on the night of June 6. The jury already knew that Darlie had been wounded, and might wonder what other purpose the doctor had for being called as a witness. Santos, with five years of emergency room work at Baylor, recited the medical details in a calm, dispassionate way. To him, Darlie had been just another patient, one of hundreds he had seen in his career.

After having the doctor describe her route from the ambulance arrival through the operating room and into the intensive care unit, Greg Davis struck swiftly, having Santos admit that the type of slash Darlie sustained along her neck "can be called a superficial wound." Everyone knew *superficial* meant it wasn't much more than a scratch.

Then Davis quickly scored again by asking Santos the results of a routine drug screen run on blood that was drawn from Darlie in the emergency room. The doctor replied that the test came back positive for amphetamines, although he could not say what kind or how much. He answered a follow-up question with the point that amphetamines are often found in diet pills. These answer did two things. It backed up a prosecution assertion that Darlie had been trying to lose weight after the birth of Drake, even having to seek help from pills. More importantly, it obliquely introduced a specter that would play a significant role in the case before the conservative jurors. They suddenly were not thinking diet pills, but *DRUGS!*

Santos then was pressed by the prosecution to give his impression of how Darlie reacted to the situation in which she found herself. This meant that he had to go beyond his purely medical expertise and give a personal opinion backed by no data whatsoever. He did this by comparing her behavior to that of other people in similar circumstances. In fact, Santos didn't even know what had happened to her before she became his patient. He said he learned that information only later, and when he saw her in bed, with her husband at her side and the large photos of two boys with her, she did not seem excited, responded to his questions in a monotone and with "blunt" reactions. "Usually, mothers get hysterical. It [the death of children] is very hard for a mother to accept, and they usually tell me I'm wrong. There [usually] is a lot of anger."

Her attitude remained aloof, he thought, even when she was discharged on June 8. "I never saw a mother act that way." The doctor said he would have preferred that Darlie stay in the hospital longer, but the family wanted to get her out as soon as possible so she could be at the funeral for the children.

For one final point, Davis showed Santos a June 10 picture of Darlie's right arm, the bottom of which was heavily bruised all the way to the armpit. The physician said it appeared to have been inflicted by some "blunt trauma" like a baseball bat. He said he had not seen any such bruising when she left the hospital, and that the type of injury indicated it had been inflicted between twenty-four and forty-eight hours earlier. That time frame would be *after* she left the hospital.

Greg Davis ended his questioning of Santos at 4:28 P.M., and he could not have picked a better time. Before the defense could start to cross-examine the doctor, there was a mass exodus from the courtroom of reporters, primarily the television correspondents. They had to rush to the trucks parked downstairs and get ready for the important afternoon news shows that were about to go on the air. Several newspaper reporters also headed for the exit to call their editors. Everybody had a hot story. Darlie had been using amphetamines, Darlie's responses to questions had been "flat" and unusual for a mother whose children had been killed, Darlie's neck wound was only superficial. The hospital's well-qualified doctor had said so. Any of the three topics surely was good material for a lead story. The only problem was they left too early and reported only half a story back to Dallas, where people were following the Routier trial with great interest. The deadlines of the news business contributed to slanted accounts.

After the reporters left, things really got interesting in that cold courtroom on the second floor as the defense autopsied the doctor's findings.

First, the business of Darlie having a "flat" response to the terrible event. The hospital admission slip was introduced into evidence and Santos confirmed that it listed her as being both tearful and hysterical. A nurse's note added that she was crying and visibly upset. At 7 A.M., another nurse recorded that she was "very emotional" and crying and sobbing about her family. Did Dr. Santos see these notes? No, he replied. He didn't read them.

And if Darlie was "flat" and unemotional, why did the doctor, when she checked out of the hospital, prescribe the powerful tranquilizer Xanax? He answered that she had suffered a major loss of blood, was diagnosed with postoperative amnesia, and had sustained a very painful injury. She had been given doses of both Demerol and Xanax in the hours following the general anesthetic of the operation. No wonder she was relaxed. In fact, the doctor soon admitted that as late as 8 A.M., he would expect someone under such a drug load to be confused, disoriented, groggy, and suffering from short-term memory loss. And police began to question her, the doctor admitted, only five minutes after she was injected with the Demerol. He added that he would consider anything someone said under such a condition to be "suspect."

Then the vital information about that "superficial" wound was attacked. In a matter of moments, the doctor revealed that was only a medical term. Actually the slice had come within a mere two millimeters, a very tiny distance, from the carotid artery. If that had been cut, Santos said, Darlie would have bled to death "within two or three minutes." The line is very thin between "superficial" and "fatal."

The big bruise that he had hinted so broadly was inflicted after she left the hospital? Santos broadened the time line and said it might have been up to four days old. Since he saw the picture on June 10, the bruise might have been inflicted as early as June 6, the day of the attack.

The questions turned to the "flat" responses Darlie

displayed. Would someone who is depressed show a similar reaction? Yes, the doctor said. He could not rule out that Darlie reacted the way he observed because she had been "deeply depressed and grieving."

Court ended for the day at 5:18. On cross-examination, Dr. Santos had rolled back almost every damaging claim he had said in his opening testimony. Luckily, the lawyer's sterling performance at dismantling the story had been seen by the jury. Unfortunately, most of the reporters had missed it and their stories on the day's events would be both harsh and unfair.

Judge Tolle had one final piece of business for Wednesday. He turned to his jury panel and joshed with a stern tone. Getting lost and being late wasn't going to be acceptable from now on. He had optimistically planned to get this trial done in only two weeks, but was already some three hours off that schedule without yet coming close the heart of the case. Through the combined efforts of the plodding prosecutors, the verbose defense team, and the evil weather, the judge's timetable would soon be junked entirely, but he gave it one last try. "Regardless of what you hear on the radio, this court will start at nine o'clock," he declared.

22

IN TEXAS, WITNESSES are sometimes called into a room and briefed by lawyers prior to going on the witness stand. In the Routier case, prosecution witnesses used nearly identical words and phrases to describe events after having been allowed to hear what others were going to say. Instead of spontaneous responses, the answers seemed rehearsed, as they indeed were. A mock trial put police officers before one another, and hospital nurses and doctors mingled freely in a Holiday Inn room in Kerrville as the prosecutors ran them through their paces before actually putting them on the witness stand.

Thursday, January 9, the fourth day of trial opened with Baylor resident Dr. Patrick Dillawn, who was followed with an emergency room nurse, a hospital security guard, another nurse, another nurse, still another nurse, and a final nurse who would be carried over to Friday. Their testimony flopped from their few medical observations into an area that was close to gossip. In fact, the most damaging comments came from nurse Paige Campbell, not over medical evidence, but by doing a parody of how Darlie Routier, who "never needed a Kleenex," sounded when she "was whining a lot."

The thrust of their testimony was to show that the defendant was not upset about the deaths of her kids and made contradictory statements to them and to police. Like a top, they went around and around the same spots, their repetition of June 6 muddied when defense lawyers constantly had them admit they flew down from Love Field together, stayed in a block of rooms at the Holiday Inn, and all met in the hotel's conference room on Wednesday to review pictures of the defendant and "talk about what we saw," while prosecuting attorneys and investigators reviewed the case with them.

The medical personnel were effective in pounding the jury with the repetition of their observations, but lost ground steadily as the defense lawyers showed example after example of how what the nurses said on the stand contrasted with what was written in their notes. By doing so, either the credibility of the notes or the nurses had to be questioned. "I think it's very clear to the jury what happened," Doug Mulder would observe after court on Thursday, when he said the testimony of the doctors and nurses was "coordinated" because it resulted from a "brainstorming" session at the hotel.

Dr. Dillawn said Darlie "was not particularly upset" and emergency room nurse Jody Fitts said she heard contrasting statements from the patient. When she entered the emergency room, Darlie was asking, "Why would they kill my boys?" but later changed her comment to "Why would he kill my boys?"

Chris Wielgosz, who only saw Darlie briefly the morning she was admitted and was the nurse who administered the tranquilizers just before police arrived, added nothing new, other than being surprised when police called him, a month later, wanting a statement. "She was crying," was about all Wielgosz could contribute. It wasn't clear why he was on the witness stand. He said there was no blood on her feet when she was admitted.

Trauma coordinator Jody Cotner, who bandaged Darlie, asked the patient what had happened, and "She told me that Damon, the little one, he was standing over her saying, 'Mommy,' and woke her up. There was blood and he was hurt, and that he followed her and she told him to lay down." Cotner said when neighbor Karen Neal brought the baby, Drake, to the hospital bed of his mother, Darlie turned her face away from the child. Cotner saw no bruise on the arm.

Nurse Dianne Holland said, "I never recall her using a tissue to wipe her face, she never cried," although her eyes would well up with tears when she touched the pictures of her children. The nurse, however, cried on the witness stand when she told of Darlie relating the story of how Devon would often pick flowers and give them to her when she was upset with him.

The nurse, however, went a step too far in her emotional testimony and introduced the defense idea that a suspicious car had been seen around the neighborhood and that the people in it appeared to be watching Darlie's house. Getting back to the medical testimony, Holland said she didn't see any bruise on the right arm, either.

Richard Mosty, with his country-boy twang, asked, by golly, if Holland could help him out on one point, this thing about Darlie never crying. Why, he wanted to know, did Holland write in her notes at noon that "patient continues to weep." And, he wanted to know, if all patients reacted in an identical way to grief, such as the loss of children. No, replied Holland, "usually they don't talk about it."

When Toby Shook, an assistant district attorney helping Davis, was given a chance to examine the witness again, the prosecutor addressed the group meeting. "I never asked you to make a story up, did I?" he asked. "No," said the nurse. Then she backtracked again on the crying, repeating that she never saw tears running down Darlie's face.

The day of wishy-washy testimony ended with Paige Campbell putting on a display about how Darlie had "whined." In doing so, however, she contradicted her own hospital notes in which she had described the patient as being "very tearful."

The jury left the room perplexed. If these doctors and nurses had been brought in to show a unified front against Darlie, they had failed, despite the Holiday Inn practice session prior to their testimony. They managed to use a lot of the same words, but could not agree on vital points, such as where blood had been on Darlie, how she acted, and even whether she had wept over her lost boys.

An outraged Mama Darlie had called her own news conference in the courthouse hallway that morning to protest the one-sided reporting from the previous day when the news gatherers had left court before hearing the full story. That triggered a complaint in court by Greg Davis that she was violating the gag order, but Judge Tolle pointed out the order was no longer in force once the trial started. Davis made up his mind to finally break the silence in which the district attorney had wrapped the case, and the defense team took the same cue. Henceforth, every day would end with each side appearing before the cameras to give the story a little spin. But Mama Darlie's anger didn't change things with the press. *The Houston Chronicle* headline the next morning read:

ROUTIER'S BEHAVIOR NOT TYPICAL FOR GRIEVING MOM, NURSES SAY

Friday, the final day of the first week, started with another defense request for a mistrial, with Mulder's team claiming the parrotlike responses from the medical personnel were the result of a "clandestine meeting" in which they had been coached. Judge Tolle denied that one, too, and it was plain that while the nurses many times would use similar words and phrases, they also had trouble keeping their stories straight. The first witness of the day was Dennis Faulk, another Baylor nurse, who testified that he, too, heard Darlie "whine," but also that around midnight on June 6, he bathed blood from her feet. Jurors had heard nurse Chris Wielgosz testify that there was no blood on her feet.

The powers of observation of doctors and nurses are somewhat limited, for they look for specific things. Wielgosz, in the emergency room, would have been much more interested in the gaping wound in Darlie's neck than her feet. Nurses tending an IV in one forearm would not be looking for a bruise on the other arm. Therefore, their notes made at the time did not necessarily match the overall recollections presented in court. Instead, they were testifying about Darlie's state of mind, although none of them were qualified experts in that field. Oddly, the prosecution did not have a psychologist or a psychiatrist on their witness list.

Faulk, however, managed to add one significant point. He said that while bathing the patient, Darlie had told him that she began to awaken on the couch when the intruder ran into the wine rack and shattered a glass. She said when she turned on the light, she saw her two boys on the floor and began to scream. This was new information and differed from what she had told police at the house and the answers she had given to Detective Patterson in the earlier hospital interviews. Darlie was having trouble keeping her details straight, but she wasn't alone in that respect. Defense lawyer Richard Mosty pounced on the nurse's comment and Faulk backed off, saying that she "became fully awake" when the wine glass broke and had really been "kind of awake" when one of the boys nudged her. That diluted the impact of the differing version, because this nurse, like the others, had a problem with consistency.

Faulk also discussed the hotel room meeting of the witnesses from Baylor, overseen by prosecution lawyer Toby Shook, in which pictures of Darlie were placed on a table. "We looked at 'em and discussed what we saw," the nurse said.

Judge Tolle got involved in the out-of-court controversy over who was telling what to the media, and whether his oft-violated gag order was again being ignored. He had already decided the order was no longer in force, and family members and lawyers alike were free to talk to the press. But he had something else in mind when he asked Mama Darlie and Sarilda Routier to step into his chambers for a brief, private talk before court on Friday. He wouldn't stop them from talking, but he hoped to soothe their anger. The judge gently patted the defendant's mother on the arm and told her that Doug Mulder and Richard Mosty and the defense team were some of the best lawyers in the state. She should believe that they would represent Darlie to the best of their ability, he said. Mama Darlie later interpreted that meeting, happily, as the judge telling her "everything is going to be okay."

Greg Davis finished with the litany of the nurses and returned to his lineup of policemen, starting with Sergeant Tom Dean Ward, a pudgy and bald veteran with twenty-five years in law enforcement and three gold stripes on his sleeves. His strength was his experience, which would also turn out to be his weakness.

Ward outlined how he had been awakened by a call from headquarters early on the morning of June 6, drove to the scene on Eagle Drive, and was assigned to the team of officers searching the alley behind the house. At that time, they were looking for evidence, he said, and "not really expecting to find a suspect."

Ward described the thoroughness of the alley search in the predawn hours, of going through every trash can, looking into every storm drain, climbing up to see over fences, checking beneath boats and cars. It was he who found a "white tube sock" with a stain that appeared to be blood behind the house at 5709 Eagle, and stood guard until an evidence-gathering officer could pick it up. After the alley search, he joined other officers in knocking on doors and talking to area residents. When daylight came, he repeated the alley search, but found no more evidence.

His story was seamless, until then. About 8:30 A.M., his attention was directed to one backyard, at 5706 Willowbrook, and he looked over a hedge to where a fresh bed of flowers was being laid out and lined with a rubber edging. Ward could see a yellow-handled screwdriver on the ground and a "kitchen butcher knife" sticking into the dirt beside the rubber molding. From his distance, he could see no blood on the blade. Greg Davis picked up an evidence bag and pulled out a muddy-handled knife, which the policeman identified as the knife he had seen but had not retrieved. "There was no question in my mind that they [the screwdriver and knife] were not connected with the offense," Ward said. Anyway, he testified, he was separated from that yard by a barred iron fence six feet tall with a locked gate. He was certain about that.

The sergeant discussed the notes he had made about his work, and how the date was left out of his handwritten version and how he misidentified the officer who collected the sock until he filled in a corrected and typed version.

Richard Mosty did the cross-examination, and struck first at the notes, knowing a weak point when he saw one. In fact, the policeman admitted, his original handwritten notes had gone missing, a fact not discovered until this very morning before he went on the witness stand. Then things became even more confused, because he did another handwritten version after typing his original notes, and saved one on a computer. It was that computerized version that he could offer the court as evidence. It had been faxed to Kerrville from Rowlett at 9:44 A.M., and Ward had begun his testimony ten minutes later. Although the original notes had vanished from police headquarters, Ward admitted that he had misnamed the evidence officer and forgotten the date. "You made an error, didn't you?" asked Mosty. "Yes," said Ward, who repeatedly would bring up the fact that he had vast experience as a policeman with a quarter of a century in law enforcement. The reason the missing document was important would be similar to a chain of evidence procedure, in which each time a piece of evidence is removed for examination, someone has to sign for it. That way, a continuous chain exists to prove the item has not been altered. Without the original notes, Ward's story of what he did and what errors were made relied only upon his memory six months after the fact.

Mosty veered to the search itself and the officer confirmed finding the sock and knowing that "we had two dead" of knife wounds. Despite the thoroughness of the first search, he missed seeing the knife in the dirt, Mosty declared and Ward confirmed. The knife, therefore, wasn't mentioned in the notes that were missing, or even in his supplemental, formal report. And when Ward knocked on the door of the house with the patch of garden in the rear, he did not ask the residents about the knife. No, Ward said, he didn't, because he didn't even see that knife until a few hours later.

The defense lawyer then attacked the prosecution's "dress rehearsal" trial for the police witnesses and Ward said it was held in the Dallas County Court House. The prosecution had someone in the chair of the judge, people in the witness box, so the potential witnesses could run through their testimony in a realistic setting. They also had a chance to listen to each other's stories.

The only significant thing to which Ward could testify was that he had found the bloodstained sock. But his effectiveness was questionable because of the way he had missed both finding or mentioning the knife, which would later have to be collected and eliminated as a potential murder weapon. When combined with the unexplained loss of vital notes in a major murder case, Ward's reminders that he had twenty-five years in law enforcement rang hollow.

That wasn't the worst. The very next witness was eighteen-year-old Gustavo Guzman, Jr., who lived at 5706 Willowbrook. A student, he had been out late the night before, and returning home, had been watching television in the kitchen when he saw police with flashlights go down the alley. Later the next day, after being interviewed by police, he went to the backyard, worried that the knife that he had been using to help his mother dig in the garden might have been the murder weapon. But it was still exactly where he had left it, and he left it again. When Mosty cross-examined the young man, Guzman testified that when he came home the previous night, he went into his house through the backyard about 11 P.M., leaving the gate unlocked and open behind him. The much-experienced Sergeant Ward had said the gate was closed and locked. During his careful search, he could have walked into the open yard and found the knife he didn't see for several more hours, the knife that he ignored when he did see it, although he knew that a knife had been used in the brutal attack at the nearby Routier home. Police did not pick up the muddy garden knife and other gardening tools until a month before the trial began.

*   *   *

and Rowlett Patrolman Steve Ferrie had an easier time on the stand, since his part in the drama was minor. An eight-year member of the force, the sandy-haired officer assisted Ward in the first search of the alley, then was assigned to guard the crime scene by standing at the front door and logging in the few people approved to enter, then later standing guard on the perimeter of yellow crime scene tape until he left for the day. On cross-examination, he told Mulder that he, too, had participated in the pretend warm-up trial exercise staged by the prosecutors.

Such a preparatory trial exercise was a tricky item for Mulder to handle. It impressed a jury to know the witnesses had been carefully briefed, and perhaps might alter their own testimony after hearing what others had to say. But as Greg Davis had pointed out to this jury, Doug Mulder had been one of the pioneers of the tactic, back when he was a prosecutor.

Friday and the first week of testimony concluded with testimony from paramedics Jack Colbye, Brian Koschak, and Larry Byford, who presented haunting and detailed stories of how they found the bloody boys and the wounded Darlie in that horrible murder scene. Colbye, a large man, was jolted by finding Damon, the small body punctured with stab wounds, and rolling the child over just in time to hear the last breath of life escape from the boy's lips and see the light fade from his eyes. Koschak and Byford described how Darlie was treated, and Koschak said when he saw the neck wound, he thought, 'That's a life-threatening injury.' But her vital signs and skin color were good, she wasn't in shock and was alert when she was bandaged and placed in the ambulance. Byford said she was anxious on the way to the hospital, wanting to know how much longer until they got to the emergency room. The paramedics brought drama to the case, but little else, since their roles were so minor.

*   *   *

There is a game plan in every trial, and it is not unusual for the prosecutors to put on some of their weakest witnesses first. That way, the jurors probably will forget about any stumbles as more powerful testimony is presented during the more heated trial days yet to come.

In the opening week of the trial, twenty-three witnesses had taken the stand, but they had little to offer in the way of proving that Darlie Routier had killed her sons. Policemen, doctors, paramedics, and nurses usually are only supporting players in such a crime, performing their assigned roles and then exiting the stage.

The Routier case was built on circumstantial evidence alone, and the experts who would be able to put that evidence into context were yet to come. But as court closed for the long, cold weekend, and Greg Davis met the press downstairs, he waffled when asked why Detective Jimmy Patterson had not been among the witnesses so far. Twenty-three people had been heard from, but the policeman who was the lead investigator in the case had not been among them. Davis shrugged away the question, as if it had no importance. It was important, however, and as time passed, the performance of Jimmy Patterson would be brought into sharp and questionable focus.

23

THE WEATHER WENT wild. Freezing rain and hammering wind scoured the hill country, gaining strength during the weekend until roads were deemed too dangerous to travel. State Police cars stopped any vehicle from entering the interstate highway system after a car went out of control on unseen ice, flipped over a median, and slammed into a bus, causing fatalities and injuries. A "Weather Emergency" was declared in the area. Mama Darlie slipped walking to the jail to visit her daughter on Sunday, sustaining a scraped nose and facial bruises and bringing deputies on the run to both help and take photographs on the spot in case she decided to sue for damages. With the skies gray and gloomy and the roads impassable, Judge Tolle sent word to all that there would be no court on Monday.

Trial resumed on Tuesday, January 14, but the weather would not moderate and wrapped the old courthouse in a freezing embrace. Half of the building's heating system failed and bone-chilling temperatures oozed into the courtroom through the eight-foot-high windows behind the jury box. Jurors and spectators alike huddled in sweaters and heavy coats, and Tolle called frequent breaks in the trial to let people warm up elsewhere. During a two-hour lunch, maintenance workers sealed the big windows with duct tape and panels of insulation, and installed a few space heaters.

Because of the problems, only one witness, Rowlett Officer David Mayne, was heard in the sixth day of testimony. Mayne's job was to collect evidence at the scene, and after he described finding a quantity of personal and financial papers in the living room, the policeman strayed from his script and lobbed the trial into questionable legal water. In pretrial meetings, the prosecution and defense had agreed not to bring up that cops had found a small quantity of marijuana in the house, because there was a question about who owned it and no indication that Darlie had smoked it. Mayne had also been among the policemen who attended the court rehearsal the prosecution had held in order to be certain of their testimony. Then, in a total surprise for all, when Greg Davis asked if the cop had retrieved anything other than the documents, Mayne blurted, "Yes, I retrieved some marijuana."

"Objection!" cried Mulder and Mosty almost in unison. The jury was immediately led from the room and the defense attorneys once again asked for a mistrial, with Mulder saying the comment was not a slip of the tongue, but a "flagrant violation" of the earlier agreement. "The witness should have known better," Mosty said. Mulder said the "dress rehearsal" trial certainly should have impressed on the officer that the marijuana was not to be mentioned. Greg Davis insisted that the statement was an accident and he had anticipated Mayne answering just "yes" or "no" to his question. Mulder said that now that the subject of marijuana had been introduced, the jury didn't know if the policeman was talking about a bale or a gram, and the defense now had the chore of explaining something that shouldn't have been introduced in the first place. Tolle denied the motion for a mistrial and instructed the jurors to disregard the cop's statement. That was tantamount to telling them to stand in a corner and not think about elephants. During the next break in the session, as jurors passed through the throng of people waiting in the warm anteroom, one cowboy loudly observed, "So she got high and killed her kids, eh?" The introduction of the subject of marijuana to a mostly middle-aged, all-white jury in conservative Kerrville was a damaging blow to Darlie Routier, no matter what the judge instructed. A family member later would say that Darlie didn't even know the marijuana was in the house and that it belonged to a friend.

The remainder of Mayne's testimony, the way he chose to take some items and leave others and the method and numbers of photographs he took, would soon fade to irrelevance, but for the moment, the impression that he left of finding such things as a handwritten will, birth certificates, instructions on who was to sell the house in case of the deaths of Darlie and Darin, and insurance policies a few feet from the body of Damon was, in the words of Greg Davis, "a lot more than coincidence."

When Mosty began to cross-examine the witness, Mayne became the latest Rowlett policeman to suddenly admit that some of his notes were missing. Since Mayne was the officer to originate the official chain-of-custody on evidence, the fact that some of his notes were unavailable was significant.

After the marijuana flub and the missing notes, the policeman was obviously in for a rough ride with the defense lawyers, and they spent some time battering him on procedures and the idea that he mishandled evidence. Soon, Mayne was wilting beneath a barrage of questions about his "improper" actions that indicated a shoddy investigation and incorrect reports. Mosty and Mulder teamed up to demonstrate that some items, such as Damon's bloody jeans and underwear, had been placed in the same bag instead of separate containers prior to testing, and blood evidence could have been transferred as they rubbed together. "That's not good police work is it, to have two items crumpled in a bag like this?" asked Mosty. "No, sir," replied the policeman, who also then had to admit he was incorrect in listing the sequence in which he took photographs, a list which could be vital in trying to reconstruct whether an item, like a lamp shade or a vacuum cleaner, had been moved during the investigation. In fact, the baffled officer who photographed the crime scene even admitted that he didn't know much about cameras at all. He also conceded that he had no particular reason for taking some of the financial documents, all of which were in the same place, and leaving others.

Tolle called a merciful halt to the wicked cross-examination to allow everyone to escape the cold courtroom for better-heated quarters elsewhere. Darin would explain that those personal papers confiscated by police had been at the office for years, but he and Darlie decided to keep them at home, since she was working less at the office. As far as the wills, he said they always updated their instructions prior to taking a trip, just in case something happened. Officer Mayne's work had been shown to be rather inadequate, but he had redeemed himself with the inadvertent remark about marijuana. Jurors riding home and listening to their car radio may have heard a news report on the day's brief session, which was followed by an advertisement for the Partnership for a Drug-Free America.

Mayne returned the next day, Wednesday, for more questioning, and Mosty jumped him again, having the officer admit he didn't "have any idea" how some items were in different positions from one of his photographs to another. The lawyer ridiculed the policeman taking papers about a dead pet, saying, "You decided that the cat's burial is important.'' The importance of the wills was then dimmed by Mosty producing a letter from an attorney to the Routiers, scheduling an office visit to discuss an estate plan with the arrival of the new baby.

Mosty concluded Mayne's testimony by having the cop admit he had gone over his testimony with the District Attorney's representatives no less than six times. The inference was after so many rehearsals, the policeman should have been a better witness. There was also the unspoken question of why a lowly police photographer had been left to make the important decisions on what evidence should be collected at the scene of such a crime, evidence that would be so crucial when the case finally got to trial.

Charles Hamilton, a crime scene officer who performed fingerprint tests, was the twenty-fifth witness for the prosecution. Unlike the image in detective novels and television shows, fingerprints are notoriously fragile things, easily destroyed and just as difficult to find in some situations. Hamilton's work would be no different than the usual results from any print specialist who processed everything from the kitchen counter to the door of the garage. The results were normal, which meant mostly unidentified and, therefore, inconclusive.

After a week and a half of testimony and twenty-five witnesses, little had been said that would indicate that Darlie Routier was the killer of her two children. Greg Davis would change that with the next series of witnesses.

Okie Williams, a loan officer at a Rowlett bank, was caught in a bind. She was a personal friend of Darin Routier, but the prosecutors had called her as a witness against him. Darin simply told her to tell the truth and not worry about it.

Williams was the Bank One officer to whom he had applied for a $5,000 loan for a vacation that had been turned down twice a few days before the crime because of several reasons, including "excessive obligations in relation to income," she told Davis. Mulder, questioning for the defense, led her to confirm the loan probably would have been granted if Darin had been willing to put up a $5,000 certificate of deposit as collateral. Since the loan interest would have been around 10 percent and the CD only paid 4.5 percent interest, that would have been a good deal for the bank, but not for the customer.

Davis used the loan rejection as an indication of how money was running low in the family, and how a fight over cash tied into the latest prosecution idea of a motive. He also had the couple's bank records admitted as evidence, saying the financial position was "a piece of the puzzle." After court that day, Davis would tell reporters, "Children are costly. Children demand attention, they demand money. If you eliminate those children, you eliminate that demand." Sarilda Routier responded to the reporters, "The man [Davis] has got a screw loose."

The jury would not find out that the loan was not for a vacation at all, but for a truck for Darlie's teen-aged sister, Dana. Darin wasn't willing to risk a $5,000 CD as collateral for a teenager who wanted wheels, but said Okie had told him the bank wouldn't consider making a loan for that purpose anyway. It was Williams, he said, who suggested saying the money was wanted to pay for a vacation in order to get a better reception from the loan committee.

It was almost as if everyone who came to the stand before Jim Cron were mere prelude, and almost everything after him was anticlimactic. Finally the curtain was going up on the real investigation. Oddly, the many members of the Rowlett Police Department who had appeared as wit-

nesses had not really solved the crime. It would be out-
siders who presented the strongest testimony. But one
good mark of a small police department is to know its
limitations, and to reach out for help when a big crime
strikes.

Cron no longer wore a police uniform or carried a
badge. He was, technically, just a consultant who had
conducted classes in crime scene investigations for the
Rowlett officers. But he was so well-known in the field
that even Doug Mulder had used his services in his own
days as a prosecutor. Now, although some dismissed him
as a "crime scene phrenologist who feels the bumps and
lumps and comes up with a conclusion," he was almost
a walking definition of the term "expert witness" and
told the jury he had been at 21,000 crime scenes in his
long career.

His testimony would take up the better part of two
days and provide the most crucial underpinnings for the
prosecution. When he told the jury that he decided after
a brief walk-through of the house on the morning of June
6 that "there had not been an intruder come through that
window," the jurors believed him. From that moment, it
would be an uphill battle for the defense.

Although Cron went over his preliminary work step by
step, describing how he examined walls, ceilings, and
floors for anything that might strike him as "unusual,"
he emphasized that no one object or any one situation
led to his original conclusion and he did not change after
spending nine hours at Eagle Drive. "It was the overall
scene," he said.

For instance, he noticed a pad of untouched dust covered the sill below the window through which the alleged
attacker had fled, and there was no blood on the window.
"It was sort of like new fallen snow," he said. "It was
obvious that nothing had gone through it." The defense
had made a great deal of a vacuum cleaner that had fallen

to the kitchen floor, hinting that it was knocked over in the fight. Cron said it looked to him like the vacuum had rolled through blood that was already spilled on the floor, meaning that perhaps Darlie herself had knocked it over to concoct a crime scene.

In his decades of police work, the silver-haired Cron said he did not think an assailant would use one knife to slice the screen window, then pick up another with which to stab the children. And, if a man was being chased by a woman whose throat he had slashed, it was unlikely that he would drop his weapon. The assailant also would probably have left behind bloody footprints, he said, but the only ones that were found and identified were the prints of Darlie Routier.

He found no scuff marks to indicate anyone tried to scale the six-foot backyard fence, no signs of anyone tracking through flower bed mulch, no indication of an attempted break-in at other first-floor windows and no indication in the backyard. "Nothing indicated an intruder."

After only a half-hour examination, he said a "Big Picture" had formed for him, based on experience, not on a single object or situation. Leaning comfortably forward, weight on his elbows, Cron told the jury the facts did not match up with what Darlie Routier had told police before she had been carted away by the ambulance. Cron had then suggested at the scene that the police bring in another outside expert, Charlie Linch over at the Southwest Institute of Forensic Science, and begin the methodical gathering of blood evidence that might be able to tell a story of what had happened inside that house. Words and guesses were one thing, blood was something else.

A juror fell sick to the evil weather and was dismissed on Thursday morning, and was replaced before the trial resumed, with Cron continuing to give a clinic in crime-scene examination, the long, slow twang exuding confidence. He said the fingerprint results showed no prints of an intruder that night, but admitted the prints are always just "a shot in the dark." Then he shifted to address the blood drops that were found indicating a "slow person" had left them, not someone in a hurry to run away from a murder scene.

Then a new piece of furniture was brought into court, a full-size mock-up of the garage window, complete with the huge rip in the screen. Placed to face the jury, it allowed them to pretend they were outside the house itself, looking in. It was partially open, just as it had been found by police. To demonstrate the alleged escape, Davis brought in Rowlett Detective Chris Frosch, who wore dark slacks and a starched white shirt, and had him duck through the window. Even Darlie had to smile as Frosch, a husky man well over six feet tall, wiggled low and went through the open window headfirst.

Of special interest was the size of Frosch, who is larger than an ordinary man. Mulder pointed out that even with his size, the detective did not touch the disputed windowsill, and therefore would not have disturbed any dust there.

Doug Mulder began his cross-examination of his old friend, Jim Cron, promptly at 11 A.M., noting they had both started their careers back in 1964 and had worked together frequently since that time. That did not mean they would not needle each other today. Mulder pointed out that Cron had not mentioned seeing a spot of blood on the garage floor, a spot that the lawyer thought was so plain that "if it had been a snake, it would have bit me." Cron explained it was very visible and looked like a "transfer stain" tracked out there by one of the policemen who had come through the kitchen. "I don't overlook things so obvious," he said.

Mulder did have Cron explain that he did not take charge of the crime scene, but only acted in an advisory capacity and made suggestions on such things as needing photographs of specific scenes. It became a serious evidentiary dance between the lawyer and the ex-cop, Mulder trying to fit the facts to match a burglary-type entrance and exit while Cron stuck with the idea of a fleeing murderer.

"You're not the kind of guy to say 'I've already made up my mind, don't confuse me with facts,' are you?" Mulder jabbed, hitting on the point that Cron had made his decision after only a half-hour walk around the house before dawn. "No," Cron shot back. "I found things to confirm my opinion."

Mulder pointed out that Cron did not examine an ice bucket or broken glass on the kitchen counter, and how a photograph showed that the broken fragment apparently had "jumped" from the floor to the shelf because someone had moved it. "You chose to ignore it because it doesn't match your story, you'd made up your mind," the lawyer probed. Cron denied that, and said further investigation gave him no reason to doubt his original conclusions.

After Mulder finished, Davis asked a few more questions himself, and Cron summarized what his conclusions were and why he had made them. The prosecutor then took his seat, correctly pleased with his best witness. "I couldn't have said it better myself," Davis observed.

24

HALENA TERESA CZABAN, the mother of Darlie's maid of honor, Basia, veered the case away from the professional and toward the personal. Instead of policemen and nurses and technicians, here was a middle-aged woman who could take the jurors inside the Eagle Drive house, and through her own eyes paint a picture of Darlie the Horrible. Before she was done, Czaban would revile the woman who had befriended her by accusing Darlie of being an unfit mother.

Part of the clash between the two women could have been due to their vastly contrasting lives. Darlie had only a high school education, but was curvy, cute, young, and blonde, with money and a family. The Polish-born Czaban was a hefty woman who wore big glasses, a tent-sized dress, and a helmet of tightly wound gray hair. She had been a registered nurse in her own country, but in America, she had worked in a factory for fifteen years, and now lived with her daughter in an apartment and did other people's laundry. She plaintively cried out at one point, "I'm a poor woman!" She did not like Darlie, did not like the way the younger woman lived or the way she raised children. Halena Czaban and Darlie Routier were from different worlds, and it didn't help that Darin finally fired Basia from her job at Testnec.

Testifying in Polish, with a Roman Catholic nun trans- lating, Czaban said she came to America in 1973 and won citizenship ten years later, living with family mem- bers in Massachusetts, Michigan, and Florida before coming to Dallas on April 6, 1996, precisely two months before the murders.

Since Basia had been Darlie's pal for years, it wasn't long before Halena Czaban was a guest in the house for dinner and by June was talking to Darlie about doing some housework and laundry for her. She began on June 4, with Basia dropping her off and giving Darin a ride to work because the Jaguar was broken. A twelve-year- old girl named Rebecca was at the house to baby-sit for Drake. Halena, spending the day doing laundry, saw Devon and Damon come in at lunchtime, and heard Dar- lie "order" the boys to either go upstairs or outside. Dar- lie took her home at five o'clock. The next day, June 5, Halena at first refused to go back because she felt that Darlie and the young baby-sitter had made fun of her. But she did return, and to her dismay, found Darlie and Rebecca together again, sitting in the family room, with eight-month-old Drake.

With that small piece of testimony, which actually said very little, the jury was escorted from the courtroom so Judge Tolle could review the upcoming piece of testi- mony. It was at that point that Czaban's floodgates of venom burst and she unleashed damning opinions that Darlie was an uncaring mother who all but tried to kill Drake, too!

Halena recounted how Darlie was seated in an arm- chair when she arrived, a blanket in her lap, and Halena asked if her leg was hurt. The older woman was horrified to discover the blanket completely swaddled little Drake. She felt the infant was in danger, and asked to be allowed to hold it. Darlie reluctantly almost shoved Drake toward

Halena and went upstairs with Rebecca. When Halena
pulled aside the hot blanket covering the baby, she said
Drake's face was very red, his lips were blue, and he was
sweating profusely. When she removed the coverlet, he
caught his breath and began to cry.

Later, she saw the baby almost topple from the glass-
topped coffee table, while the mother and baby-sitter
rested idly nearby. "I shouted, 'Oh, my God,' and caught
it," only to hear Darlie and Rebecca laugh at her. Another time, she found the baby unattended in a high chair,
where it had slipped down into a dangerous position. Halena shouted for Rebecca to come, and told the girl never
to leave the child alone like that. Darlie was upstairs and
not watching her baby.

The jury heard none of the instances of alleged abuse,
and Tolle refused to allow it into evidence, declaring it
was all irrelevant. When court adjourned for the day,
Greg Davis said the stories demonstrated "very unusual"
behavior by Darlie toward her children and could show
her state of mind a few hours before the killings happened. Family members would contend the entire episode
was a fabrication, and point out that the baby had always
liked to sleep with a blanket covering its head, and still
did. If the defense wanted to show Darlie was a caring
parent, then the prosecution might be able to bring Halena back on to repeat her stories for the jury. At this
point, however, Czaban had done no damage to Darlie at
all. "I think she's trying to get even with Darin and Darlie because Basia was fired," observed Mama Darlie.

When the jury was seated once again, Czaban testified
that Darlie had brought down her jewelry box to have
Halena look at the bracelets and rings and necklaces, and
confided that she needed to get ten thousand dollars. Czaban said the jewelry was inexpensive.

Although the jury had not heard Czaban's statements
about how she thought the baby was mistreated, they did

have an opportunity to hear the woman awkwardly speak about the mysterious car seen around the neighborhood. When Basia came by at five o'clock to pick her up, Halena said a black sports car came from the left, stopped, and a second person got into it in front of Darlie's house; then it sped away. "I got frightened a little," she said. The murders of Devon and Damon happened overnight, and a few days later Basia coaxed her mother to tell police about the strange vehicle. She told the cops she had seen it once before, in the alley behind the house when she had been over there for dinner, and thought someone was staring into the garage. When Richard Mosty began to cross-examine, he asked if she found the car to be suspicious and she replied, "Yes . . . Maybe somebody is watching."

She waffled on why it took so long to report the car to police, perhaps realizing she was helping Darlie's alibi, and Mosty asked pointedly if she had contacted the police because the strange car might be linked to the killings or "did you want to report unsafe driving?"

"I simply said what I saw," she replied. "I told my daughter they shouldn't drive that fast." Czaban went too far in trying to distance herself from stating the car might somehow be connected to the crime. "I told my daughter and she told Darin in the hospital. Cars shouldn't drive that way."

Mosty changed tactics and had Czaban explain that Darlie had been kind to her. When she first came to Texas, Darlie came by to visit and "the boys brought me flowers."

The day ended when Czaban left the stand, trailing her bizarre story behind her. She had made more points for the defense, by saying the mystery car was around, than for the prosecution, for the jury had not been allowed to hear the damning opinions that Halena held about Darlie.

*   *   *

Bibles were on the small table in the anteroom on Friday morning, opened to Psalms and Proverbs, and Darlie's aunts, who had flown in from Pennsylvania, read and prayed for their niece. Mama Darlie, after two weeks of prosecution witnesses, was feeling the weight of the ordeal, and confided, "It's hard always to be strong when you know on the other side of that door, your daughter is on trial for her life." The weather finally moderated, but the beams of sunlight brought her little warmth.

The final witness of the week was the long-awaited appearance of Barbara Jovell, known to all as Basia. She was a smaller version of her mother, with dark hair, glasses, and a severe look. Basia was to introduce several solid pieces of evidence, primarily about Darlie considering suicide and the news-tape version of the cemetery party. By doing so, she became the prosecution's second-best witness, behind Jim Cron.

Toby Shook, one of Greg Davis's assistants, did the questioning, and Basia spoke immediately of the thoughts of suicide. Darlie had told her in May, the month before the slayings, that she had taken sleeping pills out of their wrappers and had written a suicide note, only to hide them when Darin came home unexpectedly and the dog, Domain, pulled the pill wrappers from beneath the bed. Darlie, according to Basia, was feeling "really strange" and "doesn't understand why people expect so much from her." Basia told her friend she needed help. The defense objected that the incident happened more than a month before the crime and was too far in the past to matter. Tolle overruled.

A few moments later, Basia briefly discussed attending the cemetery party and cleared the way for the party tape, again objected to by the defense, which claimed that it was an edited version. Tolle overruled. Since it was a truncated version of what had happened that day, the defense said it could be prejudicial. Tolle overruled and said it showed her state of mind.

Shook then had Basia describe her background with Darlie, going back to how she met Darin in 1987, when he was only nineteen and got his job at CuPlex. A few months later, she met Darlie and was maid of honor at their wedding. In June of 1992, she went to work for Darin's new company, doing electronics testing, while Darlie kept the books. Business was good, she said, and Darlie changed, becoming ''materialistic'' and subject to fits of anger and depression, fighting frequently with Darin about money. ''She liked pretty things and looking well,'' Basia confided to the jurors. As a result, she thought, no money ''was going to Testnec, it was going to Darlie.'' Her friend had wonderful taste and accelerated her purchasing to furnish her new home, fill her jewelry box, and clothe her kids.

Business slacked off in late 1995 with fewer jobs, and money tightened, causing more frequent fights between Darin and Darlie, who had ''the more dominant personality'' and a temper that could flare. Basia warned Darin that Darlie was troubled. ''Don't you see what's going on? Something is bothering Darlie.'' According to Basia, if Darlie didn't get help soon, ''something bad will happen to her.''

Visiting the house one day, Basia said Darlie confided her thoughts about suicide and also that she was bothered about how much weight she had gained being pregnant with Drake. She also worried that if something happened to her and Darin, ''Sarilda [Routier] would take the kids.''

After the murders, Basia went to the hospital and saw Darlie alone in the ICU when Darin left briefly to check on the business, and Darlie told her the story of how she had awakened feeling pressure on her legs and saw a man with a knife start toward her throat. But in another hospital conversation, Darlie changed the details to say that the man was actually sitting on her, brushing the knife blade against her face and looking as if he enjoyed doing so.

With Shook leading Basia through the schedule of questions, he asked about the June 14 cemetery event, and when Basia described it, Shook turned on the tape. The jury was silent, but stunned by the television news tape, with Darlie and Darin acting cheerful before a field of balloons and flowers. Ironically, Munoz was in the courtroom, reporting on the case that day. On the tape, Darlie smiled and laughed and hugged people and squirted Silly String, a tarnished Madonna who was not seen as remorseful about her two dead kids.

During a break in the court proceedings, as the crowd waited downstairs, one Kerrville resident asked: ''Now who would vote to acquit?''

Naturally, the cross-examination on Basia Jovell was brutal, with Richard Mosty tearing into her own personal history in order to discredit her story.

First there was the image of Darlie the uncaring mother. Basia now said Darlie loved having kids around, gave them drinks and Popsicles, and ''was kind to all the children.'' Devon and Damon were described as polite and happy boys who had plenty of toys, food and clothing, and were gently disciplined, with perhaps a slap on the butt or a squeeze on a cheek to emphasize something. Darlie never used a belt to whip them. ''Kids loved her,'' Basia admitted. ''She is a very kind person'' who donated time and money to charities and school events, was ''a very giving person'' who bought presents for friends, and had even let Basia charge things on Darlie's personal credit card. This was very peculiar testimony from a witness who had made a clear impression only minutes before that Darlie was a materialistic, spoiled, and self-centered woman who primarily cared about herself and her possessions.

Mosty challenged Basia on the comments about no money going into the business, and she confirmed that Darin had paid big bucks for a new computerized testing machine, bought a computer on which Darlie could do the books, a new typewriter, telephones, a fax machine, and a desk. As for money being tight, Basia now said she didn't know about the company's billing receipts and expenses and had "no idea" about the cash flow of the first six months of 1996. Earlier, she had stated business had slowed down and now she didn't know anything about the accounts side of the ledger. But after saying that, she claimed that Darin, who paid her ten dollars an hour, was cheating customers by overbilling. If Mosty could emphasize such contradictions and limited knowledge, the rest of Basia's testimony might be considered suspect.

To do so, he asked the witness about her conversations with police, whom she originally told that she was not aware of any problems between Darlie and Darin, when she now said they were fighting over money. "I lied to the police," Basia admitted. Jurors had to wonder which version of Basia's story was the real one.

Concerning the suicide possibility, Basia said Darlie told her "I was going to do it" by taking pills. Mosty was carefully setting up some future questions by allowing Basia to freely outline her version of that day.

He switched to the cemetery taping and Basia toned down the impact somewhat by telling the jury the Silly String had been brought out not by Darlie but by her sister, Dana. Basia said she had not been there when a Baptist minister offered a prayer service. Mosty then touched on the different ways people observe death, and Basia said as a Polish Catholic she was used to long prayers and putting candles on graves. Had she been of

Irish descent, she may have been used to mourners getting drunk during a wake for the deceased. Having a birthday party at a cemetery went against her cultural background.

Then the jury was led from the room once again, as the defense attorney prepared to attack Basia's personal life in hopes that Judge Tolle might allow the information to be repeated before jurors. It was startling. He said she had two divorces, a psychiatric history since the age of sixteen, when she stayed home from school an entire year, had been twice incarcerated in "various insane asylums," and experienced fits of depression. Under questioning, she said she had tried to commit suicide herself when she was depressed, once put on forty pounds, heard voices, hallucinated, and was described by an acupuncturist as suffering from "manic depression." To cap that history, Basia said she had once tried to take her own life while depressed—with pills. In a discussion with a defense attorney, Basia had once said she was "afraid I'm losing my mind."

"This is the source of the suicide idea information," said defense lawyer John Hagler. The symptoms and actions that Basia herself had suffered were exactly the ones she was describing Darlie as having, "projecting" her ills on her former friend. "She was really describing herself."

Tolle said the information could not be brought before the jury because it was not relevant to the truth or untruthfulness of the testimony. The decision was a major setback for the defense team, because the jury had heard Basia, with no medical training, diagnose Darlie as suffering from depression. Had they known Basia's own background, the story may have sounded much different.

The jury went home for the weekend, thinking not about the troubled witness Basia, but about the image of Darlie, partying at the grave of her sons.

25

DARIN HAD HUNG around Kerrville from the start of
the trial, like Banquo's ghost in Shakespeare's *Macbeth*,
a sad figure always near the trial, but almost invisible,
dodging reporters and staying out of the sight of prosecutors and policemen. He had undergone some changes
since taking Doug Mulder aboard to lead Darlie's defense. Gone was the beard, except for a neat mustache.
Gone were the nugget rings, replaced by a single gold
wedding band and his high school ring with its green
stone. Gone was his belief in the system, replaced by a
feeling of betrayal and skepticism. Unable to sleep, unable to work, he held on every day until his mother,
Mama Darlie, and the other family members could de-
brief him at night and tell him what happened in court.
He was nourished by group hugs. *How did Darlie look?
Was the testimony good or bad? What was the press going to report tomorrow?* Darin was in a state of drift as
the trial entered its third week. About the only good thing
in his life was that the weather was warmer and he was
able to spend some time playing in the chilly sunshine
with his surviving son, Drake. Remembering his other
boys, he tapped his heart. "They're not buried out there

[in the cemetery]," he said. "They're in here. They're just like us."

But the toll this ordeal was taking was more than a mental and physical one. In a hotel lounge one night, he confided that he was finally broke. "I'm down to $32," he said. Almost everything he owned had been sold to raise money for the lawyers. He had refused, however, to part with a Dallas Cowboys helmet autographed by all of the members of the 1995 championship team except Deion Sanders. Darin was saving that football helmet for Drake.

He was clinging to a dream, waiting for the moment that the prosecution would finish telling its "lies" and Doug Mulder and Richard Mosty could finally reveal the true story that had been bottled up for so long. Once he and Darlie got their chance on the witness stand, Darin was sure the jury would see the truth! "Maybe in just a few more days, I'll have her back," he said. The feeling was mutual. In a private conversation in the jail, Darlie had told Darin that she had always loved him, but felt that maybe she had held a little something back. That would change when she was released. "I'm going to totally love you, like no woman has ever loved a man," she whispered.

As the third week of the trial began, Greg Davis continued his case, bringing on another strong witness, Charles Linch, a trace evidence analyst from the Southwest Institute of Forensic Sciences. Like Jim Cron, he was an expert in the aftermath of crimes. The forensic specialist was personable and confident on the witness stand, able to translate arcane scientific tests and terms into language the jury could understand.

He had volunteered his services to the Rowlett Police Department as soon as he heard about the murders, and was at the scene shortly after noon, talking with Cron and Patterson and getting a guided tour of the house. With his testing kit, he set to work on the suspected bloodstains, quickly eliminating the splotch in the garage, which he determined to have been caused by some syrupy material like Kool-Aid or a melted Popsicle. A smudge on a white sign in the garage tested positive for blood.

Linch found an "unusual" amount of blood in unexpected parts of the kitchen. The kitchen sink had been cleaned, but yielded positive results to sophisticated tests. No blood was seen on the faucet, but it, too, proved positive with a blue-green imprint when he sprayed it with Luminol and shined an ultraviolet lamp on it. Blood was found on the cabinet knobs and even inside the cabinet, which meant the only way for it to have gotten there was for the cabinet doors to have been opened.

During his three hours at the scene, the specialist directed that several things be collected for further testing, including scissors, knives, sections of carpet, and parts of the garbage disposal. He returned on June 11 to go over the house again with Rowlett officers, this time, with Greg Davis overseeing the search. Tests for blood were negative on spots in the driveway and on the gate and areas of the interior floor, he found nothing unusual around the backyard spa, and Linch had the entire family room carpet cut into two sections and taken away for a more detailed examination in the laboratory. Police spray-painted outlines where the little bodies had been on the floor. And on one section of the carpet, Linch said he found the bloody imprint of a knife, one or two steps away from Devon's body.

Darin and Darlie had also met with him that day and voluntarily gave blood and hair samples, and he collected samples from all three children. These would be used to compare with the items that had been tested or retrieved.

Linch returned again on November 21, some five and

a half months after the event, still looking for clues. Now a section of wall was cut away for tests, woodchip material was gathered from outside, and he found two more bloodstains below a kitchen light switch. His final search was made on November 26, when he tested and carted away further sections of the walls.

When he had a chance to test the blood-dappled sock found far from the crime scene, he discovered a mystery, for one of the hair fibers was either an antelope, deer, or an elk and a fiber match to a Reebok tennis shoe. He offered no real meaning beyond that, and the sock remained a mystery, now with some perplexing wildlife overtones. Linch continued his litany of positive and negative tests, but finally came to the crux of his testimony, a pair of points concerning the knives in their butcher block holder and Darlie's torn T-shirt, both of which he received on June 8.

The scientist turned seamstress briefly and stitched the holes in the T-shirt together to examine the garment as a whole. He found "defects," or holes, in five places. A puncture type was on the left front, near the collar; another puncture was on the right front, and three "defects caused by a bloody blade" were discovered on the top right shoulder. Then he mentally put the T-shirt back on the victim, Darlie, and the wound to her left shoulder matched the corresponding hole in the shirt. But he said she indicated she had no injuries to her right shoulder, where he had found the three holes. Greg Davis walked along the jury box, holding the bloody Victoria's Secret shirt for examination, and asked if Darlie might have cut the shirt in the remaining places by pulling it away from her body before puncturing it.

"That's the only way I know of that those punctures could occur without involving the skin," replied Linch.

"The shirt was pulled up?"

"It would have to be without injuring the defendant."

Another forensic brick had been thrown at the story Darlie had told officials. Science was finding things that police had not.

The tests on a knife in the butcher block were equally effective, for Linch said he found a substance, a combination of glass debris and rubber dust, on a serrated blade on one of the holstered utensils. "Did you see any difference in the rubbery material from the screen and the rubbery material you removed from the knife?"

"No, sir, I did not," Linch responded. A test cut had been made on the screen and yielded similar results.

Richard Mosty, on cross-examination, was unable to deflate the hard science that Linch had carefully recited. In fact, Linch lightened the mood himself by joking that he volunteered to help because his services are seldom sought in the heat of an investigation. "Nobody ever calls me. I'm like the Maytag man." The jury liked this fellow.

Mosty emphasized that a blond hair had been found in the screen, and DNA testing showed it did not belong to Darlie. Still, Linch felt the hair was "microscopically similar" to that of the defendant, but admitted that conclusion could easily be incorrect. "I report a scientific finding and leave it to the lawyers to draw conclusions," he said. But Mosty had no luck trying to shake the scientist's testimony on the bloody T-shirt or the fibers found on the knife, and the lawyer perhaps went too far in trying to do so. It was late in the afternoon and several jurors began to yawn. They were bored and ready to call it a day.

Greg Davis, with a few more questions, ended with a solid return to the holes in the T-shirt where Darlie had no wounds. Linch flatly stated, "In my opinion, they were self-inflicted." The prosecutor asked the experienced crime scene investigator if it was common for an adult to survive such a wicked attack on children, as Darlie had survived the fatal assault on her boys.

"I see an average of six hundred homicides a year, and I have never been made aware of an instance where an adult survives the children" with injuries that were minimal, Linch said. Mosty quickly pointed out that the wound in Darlie's neck was hardly minimal, and came close to being fatal, but Linch stuck stubbornly to his conclusion.

This day, heavy with scientific data, had not been good for Darlie, and the following session, on Tuesday, would not be much better as more men and women of the microscope, tweezer and test tube brigade stepped to the stand. The prosecution was nearing the end of its case and had relied solely on science to put Darlie Routier behind bars. For noticeably absent at this point were three names from the police department. Neither Detective Jimmy Patterson, the lead investigator, nor his partner, Detective Chris Frosch, nor their boss, Lieutenant Grant Jack, had appeared as witnesses. Indeed, the top two witnesses had been on the rent-an-expert side of the ledger: Jim Cron and Charlie Linch. The three Rowlett cops most intimately involved in the investigation were kept away from the jury.

Greg Davis continued the science lesson on Tuesday, with Bob Poole, a SWIFS specialist in ballistics and tool marks; Tom Bevell, a retired Oklahoma City police captain who runs his own forensics school; and two DNA analysts, Carolyn Van Winkle of SWIFS and Judith Floyd from Gene Screen, a Dallas laboratory. Although Bevell would return to the stand on Wednesday with much more impressive testimony, the Tuesday session was a lengthy presentation that offered neither great help to the prosecution nor openings for the defense. In short, almost everything said on Tuesday fell into the realm of inconclusive.

Poole could say only that the bloody knife that was recovered "could have" caused some of the wounds to Devon. But Van Winkle would testify that she found no evidence of Devon's blood being on the knife. Judy Floyd's test for DNA found bloodstains belonging to Darlie, Devon, and Damon on various articles of clothing and other items, not surprisingly, since all three had been bleeding. Answering defense questions, she said she also found unidentified facial and pubic hair from the scene. Such comments made little impact.

The main development of the day came in a clash of comments outside the courtroom. Norman Kinne, the First District Attorney of Dallas County, had been a regular observer at the trial and was never reluctant to grant the Dallas media an interview. At such times, he would square his shoulders and make a few certain comments about how his office was doing a terrific job protecting society in general and children in particular, apparently oblivious to the fact that the reason he was in Kerrville was that two children had not been protected, but indeed murdered. Kinne again went before the cameras during one of the breaks on Tuesday to interpret the courtroom developments and said the forensic evidence currently being presented clearly showed there had been no intruder.

From off-camera came a shout. "That's a lie!" called Darlie Kee.

Kinne sniffed, not used to having his proclamations challenged by a mere citizen. He asked, on television, if he had to stand there and be interviewed in front of "trailer trash." He later said, "Mrs. Kee started yelling at me that I was a liar, and I didn't take kindly to it."

Mama Darlie was shocked and wounded by the personal attack. *Trailer trash?* In Texas, there are few stronger epithets. Mama Darlie retreated, saying the man had no reason to stoop to gutter talk. But her teenaged daughter, Dana Stahl, had to be restrained from ''gettin' rowdy'' and responding in terms similar to the one used by the First District Attorney against the family. Dana, wearing a scarlet and black sleeveless short dress and knee-high black vinyl boots, didn't care about the man's exalted position, his coat and tie, or anything else. She was ready to get in the mud with Kinne, Texas-style showdown, nose-to-nose, right here, right now, you-'n'-me on this courthouse lawn, bubba, and I'll whup your D.A. butt all the way back to Dallas. By damn, you don't call my mama trailer trash and just walk away! Darlie sent her angry daughter home to avoid the confrontation. She didn't need two daughters in the Kerrville County jail.

In Dallas, radio station telephones lit up as talk-show callers swarmed all over Kinne's slur. It was a public relations fiasco for a prosecution team that had worked hard to spin the daily story. They wanted to appear wearing the white hats. Kinne eventually would make an on-the-air apology of sorts, particularly to people who lived in mobile homes, but the ''trailer trash'' comment was very revealing about the attitude that the District Attorney's office apparently held toward Darlie Routier.

26

BEVELL HAD BEGUN his testimony on Tuesday and it carried on all day Wednesday, after he survived a spirited assault by the defense team, which didn't want him to testify. His conclusions were just too dramatic to be allowed into evidence without a fight. He immediately hit a home run, confirming for Greg Davis that the blood trail thinned out remarkably at the utility room door, where blood had been thick enough to run down the edge of the doorway. If the intruder had had that amount of blood on his hands, it should have shown up elsewhere, at the window or the fence or the backyard, and it had not.

A few minutes later, Bevell discussed the direction of travel of some of the blood splatters he had analyzed from Darlie's T-shirt, stains that were cast off in specific directions. That opened the gate for the most dramatic moment the trial had seen from thirty-five witnesses in thirteen days of testimony.

Greg Davis went to his knees, with a knife in his hand, and portrayed Darlie stabbing her two sleeping sons. Up and back the hand arched, then down and forward. Just as he had hoped, the jurors got involved, standing and leaning over the railing to get a better view of this piece of Perry Mason theater. He held the knife to demonstrate how blood flew from the blade. "Would that stain be consistent with the defendant kneeling beside Devon, stabbing down and then pulling back up?"

"It certainly could be consistent," replied Bevell. He further stated that he had been able several times to duplicate similar stains on a similar garment by performing an over-the-shoulder stabbing motion in one of his tests. Davis showed the jury the shirts Bevell used in his reenactments to demonstrate the relationship with the stains on Darlie's shirt.

As the circumstantial evidence mounted, the strain was taking a toll on the family. The little group of women outside the courthouse door, led by Mama Darlie and Sarilda, added singing to their Bible reading, and as the lawyers worked they could hear the soft strains of hymns, such as "Love Lifted Me."

Richard Mosty quizzed Bevell thoroughly, but managed to recover little ground, even by needling the forensic specialist , claiming that "You come to your opinion and then perform a demonstration that supports your opinion?" Mosty did uncover that Bevell's tests did not include the notes that would have accompanied a truly scientific experiment, that the photographs of the crime scene he used to replicate the attack may have been incomplete, and that the expert had "no understanding" of how the bloodstained sock was found three houses away from the crime scene.

Mosty gave a hypothesis. Suppose an intruder came in, found two socks and used both of them to hide his fingerprints, and that the second sock was not found. "You can't rule out or rule in that there was only one assailant, can you?"

"Not conclusively, I sure can't," said Bevell.

The defense attorney knelt on the floor and gave a try

at staging his own demonstration of the stabbing, but Bevell would not agree that there wasn't enough room to hold the knife high or that the blade inflicted short jabs. Bevel stated that if the knife was used in the way the lawyer was doing, "[Y]ou won't inflict the wounds that were on those bodies." When he continued his meticulous cross-examination and showed a video of Bevell performing his experiments, discussing it at length, the jurors were looking hopelessly bored. Yawns spread like a plague. When Mosty arose, he was surprised.

"I cut my hand," he said. Nothing was going right.

"Good point, sir," Bevell chimed in, giving the defense attorney an opening.

As he tended the cut, all juror eyes upon him, Mosty interjected, "It is a good point, isn't it? Because in that scenario, with Mrs. Routier having blood on her hand, her hand would have slipped, wouldn't it, and there would be a cut on her palm?" No such wound existed.

He threw out more questions and alternatives. Could the blood spots that put Devon's blood on Darlie's back be consistent with a paramedic going from Devon to Darlie and touching her? How about a paramedic snapping off rubber gloves with Devon's blood as he approached her? How about the blood spurting from Devon's chest as his father performed CPR and the child's fountaining blood slathering Darin's entire upper torso? He read from a manual written by Bevell to demonstrate that the author did not approve of some methods used in this investigation. He had Bevell confirm he was charging $1,500 per day or $125 per hour for his testimony.

Davis, on a final few questions, had Bevell testify that his tests showed the knife imprint found on the carpet was caused by the blade being placed there, not dropped, as Darlie claimed. Davis had charged that the mother put the knife beside the dying boy after cutting herself. Then the prosecutor asked about whether the sock's location would be ''consistent with the assailant wanting to disassociate that sock from the crime scene?'' Bevell said that was correct. Further, he was asked, what was the most likely reason that Devon's blood was on the back of Darlie's shirt? ''In my opinion,'' declared Bevell, ''it's more consistent with the action of the knife coming over the shoulder to deposit it on the back.''

After court, Mosty told the press that the prosecution had failed to ''put the knife in her hand.''

When the day's testimony ended, the jurors went home with one single image in their mind—Darlie on her knees beside her boy, stabbing him repeatedly with a butcher knife, trails of Devon's blood flying from the seven-inch blade to paint an incriminating scarlet path down her back.

On Thursday, January 23, the prosecution was ready to wrap up its case with one final witness, still another out-of-town expert, FBI criminal profiler Allen Brantley, a specialist in criminal investigative analysis. Greg Davis planned to use Brantley's expertise to summarize the case. Like most FBI agents, the thin and bespectacled Brantley was schooled in how to address a jury. They always remain calm and exude professionalism, look directly at the lawyer when a question is asked, but turn if they must to look directly at the jurors when answering. It can be a disconcerting trait, but it is effective.

Doug Mulder and his team of defense attorneys fought to prevent him from testifying, and while the jury was out of the room, Brantley gave the reason why. ''It's my opinion that this crime scene was staged and that both Devon and Damon were killed by someone that they knew, and someone that they knew very well.'' Mulder and his colleagues said Brantley was going to give personal conclusions and not scientific fact, had prepared no report in advance of the trial, and that his testimony would confuse and mislead the jury. But Judge Tolle said the information was relevant and its value outweighed the possibility of it being prejudicial.

With the jury ready, Brantley recited his educational and professional qualifications. He had been with the FBI more than thirteen years and currently was assigned to the National Center for Analysis of Violent Crime. Then he set to work explaining his analysis. His facts were based upon crime-scene photos, investigative reports and a study of victimology.

The killings took place in a low-crime area, the house was surrounded by other residences, a car was parked out front, a light was on downstairs, the neighborhood was hard to penetrate by car or foot, unknown obstacles would confront someone trying to escape, and a large animal cage was inside the garage. All of the things would deter a prowler, he said, basing his conclusion on the FBI interviews of hundreds of violent felons to learn what they look for prior, during, and after an attack.

Other items didn't mesh with normal crimes of this sort, he said. The garage would have to be negotiated in the darkness, the offender focused on the children and not the mother, that adults are usually "dispatched" before a killer turns on kids, and that it was unlikely that an assailant who had just stabbed two little boys to death would be chased away by a small woman, or leave her alive.

Devon and Damon "were probably the most low-risk victims that there are," Brantley observed. Young, white, and protected, they were not in the orbit of drug abuse, robbery and sexual assault. Therefore, he concluded, the motive to kill them had to be personal. And there was no doubt in his mind that, because of the severity of their wounds compared with their mother's, the children were the object of the attack.

The lack of breakage and disruption of furniture at the

crime scene also indicated that someone had a "propri-
etary interest" in those things, particularly when compared to the horrible deaths inflicted on Damon and
Devon. The overturned vacuum cleaner appeared to him
to have been thrown down deliberately, not knocked over
in a fight. It was "very, very curious" that there was no
bloodstain on the fence or gate. Only one wineglass was
broken out of a wine rack filled with glasses and bottles,
blood droplets didn't extend beyond the utility room, and
the debris-bearing bread knife found in the butcher block
rack was strange. "Why would an offender break into
the home and get the knife and cut the screen and put it
back? That is ludicrous," Brantley declared.

Doug Mulder was sarcastic in his treatment of the East
Coast expert, downplaying the appearance of professionalism by asking, "Do y'all keep statistics as to when
you're wrong?" Brantley said, yes, as a matter of fact,
they had started keeping such data recently, but he measured the success of the FBI program by the number of
requests the agency gets for help. "Consumer satisfac-
tion," he said. Mulder began his next question by saying,
"Professor . . ."
He asserted that Brantley worked backward in this
case, starting with a suspect that had already been identified. Brantley granted that he knew Darlie had been
charged, but considered all information available.
Then Mulder gave Brantley's professionalism a slap,
asking if he knew how many weapons were involved in
the crime. Brantley said the bread knife was never submitted for FBI testing, that Linch and he didn't discuss
where the debris was found on that blade, and that Brantley had not personally examined the slit screen.
"Did you know that there has been testimony that
none of Devon's blood was on the knife?"
"My understanding was that they had the blood types

of both boys on the knife," responded the agent, surprised at the DNA results.

Mulder asked if he assumed both boys were killed with
the butcher knife, and Brantley said yes. He had assumed
the blood of both boys was on the blade. The exchange
put a dent in the FBI expert's testimony. If he was wrong
with that assumption, might he be off with another?

Minutes later, he again was struggling with the issue
of the sock. "It's my opinion that sock was part of the
staging of this event," said Brantley. "That sock was
planted after the boys had been stabbed." But, like every
other witness, he was unable to say when or how.

"Did you know that someone was trying to get in the
garage on June 5?" Mulder probed, a reference to the
testimony of Basia's mother. He drew an immediate objection from Davis, which was sustained by the judge,
while the FBI man looked puzzled.

The jury was excused while the defense team made a
final charge at the FBI windmill. Richard Mosty said the
agent had never even been inside the house and based
most of his conclusions on news reports. He asked for a
mistrial, but Tolle said the witness's testimony was based
upon exhibits and denied that motion. Another motion
for a mistrial on another legal point was defeated. The
defense requested a directed verdict from the bench that
the state had not proven its case. That motion was also
denied.

At 2:55 P.M., Greg Davis announced that the state was
resting its case.

The game was half over and Detective Jimmy Patterson was still on the sidelines.

27

THE FAMILY WAS not only ready but eager to begin the defense of Darlie. Darin came out of the self-imposed exile and made his first appearance at the courthouse, drawing a massive amount of attention from the press and spectators. "The lies have gone on long enough," he told reporters. "The jury's been hearing from people who knew her for minutes or hours. Now they'll hear from people who've known her for years."

His mother, Sarilda, remained equally firm on behalf of her daughter-in-law. "I've never doubted her for an instant, and if anybody tells me she did it, I'd slap their face." For Mama Darlie, it was time to let Doug Mulder have a chance to earn his expensive fee. She had given Mulder another payment recently that had required her to get a grace-period extension on her mortgage, and told him, "Here's my house payment. I'm going to be sleeping on your couch soon." But to her, there was no question the fee was worth every penny. "If Doug Mulder told me to go stand in the middle of the street in front of the courthouse and strip, I'd do it, if it would help Darlie."

And so it began, shortly after the state rested its case, with the defense starting slowly and softly, putting on four witnesses before the court session ended Thursday. It was as if Mulder was playing poker, showing just enough of his cards to let the opposition know he held some strength. For three weeks, he had dominated the court by doing little, even when he was just sitting at the defense table with his fingers steepled, his eyes following every move, giving the appearance of some predatory creature ready to pounce. His reputation preceded him, and everyone felt that the real Doug Mulder was about to emerge from a chrysalis, awake and on the attack. He let other members of the defense team begin the strategy of softening the image of Darlie Routier.

The first defense witness was Sherry Moses, one of Darlie's aunts from Pennsylvania, who wasted no time in describing how good a person and mother her niece was. "She's just always such a gentle mother, always very patient," Moses said, her voice quavering. "She never spanked them, she was always so gentle and soft-spoken with them. . . . Her patience was incredible. All her babies were special to her."

Defense lawyer Curtis Glover directed Moses to describe Darlie in the hospital, where she met her niece about midnight the day after the murders. Darlie, she said, was sitting in bed, "numb [and] just in agony." Sherry saw the big bruise on her arm right away. By the time Moses observed Darlie at the private funeral home viewing, the bruises had darkened even more and Darlie had become even more emotional. "I could hear her screaming when she saw her boys. She was damning the person who did this to her babies. It tore our hearts out to hear her pain."

Then she was asked about the graveside party, which Moses attended in its entirety, and the witness brushed away any idea that it was an extraordinary event. "To me, it was just a final tribute to Devon."

This type of testimony was a direct challenge to the

long list of nurses and medical personnel who had said there was no bruising and that Darlie acted uncaring and aloof. Greg Davis did the cross-examination, but spent little time with the witness. He asked why she never inquired why medical personnel didn't attend the bruises and if she would agree that "it's possible the defendant behaved differently with the children when you weren't around?" Moses shot back, "No, I do not agree with that."

Davis emphasized that Darlie loved beautiful things and put a lot of money into the house, and Moses agreed. She also vehemently denied telling a prosecution investigator that Darlie had said she could identify an attacker. On the attack itself, Moses told Davis that there was "a lot" Darlie could not remember. "She just said she'd been sleeping," Moses said. "Damon nudged her and she saw the man leaving. . . . She wasn't aware that she was wounded until she turned on the lights and saw the boys." Darlie had also told Sherry of remembering a "sensation of struggle."

The next witness was even more interesting. He was David Rogers, the pastor of Shepherd's Heart Fellowship Church in Mesquite, a minister for about twenty years. He had not known the Routier family prior to being contacted by a mutual friend before dawn on June 6 and asked to pray for them. Rogers went to the hospital at ten o'clock and visited with the family, but didn't speak with Darlie. Later, he would become close with her and talk with Darlie fifty-one times while she was in jail.

He first met the defendant at the funeral service, where he had been asked to officiate, and Darlie arrived with Darin and Detectives Patterson and Frosch. This time Preston Douglass was handling the defense team's questioning, and he had Rogers establish that he had officiated at dozens of funerals and was very familiar with how grieving parents act. How about Darlie? "She was grieving appropriately,'' said the minister. ''I observed a mother who was grieving and heartbroken and anguishing over the loss of her children.''

Douglass asked him about the party, and the pastor said it did not strike him as ''abnormal.'' He also observed the arm bruises that ''appeared significant.''

Sherri Wallace assumed the cross-examination for the prosecution, and needled the pastor about being difficult to contact. Rogers said he had been apprehensive about speaking with an investigator. When she hinted that Darlie wasn't crying upon entering the funeral home viewing room, Rogers contested the statement, saying he saw tears on the face of the defendant. ''She never whined in my presence. Her displays of grief were genuine and real,'' he said, a comment that was a direct slap at the Baylor nurses who had repeatedly used the term ''whined'' in describing Darlie.

The prosecution made a foray against the use of the rap song ''Gangsta's Paradise'' at the funeral of the little boys, but Rogers shrugged that off, saying he was told by Darin that it was the kids' favorite song. Wallace asked a leading and loaded question, designed more for jury consumption than an answer: ''Did you feel the pocket knives in the coffin of two boys who had been stabbed was appropriate?'' Rogers would not agree with her insinuation, and said he wasn't aware that tarot cards were also put into the coffin. Later, the prosecutor would say the use of ''Gangsta's Paradise'' was an odd choice for a funeral, even if it was the favorite of the slain children and was an anti-drug message. ''I've never seen a Baptist hymnal with that one in it.''

The early witnesses were passing in quick succession, for the sooner they got off the stand, the better for the prosecution, which had spent three weeks building momentum and didn't want it derailed by tears and good words for the defendant.

Next up was Dana Godfrey, a friend of Darlie's for about eight years who described her pal as "a sweet, caring, loving person from the first day I met her." At the hospital, Godfrey found Darin "in shock" and Darlie holding pictures of the boys in her arms, crying and rocking back and forth. Godfrey removed the pictures from her hands and told Darlie to try and rest. "There was no faking . . . I saw the real Darlie and she was heartbroken."

On cross-examination, Greg Davis was brief. Godfrey had said she was taken aback that blood was still on Darlie's hands, arms, and neck. "It looked like they didn't clean her up very well." Davis wanted to know if she told a nurse that, and Godfrey said she had not, but did tell a nurse to give Darlie something to calm her down.

The last witness of the day was Cara Byford, known to her friends as Jeannie, a resident of Plano who works in the same office as Mama Darlie Kee and had known and socialized with Darlie Routier, who was about her age, for four years. She also described the defendant as "kind-hearted, one of the nicest people I've ever met," usually upbeat and happy.

Jeannie also saw Darlie in the hospital, holding pictures of the children and crying. She was "very hurt and painful. She missed her boys." The witness also noticed bruises on the arms that were so significant she didn't feel it necessary to point the problem out to a nurse. At the funeral home viewing and later at the graveside party, she believe Darlie had behaved appropriately to how a grieving parent should. When Jeannie was allowed to read a poignant poem in court that she had given Darlie, not only did the defendant begin to cry, but several jurors also appeared to be emotionally moved. Was the personalization of Darlie Routier working?

Greg Davis dealt quickly with this witness, too. Time

was running out for the day and the prosecution needed to move on before this emotional testimony eroded the purely cold and scientific arguments put forward by their hired experts. But it wasn't easy. When he probed, ''Wouldn't you agree that even a kind-hearted person can reach a point where they can't cope?'' the witness shot back, ''Not in this case!''

That night, a full moon came up over Texas and that, along with the warming weather, seemed to be an omen for the Routier family. Maybe, finally, better things were on the horizon.

But that hope was dashed the following morning when the first witness fell squarely into a devastating prosecution trap. Darlie's friend Julie Clark of Rockwall had received a number of letters from Darlie while she was in jail, in her large and distinctive handwriting. On cross-examination, the prosecutors had her confirm the same handwriting appeared in a leather-bound diary that police had confiscated from the Routier house.

Davis put the diary into evidence and read a startling passage: ''I hope that one day you will forgive me for what I am about to do. My life has been such a hard fight for a long time, and I just can't find the strength to keep fighting anymore,'' read the final entry, dated May 3, a little more than a month before the slayings of Devon and Damon. Davis also read a passage in which Routier wrote that she was a ''miserable person'' and pleaded for the forgiveness of her family. ''Do not hate me.'' According to Davis, the depressing words showed Darlie's state of mind and backed up the earlier testimony of Basia concerning a scheme by Darlie to commit suicide.

Doug Mulder protested the passages were taken out of context and the whole body of the work needed to be considered. The ''private'' journal, he said, was never meant for public consumption. Greg Davis didn't see it that way at all, and during a break in the trial, he showed it to reporters while Darlie watched, and at one point told the news-gatherers, "Y'all need to look at the whole thing. There's a lot more in there."

To support that, Mulder read some of the other passages to the reporters. "The time is getting near. Soon we will have another wonderful son," said the entry for October 1995, the month Drake was born. On April 21, "The time has come and gone so quickly. He is a wonderful baby. He is so much fun—happy all the time. He smiles at everyone. I'm a very proud mother of three wonderful, gorgeous boys." The entry for that day ended with a proclamation that she and Darin need to be strong and "watch over and protect the children, for they are our future." Mulder said he would read other journal entries to the jury later in the trial.

Julie Clark, on other matters, testified that Darlie had "some good days and some bad" as she suffered postpartum depression following the birth of Drake. But she had fully recovered and, in Clark's view, never stopped taking care of herself or her family. "After she had her period, she got better and seemed a lot happier. I don't want to be rude, but as far as her sex drive, it made a tremendous difference."

Clark also disagreed with the prosecution idea that Darlie snapped because she was unable to lose weight after the third birth. "She could still get into the jeans that she had before Drake," the friend insisted.

LuAnn Black, another of Darlie's aunts from Pennsylvania, had watched the trial daily from the spectator section and now found herself on the witness stand, where she also cast a vote for the defendant's behavior. "She loved her children very, very much," Black assured the jury.

The final witness of the long week of testimony was

Karen Neal, the nurse and neighbor and friend of the Routiers, who had been awakened the morning of the murders by Darin pounding on the door at 2:35 A.M., crying, "Help! I need your help! Someone just murdered my children."

Karen had seen Darlie only briefly at the house that morning as paramedics took her away, but soon after, she visited her friend at the hospital. "She tried to reach for my hands and started to cry," Karen testified. "She appeared very upset."

Drake was in Karen's arms and Darlie said, "Let me hold him," but couldn't reach out because of the hospital tubes and bandages. So Karen placed the baby on Darlie's stomach and Darlie held him by the fingers. "Was the love between the mother and child apparent?" she was asked. "Very much so," Neal responded, adding later that Darlie was "very compassionate, very outstanding with her children" and that many neighborhood kids regularly went to Darlie's house.

The neighbor backed up the earlier testimony that "Gangsta's Paradise" was "definitely Devon and Damon's favorite song" and there was nothing wrong with playing it at the memorial service. As for the postpartum depression, Neal said Darlie did not seem to suffer any worse "than I did after I had my children."

But perhaps the most important part of her testimony was bringing the mystery car back before the jury. She had seen "a small black car" parked in the street, right in front of her house and angled across the street toward Darlie's, a week before the murders. The windows were tinted. When Karen approached the vehicle, she said "he sped off."

Under cross-examination by Assistant District Attorney Toby Shook, Karen said she thought the driver was a male with dark hair, but could not determine his race or if he was alone, and that she had seen the same car in the neighborhood several times over the past month. And, she testified, she was "very concerned that someone would be sitting there staring at the Routier home." When she eventually told Darin about it, he also grew concerned, she said.

The judge called it a day at noon after explaining to the jury that the early halt was because a witness was unavailable, but no one was at fault for that. He may have soothed the jurors, but the point was an open question.

Mulder had planned to start Friday off with the man the prosecutors never put on the witness stand—Detective Jimmy Patterson. But when the defense attorney sought the policeman, Mulder learned the Rowlett cop had been given permission by the prosecution to return to Dallas after the state's case was rested on Thursday. That meant the defense had to shuffle its witness list, and instead of being able to interrogate Patterson, they had to begin Friday with Julie Clark, who stumbled into the diary trap. It was a major tactical loss. Mulder promised that on Monday morning, the elusive Detective Patterson would finally be on the witness stand. "I don't think there's anything sinister about it, but it gives them a chance to prepare him to testify," he said. Davis protested that Mulder mentioning the detective's absence in open court gave the jury the impression that the prosecutors intentionally had made the lead investigator unavailable, as if they were hiding something. To court observers, the question of why Patterson could not have spent one more night in Kerrville was a valid one. Now the prosecutors had an entire weekend to get him ready for what was certain to be a dicey appearance.

28

JIMMY LEE PATTERSON, a cop for more than seventeen years and a detective for eight, was the first witness of the last week. Doug Mulder considered Patterson to be the weak link in the investigative chain, and got the detective to admit immediately that he had not even testified in the now-famous mock trial held by the prosecutors. After his poor performance in earlier hearings, his lack of participation in the training session staged by the prosecutors indicated that he was not likely to be called as one of their witnesses.

"I'm not going to remember everything," Patterson hedged after denying that he had spoken with Karen Neal about the little black car in the neighborhood. But he said Barbara (Basia) Jovell had told him about such a car when he talked with her at 3:54 A.M. on the day of the murders.

Asked for any notes he took concerning the hospital interviews, Patterson had to return to the witness waiting room to retrieve them, and they were not notes, but his reports, some of which carried no dates. He said he took no handwritten notes, and Mulder pounced. "Oh, you took mental notes!"

He said he went to see Darlie at 6:11 A.M., for the

second time giving a precise time—not about 6:10 or 6:
15—but an exact minute, just as having talked with Jovell at precisely 3:54 A.M. If he was taking only mental
notes, he was very exact. He was told Darlie had just
come out of surgery, but did not know if she was med-
icated at the time. "I asked her if she was okay and felt
well enough to talk with us," and she answered all the
police questions for about twenty minutes. Frosch stood
by taking notes, but didn't jot down the time of the interview. "She told us . . . she had awoken to find an intruder over her . . . she saw a knife, she struggled with
him . . . he was wearing a black cap." The assailant was
described as having shoulder-length straight brown hair
and also wearing a short-sleeve T-shirt and blue jeans.
He had no visible scars or tattoos and Darlie could not
describe his face, the detective said.

During a break in court, Patterson went to hunt
Frosch's handwritten notes of the interview, but reported
he could not find them. "I don't have those," he said.
Instead, he reviewed Frosch's supplemental, typed notes.
Asked whether they had used a tape recorder for the interview, Patterson explained that "we don't do that."
Mulder then produced a stenographer's notebook which
contained the handwritten Frosch notes, and Patterson
spent five minutes reviewing it, saying it was the first
time he had seen those notes.

"Did she tell y'all the man was possibly black?"
Mulder asked.

"No," the detective said, and Mulder followed with
why, then, did that comment appear in Frosch's notes?
Greg Davis intervened with an objection and the judge
sustained it, telling Mulder he could call Frosch as a witness to ask about his notes, and Mulder replied that he
intended to do so.

"You made no handwritten notes when you talked to
Darin?"

"No."

"You made no handwritten notes when you talked to Darlie?"

"No."

Mulder questioned him more about the mystery car, and Patterson sparred with him about what time various bits of information concerning it were received, but admitted that he had spoken with at least two people about such a vehicle in the early hours of the investigation. When the lawyer began to question Patterson about what he observed back at the house on Eagle Drive and got in another dig about the lack of notes, Judge Tolle ordered Mulder to move on: "I think we've established that he didn't take any notes."

On some points at the crime scene, the lead investigator said that he was "just going on what James Cron told me" and could not personally verify if some of those observations.

Mulder edged closer to the exact point he wanted to make with Patterson, having him describe meeting with Darlie again at the hospital on June 7, then at the police station on June 8, where she was read her Miranda rights and gave "a voluntary written statement" ten pages long. Patterson didn't recall whether Darin gave him the keys to his house and business, because "someone else went over there and done that."

The lawyer read a portion of the statement aloud, admitting that she and Darin "had a few words between us" the night before the murders, but Darin had kissed her good night and said he loved her. Later that night, "I felt pressure on me," Damon was leaning on her right shoulder and the man was walking away. She heard glass break, saw the knife on the floor and ran back through the kitchen, realizing that blood was all over the kitchen. She said she told Darin, "he cut them" and "tried to kill me." She wrote that she put a towel to her own neck and a towel onto Damon's back, saw the glass coffee table had been knocked halfway over and a flower arrangement was toppled. Darin told her the boys were dead. "After that I just remember screaming and showing Darin my neck."

One very important point was that Darlie wrote that she had called for her husband as well as phoned the 911 emergency number. Critics had zeroed in on the earlier reports that she just called for police help, saying that the normal first reaction should have been to scream for help from Darin. On June 8, when the report was written, she acknowledged doing just that.

Patterson did not speak to her while she wrote the statement, he said, and denied on the stand that she was his prime suspect at that point. He told her the police had "a lot of leads."

Mulder asked if the detective personally checked the security light in the back yard. He had not and did not know where to walk to make the motion-sensitive light come on. He said he had not read a police report about the light, but later backtracked and said it stayed on for eighteen minutes. When Mulder questioned the change, Patterson replied, "Well, but I did read the report. It was just my mistake."

Then the defense attorney inserted a critical point by having Patterson confirm that two detectives hid unseen microphones at the grave site of Devon and Damon "in case someone confessed." After a short lunch break, Mulder honed in on the graveyard spying, asking if Patterson was aware that planting the microphones might violate federal and state laws. "Are you telling me that you folks planted microphones at the graveside where people went to pray and grieve for the dead?" asked Mulder with a disbelieving tone.

Patterson was immediately alert, and refused to answer.

"Did you know you were violating state and federal laws?"

"I won't answer questions about violating laws," the detective said. "Until I get legal counsel."

"You are going to answer my questions," Mulder shot back.

"No one's read me any statute that I violated any law. If I violated something, I'm not going to answer you."

After a few more thrusts, the judge said the issue would be handled later and ordered Mulder to move forward to another subject. When Patterson was handed a transcript of his prior testimony, his hands began to shake nervously. The lawyer badgered him about a few more points, then Patterson was allowed to step down to consult a lawyer of his own before resuming his testimony.

The episode was not yet over, but was a clear win for the defense. The work done by Patterson was shown in an extremely bad light, and now the lead detective was refusing to answer questions about whether he, himself, had broken the law. The jurors watched in awe.

Mary Angela Rickels, a small, slim woman, wore a light blue suit with white shoes, a combination that violated the fashion sense of some women in the courtroom, according to their comments later. Who would wear white shoes in January? Tsk-tsk. However, Rickels wasn't there to discuss her wardrobe, but to tell what happened about 1:30 A.M. on the morning of June 6 at her home in Rowlett on Miami Drive, just a few blocks east of Eagle Drive. Geographically, the streets are close. A car coming north on Dalrock Road, upon reaching Willowbrook Drive, could turn right and be one street away from Miami. A left turn would put the car at the curve where Eagle Drive meets Willowbrook. It is the same general neighborhood.

A mother of three teenagers and a fifteen-month-old

child, Rickels suffered a stroke after her baby was born. Her husband worked the overnight shift for a cable company. She testified that she was watching television at 1:30 when she heard "somebody at the door, and my first thought was that it was my husband coming in." The noise, "hittin' on the door," continued and when she snapped on the porch light, Rickels saw two men, who immediately ran away. One was stocky and wearing a knit cap over blond hair that could be seen beneath the edges, and a dark jogging suit. The other man, she said, was tall and thin. Once they ran away, she checked the locks and resumed watching television.

Only a few minutes later, she heard a "tapping" sound at her daughter's bedroom window and peeked out to find the same men there again, this time with either a knife or a screwdriver. When she turned on the lights, they fled once again. Although she told her husband and others, she did not report the incident to police until several days later. "Were the police interested in what happened to you?" Mulder asked. Rickels shook her head. "Not at all."

Toby Shook, for the prosecution, had the witness say that she was watching a horror movie that night, and redefined the front door noise as a "jiggle." Shook actually rattled the knob of a courtroom door to produce a loud, rattling sound, and the witness said the noise continued for several minutes.

What about the second man?, he asked. She said he wore a dark cowboy hat, a Western shirt, and jeans.

In front of the house, she said, was a strange car that she described as a dark blue, small, and boxy vehicle. It was seen there at 2 o'clock and was still there an hour later. Shook pinpointed the day she reported that attempted break-in as June 11, five days after the Routier children were killed.

Finally, the prosecutor zeroed in on Rickels' health.

She had suffered three heart attacks in 1996, including one in July, and her younger brother had died on June 3. She was taking a number of medications, including an antidepressant, and her monthly drug bill was some $1,600.

The witness's testimony could be powerful if the jurors believed her. Or it could be dismissed if they thought she was simply hallucinating under the influence of drugs and a scary movie. How could you take someone seriously, some women opined, who wore white shoes in January!

The next witness would have to be carefully handled by the prosecution, for Sarilda Routier projects the image of a totally believable person. Wearing a plain black suit with a high neck to match her dark hair, Sarilda had never hidden the fact that she loved and believed Darlie. Today would be no different, and the prosecutors did not want to be seen by jurors as picking on a woman who had lost two grandchildren to violent death. In fact, when she was asked how many grandchildren she had, her response was not that she had only two, Drake and Dillon, the son of her other boy, Deon. She responded simply and powerfully that "I had four."

Asked to describe her relationship with Darlie, Sarilda Routier gushed, "She's really a girlfriend of mine." They spoke frequently. "Darlie's a daughter-in-law that everyone would want to have. Y'all would be lucky to have her as your daughter-in-law."

"Do you think Darlie is selfish or materialistic?"

"I most certainly do not," replied Sarilda. "Darlie liked nice things, Darin liked nice things, and they worked hard. I don't see anything wrong with that." Darlie was, she said, a wonderful mother who could deny her children nothing, "and that's the truth."

Asked about Darlie's grief, she snapped, "I'm offended by anyone saying it wasn't there. It was appropriate at every step.'' And her family's goal right now was ''getting Darlie home and getting this awful mess straightened out.''

Greg Davis knew a no-win situation when he saw one. He would approach this hostile and dangerous witness with extreme care. What lawyer in his right mind would want to be seen badgering a mother-in-law who thought her daughter-in-law was a saint? ''Mrs. Routier, I know you loved your grandchildren,'' he said. ''I'm sorry you had to come down here. I have no questions for you.''

But he would have plenty of questions for the next witness. Sarilda's oldest son. Darlie's husband.

If anyone was expecting a lightning bolt with his testimony, they would be disappointed, for the simple reason that Darin was asleep upstairs in his house when his sons were killed downstairs. He didn't see anything until after the fact, and was 100 percent in support of his wife.

At age twenty-nine, tall and well-built, his hair cut neatly and wearing a dark, conservative suit, Darin Routier was a walking reminder of just how young he and Darlie really were. They were not wild kids who had spurned society, but instead had embraced the standards of their day, prospered through hard work and used their money to buy material possessions on a scale unusual for their ages. In others words, they represented what many parents wished their own kids were.

He recited his work and personal background, then Mulder had him address the prosecution contention that he was broke. For 1995, Darin read from a tax return, he reported a gross income of about $264,000 and netted about $100,000 for himself. Most of the equipment in the business was paid for, including about $11,000 worth of new material—a new laptop computer and desktop computer and miscellaneous gear. Basia had been the only full-time employee, and he thought she was jealous of

Darlie and wanted more than the $10 an hour he was paying. In fact, he said, Basia had been terminated from her last two jobs and was making more from him than she ever had before.

He gave himself a salary of about $1,000 to $1,500 each week "depending on the bills," had paid $10,800 in cash for the Jaguar, and the boat payment was about $340 a month.

Concerning Darlie's postpartum depression, he said that she called him at the office on May 3 and he went home, finding her on the bed, weeping and writing in her "private diary," which he did not read. "She just said that she was really feeling bad." He pondered the situation and realized "she needed me to spend more time with the kids, and it hit me that she didn't want me to work so much." He said the situation was a one-time thing, that "we had a good long cry and the next day she perked up." A few days later, Darlie resumed having her period for the first time in months and immediately felt better, he said.

His wife was, in his opinion, "[t]he most loving, caring woman I've ever seen with her kids. Our whole lives revolved around those babies."

As he went over the events of June 5, when the Jag broke down, he said he drove Darlie's Pathfinder to work and when he returned home with Darlie's sister, Dana, "a black car came behind me" going a bit fast for the residential neighborhood. Darlie told him that Halena also had mentioned something about a black car parked in the alley and someone looking into the garage, and that Karen Neal had mentioned a black car about a week before.

The family had dinner together and he took Dana home, then returned. The baby was sleeping on Darlie, and Darin confirmed the infant liked to sleep under blankets in "complete darkness." He and Darlie talked until midnight about many things, the broken car, a trip she had planned to Cancún with a girlfriend, his tenth high school reunion, and his sister's upcoming wedding.

Back on finances, he said he had some $7,000 in his business account and another $18,000 to $20,000 in accounts receivable. "I had plenty of money," he said, shrugging off the prosecution claim he was down to his last few bucks, and with his work for big companies, he expected to continue to prosper.

He awoke upstairs to the sound of breaking glass, then Darlie's screams, "I mean screaming so loud you wouldn't believe it." He found her at the bottom of the stairs, yelling, "Devon! Devon! Devon!" Darin found the boy with huge gashes in his chest and thought the toppled glass table top had fallen on him. He didn't realize that Damon was also hurt until he lifted the child's T-shirt and saw the wounds.

Darlie was running back and forth getting towels and brought them to him. "She was trying to stop the bleeding, to hold his chest together," he said with a sob, and at the defense table, Darlie put her hand to her mouth. "She had the phone in her hand, she kept running back and forth getting towels and screaming."

Then he was asked about the first cop on the scene, Officer Waddell. Darin looked contemptuous. "As soon as he walked into the room, he froze. He wouldn't help me. I never saw a gun." Chaos followed the arrival of other people, and amid the yelling, Darin saw one of the paramedics replace the glass top on the coffee table so he would have a work surface, and another knocked down a lamp shade. Darlie, he said, was standing beside the vacuum cleaner, using it like a cane for support. He later saw it was laying down in the kitchen.

Darlie, he testified, had fetched three or four wet towels from the kitchen. That item could explain how blood got smeared into the sink and around the cabinets.

Darin's testimony was tying together a lot of loose ends for the defense, and after a twenty-minute break, Mulder continued with his best witness so far. Darin spoke of the hospital, when his wife was sedated and groggy and on an emotional roller coaster. Her actions were appropriate, there were bruises on her arm, and she kept asking to see Drake. "Karen took the baby in and Darlie held him by his fingers. When we got the pictures [of Devon and Damon] she just fell apart."

Darin shook his head slightly, disgusted, remembering the cooperation with police, when he gave them his keys to everything, permission to do whatever they wanted and they told him they were pursuing "hundreds" of leads. He felt betrayed and that they had lied to him.

He and Sarilda planned the funeral and the use of the rap song was chosen because it was the boys' favorite. When asked if it was appropriate, Darin responded that "it was not appropriate that they were killed, either." They were buried together because "they died together and they went to Heaven together." Some items the boys treasured, from silver coins and stuffed animals, not just pocketknives, were placed in the coffin.

Darin added another piece of vital information and said Darlie was right-handed. Her throat wound was more consistent with her being left-handed, if she inflicted it herself.

Greg Davis was not as polite with Darin as he was with Sarilda, and started his cross-examination by challenging the new appearance, saying Darin had changed it "dramatically." Then he threw a curve ball, one for which neither side was really prepared, as he addressed the curious sock. "That sock's yours?"

"I don't know that," Darin responded.

"You told Corinne Wells it was your sock on December 3, that it had come from your utility room."

Darin scrunched his forehead, clearly not remembering Corinne Wells. He recalled that he had spoken with the couple who now lived in his previous house on Bond Street for about an hour and a half one evening in December, going over there to see if the screens had ever been cut there. "You told her it would take only 27 seconds for Darlie to have put the sock down the alley?"

"No, I did not say that," Darin said.

"Isn't it true there were a lot of things troubling your wife back then?"

"No, sir."

Darin then contested the reports of CPS worker Jamie Johnson, who interviewed Darlie in jail, saying that she was "prying" and, under further questioning, said, "She is becoming a liar."

The wrangling continued. On business, Darin insisted that although things were "comfortably slow" during the summer, he had already made $110,000 in the first five months of the year. Davis pressed whether "living large has its costs." Darin defended his lifestyle, although admitting Davis was "somewhat" correct in saying they were caught up in a materialistic binge in 1996.

The husband treated $10,000 overdue in taxes, a $12,000 credit-card debt, and the Jaguar repair bill as inconsequential in light of his income.

Back to the crime, Davis lunged.

"She slept through Devon being stabbed in the chest?"

"Yes, sir."

"She slept through Damon being stabbed four times in the back?"

"Yes, sir."

"Wouldn't you agree that your wife's story means she slept through her own stabbing and didn't wake up until her middle child woke her up on the couch?"

"Yes, sir."

When Davis badgered him about his memory changing, improving over time and reflecting only now that Darlie had brought him towels while he was doing CPR on Devon, Darin replied, ''Mr. Davis, I've thought about this for 265 days.'' He stuck with his latest version and denied changing his story to match a need to place Darlie by the kitchen sink. ''She was going back and forth from Devon and Damon rendering aid.''

The court day had been long and wearing, and Darin's testimony was not close to the end. Judge Tolle called it a day at 5:15 P.M., giving both sides some breathing room while the case reached its dramatic peak.

29

THE CROSS-EXAMINATION OF Darin continued the following day, with Greg Davis attempting to prove that a sword of debt had threatened the young couple. Davis produced records that Testnec had recorded receipts of $74,000 for the first five months of 1995, and had paid out $77,297. The company's landlord had warned Darin he was a month behind on the rent. Darin insisted there was no financial trouble beyond the ordinary run of any small business.

The prosecutor then picked some more at the written statement Darin had given police, pointing out how it varied with his latest testimony, including the vital point that he never told police that Darlie gave him towels for the boys. Darin admitted he "skipped right over" that part.

"Another detail you left out?"

"Yes, sir. But that doesn't mean it didn't happen."

"Is there anything in your statement about your wife putting a towel on Damon's back?"

"No, sir, there's a lot of things missing."

Davis was trying to prove Darin was lying and had changed his story to match the facts, and asked how often he and Darlie had discussed what happened. "We've talked about it a lot—two hundred, three hundred, five hundred times—and she says the same thing over and over again. It's like a broken record,'' the husband replied.

The prosecutor questioned him about his conversation with Corinne Wells, but Darin eventually responded, ''I don't remember what I said to her,'' shutting down that line of questioning.

Davis touched on specific subjects, such as the placement of Darlie's jewelry and whether a cat was caged in the family room, next to the couch. ''If a stranger came into the room, that cat would raise a ruckus?'' Davis asked. ''Personally,'' replied Darin, ''I wish that cat could talk. We wouldn't be here now.'' Davis countered, ''I think we probably would.''

Once again, the prosecutor took a swipe at ''Gangsta's Paradise,'' as if the case was about musical taste, and a frustrated Darin responded, ''Mr. Davis, I didn't write that song. . . . They listened not to the words, but to the music. If they had loved Barney, we would have played Barney.''

Mulder had a brief redirect session, with Darin confirming that his house payment, American Express, and other bills were up-to-date, in order to again blunt the prosecution claim that he had been on the financial ropes.

He also explained that old socks, such as the tube sock with holes in it that had been found, would have been discarded onto a ''rag pile'' that was really a basket atop the washing machine.

Davis bounced back with a letter from Mellon Mortgage in May 1996 saying that the house payments for April and May were overdue and the loan was in default. Darin said the payments had been made, as well as the June payment, which had not yet been mailed because it was due on the fifteenth of the month. Now, however, he admitted, ''I am broke.''

Turning sarcastic, Davis finished his questioning. "There wasn't any intruder that night, was there, Mr. Routier?"

"There was an intruder."

"A lucky intruder?"

"I don't know what you mean."

Davis launched a series of comments that the man was very lucky because the window was open on that hot night, the alarm system was off, Darlie was asleep during the attack, and that he found a sock and left no blood trail of his own "This intruder is a real lucky guy, isn't he?"

"Yeah," Darin snapped. "And I want him dead!"

Mulder finished up with one simple question. "Have you ever doubted your wife's innocence?"

Darin squared his shoulders. "No, sir."

And Mulder would agree the intruder was a lucky man. "He was lucky the police never pursued him."

The conclusion of Darin's testimony was actually an anticlimax, for the major development of the day took place out of the jury's presence before the usual starting time of court. A decision had to be made about Patterson's sudden stonewalling over the planting of microphones on the grave. By Tuesday morning, both Detectives Patterson and Frosch had lawyers and were taking the Fifth Amendment against incriminating themselves, normally a refuge for potential criminals, for under Texas law, illegally intercepting a conversation is a felony.

The Dallas County prosecutors claimed the bugging of the graves was irrelevant and improper impeachment of a witness. Doug Mulder responded, "Felonious conduct on the part of the police is always admissible, relevant material. It goes to the integrity of the investigation!" Richard Mosty contended the police methodology and how the overall investigation was conducted was demonstrated by the covert cemetery eavesdropping.

Judge Tolle squashed the blooming furor and ruled the tactic was indeed improper. "The actions do not reflect on their character for truthfulness," he said, particularly since there was no attempt to bring the police videotape into evidence. "Are you telling me that if I recall Detective Jimmy Patterson, I can't go into this at all?" asked an astonished and stymied Mulder.

"That's correct," said the judge.

"They targeted her and violated state and federal law and we can't go into that?" Mulder declared. The judge nodded. "The ruling stands."

Mosty chimed in that such a block prevented the defense from finding out who planned and participated in the "felonious" police conduct. "We want to know everyone involved," he said. "They never did anything but target Darlie Routier, and they wanted it so bad they were willing to do illegal activities."

The judge wrapped up the hearing, still firm. Frosch and Patterson would, on the advice of their lawyers, assert their Fifth Amendment rights to say nothing that might be incriminating against themselves. That meant, since the jury was out of the room, the Rowlett detectives would not be shown in such questionable activity. It was a major setback for the defense, which wanted to hang the two policemen up for some legal target practice. Instead, they had to settle for Patterson's shaky performance of the previous day and the jury's possible understanding that something improper had been done by the cops. It was hardly the dramatic moment for which Mulder and Mosty had planned.

The defense then followed with testimony from a pair of expert witnesses of their own, forensic pathologist Dr. Vincent DiMaio and Dallas psychiatrist Lisa K. Clayton, who would say Darlie didn't match the profile of mothers who kill their children and could not have inflicted the stab wounds that she suffered.

Clayton interviewed Darlie in jail for a dozen hours over a half-dozen sessions arranged to screen out deception. The doctor, who works often with Dallas inmates, said she doubted the Darlie actually slept through the attack, but described her as suffering from "psychic numbing" and "traumatic amnesia," a condition which prevented her from remembering details of what happened, not unlike someone who is badly injured in an automobile wreck but doesn't remember what happened. "Her assumption is that some of it may have happened while she was asleep. She doesn't understand it. She wishes she could remember."

Darlie's answers to police questions were affected by the drugs she was given at the hospital in a peculiar way. Clayton said the combination of Demerol and Phenergan and other medications would have been "disinhibiting" and almost act like a "truth serum." Rather than lying to police, she was more likely to have confessed, the doctor said.

The psychiatrist said she had testified as an expert witness about a hundred times and had interviewed more than a thousand people charged with crimes, including between seventy-five and one hundred accused of murder. Her work as a jail psychiatrist, she said, gave her an ability to figure out when an incarcerated patient is lying to her, even down to noting how often the person blinks and their posture. Darlie, the doctor said, was telling the truth.

The psychiatrist also defended the cemetery party, which she pointed out followed a somber prayer service. The Silly String which caused such an uproar was not Darlie's idea, and "the events at the cemetery which some people have misinterpreted was an appropriate form of grieving." Further, she said that Mama Darlie had told her daughter to stop crying at the cemetery because she was upsetting other neighborhood children who had come to the event.

"Everyone grieves in different ways," said the doctor. "There is no appropriate way to grieve." Rather than being some outlandish reaction, Clayton said the celebration was in the context of the family's Christian beliefs that death is not a permanent separation from loved ones. She found the family's actions to be almost "pathetic" in denying that the kids were really dead and gone.

The psychiatrist also placed the thoughts of suicide, a lynchpin of the prosecution, as being misread and out of proportion. "My opinion is that Darlie was not imminently suicidal. It was more of a gesture than a genuine attempt. She was never actually going to go through with it." When she began to menstruate again, her spirits lifted dramatically, but even when she wrote "the so-called suicide note," it showed "love and compassion for her sons."

Greg Davis was critical and suspicious of all of the conclusions, which he said presented a rather "convenient defense."

"Instead of traumatic amnesia, I think probably it ought to be called selective amnesia," he said after court. "It sounds to me like, 'I'll remember the things that won't send me to death row and forget the things that will.' "

The cross-examination by Toby Shook only brought forth more strong opinions from Clayton, who traced Darlie's repeated version of what she remembered on the night of the murders, and said Darlie was consistent in discussing Damon awakening her, following the intruder, wetting towels for the wounded children because she felt helpess about not knowing CPR. Darlie was so dizzy and out of breath that she was in a daze and didn't remember much after Patrolman Waddell arrived, hardly anything of riding in the ambulance. Her next clear memory was asking Mama Darlie if the boys were dead. "Her memory was very patchy and spotty before her arrest," Clayton said. "I think that for anyone in that situation, there may be some normal discrepancies."

DiMaio, hired by Darlie's first lawyer, Doug Parks, had as many credentials as anyone who had come to the witness stand, and his animated speaking style captured the jurors' attention. The Chief Medical Examiner of Bexar County for the past sixteen years, he was once the Deputy Chief Medical Examiner for Dallas County and is the editor-in-chief of the *Journal of Forensic Pathology*, with several books to his credit.

He wasted no time in disputing the findings of other doctors and said Darlie could not have made the cuts on herself, such as the one that just missed the carotid artery. "Another millimeter or two and she would have been dead," he said, confirming the earlier assessment of the emergency room surgeon. The doctor stated that, "based on the location and pattern of the wounds . . . it's more probable that they were inflicted by someone else." The fact that she is right-handed was inconsistent, he said, with making the long wound on her neck, which ran downward from right to left. The idea that she would not hold the knife in her dominant hand "doesn't make any sense."

The Medical Examiner took his conclusions a bit further with another important point of disagreement. "If she had been dead and I had performed an autopsy, I would have put this section as 'two penetrating wounds, right forearm,' and in parenthesis, 'defensive.'" Since he said he had performed more than 7,000 autopsies and supervised 21,000, the sheer volume of his work was on a par with Jim Cron's crime scene investigations.

To demonstrate how he thought the cuts were inflicted,

DiMaio held a metal ruler against the throat of defense attorney Doug Mulder and pulled the edge across the shirt collar and tie, bringing slight laughter from several jurors, but causing Darlie to tremble and lapse into tears.

DiMaio also said photos of Darlie on June 10 showed the sort of severe, purpled bruising associated with blunt trauma and said the bruises appeared to be several days old, with the coloration consistent with having happened on June 6. "This is a blunt-force injury and it's deep down into the muscle." He even laughed aloud when asked if the bruises could have been self-inflicted.

He also had an answer for the puzzle given by the prosecution witnesses who said there were cuts in Darlie's T-shirt that did not have matching cuts in the skin. "It happens all the time," the Medical Examiner said, particularly when the clothing is pulled away during a struggle.

When Judge Tolle rapped his gavel and court concluded, Doug Mulder was feeling good, and told reporters this had been the best day for the defense yet. He was right. In fact, if jurors had been listening carefully, some of the mysteries of the murders had been powerfully addressed.

30

IT WAS BITTERLY cold in Kerrville when Darlie Lynn Routier took the stand in her own defense on Wednesday, January 29, at 9:50 A.M., wearing a pale green jacket with a lace fringe on the lapels over a white blouse, and a green checked skirt. Her blonde hair was pulled back into a tight bun, with a tiny wing of hair dangling softly against one cheek. After four weeks, this small woman was the one person everyone wanted to hear.

Doug Mulder lead her quickly through her life to Eagle Drive, being born in Altoona, Pennsylvania, moving to Lubbock with her parents at age seven, then back to Pennsylvania at eleven and finally back to Lubbock at thirteen. She has two sisters, Dana, ten years younger, and Danelle, twelve years younger. She recounted meeting Darin at the Western Sizzler when she was fifteen, and how they got engaged in Colorado, married in Lubbock, and honeymooned in Jamaica. This was routine information, but still exciting, for up until this point, Darlie and the family had not discussed her background. It was like opening an egg and seeing what was inside.

Darlie traced her own work history and how they began their own business, and moving into the house on Bond Street two days before Devon was born. Damon was born while they lived there, too, and the growing family moved to Eagle Drive in 1993, by which time the business had shifted from their living room into a commercial building.

"Darin and I spent all of our extra time with Devon and Damon," she said, but they liked to explore different exotic restaurants as one way of expanding the universe of their children. "It was very important to me that Devon and Damon understood people from different cultures." They stayed in close contact with both families, going back to Pennsylvania once a year and making more frequent trips to Lubbock.

When Drake was born in 1995, his brothers came to the hospital, excited to see the baby. "They were very proud of him." She embellished the story with small details, like how the boys goofed around with some of the hospital's rubber gloves on their heads. Already Mulder was doing what was required, turning Darlie Routier from the ogre portrayed by the prosecution into a human being, into a real person, into a mother who loved her children. The jurors paid rapt attention to the young woman with a soft drawl.

Mulder attacked the theory that she went through a depression in April and May of 1996. Darlie said she had stopped breast-feeding the baby and was taking diet pills to take off "maybe twelve to fifteen pounds," and had lost almost all of it by May.

"Those pills didn't alter your life, did they?" asked Mulder.

"Not at all, that's why I took them, they didn't have side effects," she said. However, she confirmed that she turned moody on a few "really rough" days.

Mulder zeroed in on the depressing aspects of her private journal. "It was silly," she said with a glance at the jury. "I'm very embarrassed I even have to get up here and tell you people about this." She continued, "I did

not attempt to take my life.'' In her version, she called
Darin on the phone, told him she wasn't feeling well and
that he needed to come home. He did and things calmed
down.

Darlie began the journal when her grandfather died
about two years earlier, and since his death was on her
mind, her grandmother suggested writing down her feelings. ''It helps you stop and reflect on your life.'' She
began to read aloud.

''I see myself getting older each day,'' she wrote on
September 7, 1995, confiding that she had a few dreams
of death, but realizing ''my life is good and I have much
to be proud of.''

Then came a startling entry on September 15, when
she admitted that her stepfather had tried to fondle her
and that ''it was very hard to forgive him.'' She wrote
that Mama Darlie, since divorced from that husband, had
undergone therapy that Darlie hoped might ''make her
heart a little softer.'' She also reflected at the time, with
Damon off visiting his grandmother Sarilda, ''that without all my babies, I do not feel complete.''

Tears followed her words and when she read the October 1 entry, she was crying so hard it was difficult to
hear her read, ''I really love Darin with all my heart, but
sometimes I feel I'm missing something. I know I have
a lot of responsibilities, but a little craziness couldn't
hurt. I'm young and I want to feel it.''

When she reflected on the birth of Drake, Darlie
stopped crying as she read the words she jotted down on
April 21, 1996. ''He was a beautiful baby. I'm the very
proud mother of three wonderful, gorgeous boys.'' Her
thoughts roamed to her sister's youthful impetuousness
and a hope that God would ''put His hand down on my
marriage'' and help the boys grow up ''to see past color,
to see past rich or poor, and that we all need each other

to survive.'' She wanted God to ''watch over and protect the children, for they are our future.''

On April 29, she joyfully noted that she and Darin, after attending a friend's wedding, decided to renew their own vows on their tenth anniversary. Devon and Drake would be ring bearers and Drake would wear a little tuxedo.

Mulder interrupted to have her explain to the jury that she had never ''planned to produce this [journal] in front of the whole world.'' Darlie seemed mortified as she read about the suicidal thoughts. Darin came home to find her crying on the bed, and she told him, ''I didn't like the way I was feeling the past couple of days.'' Her husband also began to cry and asked Darlie how she had planned to do it, and she replied, ''I had thought about taking some pills.''

Her attorney stopped the reading to ask how the situation was resolved. Darlie looked up and said she was better, but remained weepy for another few days. When she began to menstruate again, seven months after the birth of Drake, ''It made a big difference.'' Changing hormones have often been blamed as the cause of female depression.

Mulder had Darlie tell about family life on Eagle Drive and how neighborhood children thronged to the house. After Drake was born, she laid down some ground rules, among them that only one friend visit the house at a time, and that all the kids had to take their shoes off upon entering, which she did in other people's homes out of ''common courtesy.'' No kid drinks or food were allowed in any room that had carpets, which kept them playing in the game room a lot. She and Darin liked to take all three boys camping and to theme parks.

The questions turned to June 5, the afternoon before the deaths of Devon and Damon, and Darlie explained that Basia's mother was visiting and called her attention to a dark car in the alley. "I just caught the tail end of a black car in the alleyway—he scooted out of there pretty quick. . . . Halena told me the car had been stopped and looking in the garage."

Darlie described receiving anonymous telephone calls, with silence on the other end when she answered. She was not alarmed because she thought friends of the kids were responsible.

Darin came home from work about six o'clock on June 5, walking in with Dana just as Basia and Halena left. The boys were playing with friends in the backyard. At dinner that night, the kids ate at their own table, then the boys went back outside.

The dinner conversation covered many points, including the Jag, which had been in the shop for two days, and would leave her stranded if Darin took the green Pathfinder to work. Usually, the Jaguar would be parked in the rear, and she agreed with Doug Mulder that its absence might indicate to someone that Darin was not at home. After dinner, Darin fixed the back gate, a chore that Darlie wanted done so she could get on with her plans of breeding dogs and cats.

Meanwhile, she and Dana had been in the garage, pricing articles that she had been putting aside for months, destined for a garage sale. As they worked, they discussed weddings—Dana's own pending nuptials, the renewal of vows for Darin and Darlie, and the coming wedding of Aurenda, Darin's younger sister.

About 9:30, she brought the boys inside, refusing to let Devon bring a friend over because the boys were in trouble after splashing most of the water out of the hot tub. When they put on dry clothes, Darlie vacuumed the mess they left next to the sliding glass door and left the vacuum beside the bar. While Darin took Dana back to her apartment, the boys hauled their blankets and pillows into the living room. By the time Darin got back about ten o'clock, Devon was already asleep in front of the television set but Damon was still awake. Darin took the fussing baby upstairs to give him a bottle and to watch the news, which Darlie seldom watched because of the "negative stuff" on the programs. With the baby in bed, Darin came back downstairs and they talked a while longer.

Mulder stopped her and changed gears, just as a trucker might slow down a big rig as it gathered momentum on an open road. Darlie held the room in the palm of her hand, and he wanted to exploit the moment.

He handed the jurors two copies of the transcript of the 911 call, not only the prosecution's pages, but a defense version, too. There were differences in the language, and the sources. Darlie explained that she was confused because she had been talking to three people at one time during the recorded conversation—the operator, Darin, and Patrolman Waddell. From the tape, she could tell that it was Darin, and not Waddell, who said, "Get the rags." An easy identification, because "I know my husband's voice."

The tape is played again in court, and she reads along, apparently crying and wiping away tears. Other women in the courtroom also dab at their eyes as her screams fill the room. Then Mulder stops the tape and plays it again. Darlie finds another error. "I didn't say 'fighting' . . . I said 'frightened'." The lawyer then played the tape a third time, hammering home the panic in her voice as he asks the jury this time to read only from the defense transcript as the words pour from the tape deck.

The repeated screams ended a grueling morning, and the court broke for lunch a bit early, at 11:45 A.M. An exhausted crowd filed out to discover that the sun was breaking through a thin layer of high clouds, chasing away the cold. Everyone soaked up the warmth, as if it could relieve the chilling effect of Darlie's screams on

the tape. The session resumed at 1:15 P.M., with Mulder
still questioning his client.

She continued discussing the evening of June 5, and how
as Darin lay beside her, they spoke of "many things,"
including the trip to Pennsylvania planned for June 14,
only a week away. They already had the tickets. Business
talk faded into a discussion about getting rid of the boat,
which wasn't being used as they had planned. There was
no argument at all, she insisted, just a normal conversation between a wife and her husband.

At some point, she decided to sleep downstairs instead
of taking the boys to their room, and Darin fetched her
a pillow and blanket. "We were kissing for a little bit"
and then Darin went upstairs, leaving her on the couch
in front of the sliding glass door with the television set
on behind her. The alarm was off. "I went to sleep, I
was tired," she recalled. "Both of the boys were asleep."
The court-watchers edged forward on their seats, knowing what was coming—a tale of murder.

"The next thing I remember is Damon hitting my right
shoulder, saying 'Mommy, Mommy.' I looked up (you
gotta remember I'm not completely awake) and there was
a man walking away from me. I heard a noise like glass
breaking [and] I went to the kitchen. Damon was behind
me, I put out a hand to keep him back." She then reported she saw the man go into the utility room, out of
her sight. With only the light of the flickering television,
she followed, realizing when she reached the kitchen island that "I had blood on me."

"I kept going, saw the knife in the utility room. It was
an instinct to pick up the knife, it was an instinct, I didn't
think about it," she sobbed in a breaking voice that grew
in volume. "I saw Devon, and he had cuts that were so
big. I could see big cuts through Damon's shirt."

*   *   *

She turned on the kitchen light and grabbed the telephone when Darin rushed downstairs to help. Darlie said she grabbed towels from a drawer and wet them in the sink because she didn't know what else to do, then went to Damon.

"I put a towel on my baby's back," she said on the stand, her voice the only sound in a courtroom in which everyone except the professionals seemed to be holding their breath. "I told him to hold on. He said, 'Okay, Mommy,' and that's the last thing he said to me.'' Reporters wrote hurriedly in their pads, and the prosecution lawyers were making equally rapid notes.

Darin, she said, was performing CPR on Devon, and she felt helpless. "I didn't know what to do, I just put the towel on top of his chest wound . . . I ran [to the door] and screamed for Karen across the street," then got more towels, urging the boys to hold on. The blue eyes, wet, looked at the jurors. "We were frantic, you can imagine, both of your babies dying in front of you, what do you do?" Mulder let her roll. This was the best chance Darlie would have to pull the jury into her corner.

When Waddell arrived, she was by the kitchen bar, leaning on the vacuum, "dizzy and not breathing real good." A glance in a mirror showed the gash in her neck. But when she sat down, she took the vacuum with her, and she firmly asserted that it was never at the far end of the kitchen, where police had said it was found.

In the chaos that followed, Walling and Waddell "ran through the kitchen" and Darin sprinted for the Neals' house to get Karen as the paramedics trooped in. Her voice rose, almost in hysteria, as she told of seeing Damon's eyes open when he was turned over. Darlie had only vague memories of being tended by the paramedics. "When I stood up, Darin said something to me about my panties were gone," she said with a rush. "That was the first time I realized they were gone." At the front door, she gave a description of the assailant to Sergeant Walling.

With hardly a pause for breath, Darlie picked up her story at the hospital, where she cooperated with police "as much as I could." Family members and friends came to see her, but she didn't remember much, beyond Karen bringing the baby Drake in and Darlie feeding him a bottle on Saturday, shortly before she was released. She did recall her arms were bruised, but thought it was a result of needles. Darlie also said her mouth was sore, "kind of raw inside," possibly because "the man had his hand over my mouth while he was attacking me." But mostly, she didn't remember much.

Darlie also said a psychic had come to speak with her and Darin. "It's not something I believe in or practice, but I think when you're a parent and desperate to find answers, you'll do almost anything." Along with repeated dreams, and the psychic's comments, and discussions with many friends, Darlie had come up with some vague ideas about what might have happened. Not facts, just a hunch.

When Mulder broached the repeated attacks on "Gangsta's Paradise," Darlie scoffed. "I think that it's been made way too much of an issue," she said, adding, "I sang to them all kinds of songs, including 'Jesus Loves Me' to Drake every night." Another song played at the funeral, which didn't get the attention of the prosecution, was "I Will Always Love You."

She stopped crying, and in a voice loud and firm, Darlie Routier told the jury she did not attack her children. "They were the most important thing to me."

Assistant District Attorney Toby Shook, not Greg Davis, handled the cross-examination of Darlie, and led her through several minor questions, including still another swipe at "Gangsta's Paradise," before getting to his first major target, the thoughts of suicide. It was mentioned in her diary, Shook asked, but "[y]ou weren't going to commit suicide?"

"No, sir," Darlie replied instantly. She "was feeling depressed and moody" when she started writing about 3:30 that afternoon. She thought about taking the pills, but never actually took them out of the wrappers. Darlie downplayed the entire episode, saying if she had been serious, then "I wouldn't be here today."

"I had decided it was silly and stopped and called Darin."

The prosecutor wanted to know why she had been feeling desperate, but Darlie replied she couldn't answer that. She didn't recall, acknowledging only that she was "feeling pretty depressed," but countering that she had never thought about suicide before that day.

Then Shook wanted to talk about the alleged molestation by Denny Stahl, her mother's second husband. The first time it happened, she replied, she was only eight years old, but the police were never summoned. When she was an adult, Darlie allowed her children to visit the man she accused of molesting her.

The attorney attacked her character, questioning how she partied with a group of other mothers, including her own, on Mother's Day of 1994, when a male stripper was hired to perform at her home, and in 1995, when they had a slumber party at a downtown hotel and seen male exotic dancers in Dallas.

"Did you attend church regularly?" he asked. "No, sir," was her reply.

Then he moved on to discuss the graveside party, asking if she went from house to house in the neighborhood to invite people. Darlie recalled going to only three homes, but making many telephone calls to invite people to attend. "I was still on some medication" but didn't think there was "anything to blame" in her behavior.

Earlier, Shook had Darlie say that Darin had fixed the broken gate, and now he asked about whether the garage window had been open the entire week. Darlie said it was both open and closed during that time, but mostly it was open and unlocked.

"The murderer of your children is not your husband?" he asked.

"Yes, sir."

"So what it boils down to is, either you killed your children, or a man came into your house and killed your children."

Darlie's voice changed to a firm, almost haughty, tone. "Sir, I did not kill my children."

"It has to be one or the other," Shook insisted.

"Sir, I did not kill my children!"

Shook pestered her on the point, asking why she thought the intruder might leave without killing her, the only witness.

"I think that he thought that I was dead."

"Do you think you slept while that man stabbed your boys?"

"I don't know."

"You're a light sleeper, aren't you?"

"I would not necessarily call myself a light sleeper." She explained that the baby's crib was noisy when the infant turned over and might awaken her. Moments later, she compromised and said that "to some degree" she was a light sleeper.

Shook pointed out that Damon was asleep within one foot of her when attacked, and she said she heard nothing.

"Again I have no idea . . . I do not remember . . ." sleeping through Damon's stabbing, she said. "I have no idea what happened that night."

"You would have woken up when he [the attacker] started beating you?"

"I have no idea."

Would she have slept through having her own neck slashed?

"I cannot remember." Several other questions brought the same answer.

To build upon her insistence that she didn't remember much, Shook queried her about the description of the assailant, and Darlie told the attorney "he was a taller man, with dark hair."

"How tall?"

"I cannot give you an exact . . . above six feet." Shook asked her to compare the intruder to Detective Chris Frosch's build. A white man? "I don't know that for sure."

Then he pushed on why she ran after someone so much larger than herself rather than screaming for her husband. "I did yell out for Darin," she replied.

Back to the description, Shook had her identify a man named Glenn Miles. She said Miles had said some things to Basia that "weren't very nice" and his wife had telephoned Darlie to discuss the problem about a year or so ago. "He threatened me over the phone," Darlie said, adding that she had never seen him and didn't know if he would look like the intruder.

By now, almost everyone in the court was wondering just where Shook was heading with all of this. Who was Glenn Miles, anyway?

"Do you think you'd recognize Glenn?"

"I don't know."

"Well, we'll give it a try."

Through the doors came Detective Frosch and a man not nearly as tall and quite chunky. They stood side by side, in stark contrast. Darlie agreed they didn't look anything alike, and that Miles could be eliminated as a suspect. Shook let the demonstration rest there. He would return to Glenn Miles later.

The attorney now began asking her about her two-hour interview at the police station with Bill Parker, and how, when he confronted her about killing the boys, she repeatedly said, "If I did, I don't remember it." On the witness stand, Darlie denied it. "No! I did not say that."

Darlie was then asked about the written statement she had given to Detective Patterson and Shook noted that a number of things in subsequent comments were not included. "As far as wetting towels—that's not mentioned."

"No, sir."

"Going to the kitchen sink—not mentioned."

"No, sir."

The vacuum cleaner? "No, sir."

"You didn't mention going to Devon, did you?"

"No sir."

Shook handed her the statement and she read aloud, "Darin started giving Devon CPR while I put a towel on my neck and a towel on Damon's back."

"There was nothing about putting a towel on Devon?" asked Shook.

"I didn't know that was important," she said. "I didn't know what I was doing. I was trying to do the best that I could in the situation I was in."

Shook wouldn't let up. Didn't she understand that wetting the towels before putting them on the boys was not a good idea? "I didn't know that," replied Darlie.

Well, what would her common sense tell her?

"At that time, there was no common sense" and, "I was doing a lot of things at once."

"But you never applied pressure to Damon's wounds?"

"No, sir, I didn't," she said. "I went over to Darin and helped with Devon."

Still, Shook persisted with a seemingly infinite number of points that didn't match or had multiple meanings.

Darlie said she used the word "frightening" and meant "frightened" although the 911 tape transcript read "fighting," and she denied telling Waddell she fought with the intruder. She "didn't remember" telling paramedics that the garage window was broken with a bat. She recalled feeling pressure on her right leg that night, but did not remember showing a nurse the cuts on her hand and saying they came from the knife.

Darlie insisted that, "As of right now, I do not remember this attack." As for the hospital, she drew a blank, hardly remembering even seeing her relatives there.

"I think if I lived to be 100, I wouldn't be able to tell you a lot of things about that night," she finally said, and Shook closed that page of his questioning.

Shook then wanted to know more about why she was on that couch in the first place, and Darlie denied it was because there had been a fight with Darin. Business had been slow in April and March, but while she would acknowledge that "money was tight," she also noted that the bills were being paid and shrugged off Shook's statement that they were two months behind in the house payment. It was only one month, she said, and it was late, not missing.

Judge Tolle interrupted the ongoing sparring, and gave everyone a fifteen-minute break. Doug Mulder used the time to talk to his client, giving Darlie a piece of his lawyerly mind. She was falling into the prosecution trap, he said, and the jury was seeing her as argumentative and hostile. He wanted sympathy from those jurors, not a negative reaction to a know-it-all performance on the stand. If sympathy meant tears, that's what he got. When the trial resumed for its final hour of the day, Darlie was almost a puddle of emotion, wiping tears from her face and blowing her nose on a fistful of tissue. Jurors walking into the room saw her looking small, vulnerable, and whipped. Mama Darlie would later describe the exchange between her daughter and the lawyer as a "fight."

With Darlie back on the stand, Shook, who has the body of a weightlifter, was now cast in the role of picking on a defenseless woman. He didn't vary his attack, and struck her hard, and from an unexpected quarter as tears flowed freely.

First he had Darlie confirm she told a radio talk show host that "I know what happened in that house that night." Then Shook pulled out a copy of a letter Darlie wrote on November 1 to a relative, in which she stated, "We believe we know who did it. I really believe he did it . . . I saw him and I know it's him."

Who was it, asked Shook? Glenn Miles? When Darlie said no, he followed. "Then who?"

"Some other man in the neighborhood that people were telling me about."

Shook produced a letter to Karen Neal. Darlie had written, "Karen, I know who did it." Darlie's face was falling apart as she wiped at the tears. "Sir, at the time, I was hoping . . ." the rest of the sentence was lost in emotion. Out came another letter to Karen. "I believe Glenn did it. This man is very evil and I told the police about him."

Suddenly Darlie got a little tired of all this hammering. Those were her letters, things she wrote from her heart. *Private things!* She demanded to know where Shook got them. He totally ignored her and shot back with still another question.

So much for the tears. She was mad. "First, I want to know where you're getting my letters!" Darlie said.

Shook told her they came from her jailers.

"Isn't that illegal?" an astonished Darlie asked.

Shook glanced at her, and softly replied, "No, it isn't." A rumble of laughter came from the courtroom, which was packed with about 150 spectators. Shook began with a new series of questions from his stack of copied letters. Darlie interrupted, saying that she didn't see dates on them and she always dates her letters.

"Do you think we made these up?" He was playing to the jury, replying in a very quiet voice, making them lean forward to hear. Toby Shook was sweeping them up in the questioning, trying to show how Darlie could change from one mood to another so quickly, in the blink of an eye.

No, she replied. She was just wondering about those dates.

Shook was on cruise control now and read from another letter that discussed "the other man" in the neighborhood who "left the sock directly in the path of his own home. We know he was outside at 2:30 A.M. Devon and Damon knew this man."

And who would that be? Shook wanted to know.

Gary Austin, responded Darlie.

What does he look like?

"I don't know." She said she had been told the man could stand on his balcony and see into the Routier backyard. Her voice was rising, breaking, and this time the emotion was true. She felt as if she were being swamped by a tidal wave. Toby Shook was *not* a nice man.

Shook, pacing like a stalking tiger measuring Darlie as dinner, handed her a photo that disputed the line of sight from the questioned balcony to the backyard and the covered spa. "Sir, at the time I was just hoping. I had been told a lot about two different people," she said. Shook looked up. That was just a lie, wasn't it, he stated. "It's not a lie," she proclaimed, the tears gone again and her voice harsh. "It's not a lie. It's what was told to me."

He produced one of Darlie's letters, in which she wrote: "I know who did it. What makes me angry is that he's running around free."

Another letter: "I'm praying they'll be able to get a confession from Glenn."

Another letter: "We know who did it and we're trying to get more on him."

Finally, Shook stopped reading the letters, leaving Darlie weeping and hurt and insisting she was just repeating things that had been told to her by other people.

Doug Mulder had a train wreck on his hands. Darlie was breathing as if she had just run a mile, and her face appeared fragile, as if it were about to break. He may have wanted her to show emotion, but this was too much. The task was to calm her and regain some ground in the few minutes he had left.

Recalling an easier part of the cross-examination, Mulder had Darlie explain that the only reason she let her sons visit the stepfather who had allegedly molested her was that her sister, Dana, was going to be with them all day.

He next dealt her the name of the second mystery man, Gary Austin, and asked what she had heard from other people about the man. Shook objected and the judge ruled against any "hearsay" testimony.

So Mulder moved to the vital point that had almost destroyed his client on the witness stand. "Darlie, why did you write those letters?"

Her voice was tiny. "Because at the time, from what I was being told, that's what I thought."

One last pitch, and it didn't accomplish what the defense hoped. Mulder wanted to show that she had been assaulted on the night of June 6. "Were you involved in a fight or altercation?" he asked.

"Look at me!" It was a tearful shout. "Anyone with any common sense can see that." Jurors stared at her with stone cold eyes.

Toby Shook had a final chance at a few questions and

he needled her one last time. "In your letters, you said, 'I saw him, I know who it is.' " Darlie made a slender reply about hoping to accomplish something, but Shook didn't really care what she had to say. He had gotten to flash the letters one last time.

Immediately afterward, the defense rested its case.

After court, Mulder spoke briefly with reporters, trying to put a positive face on what had just happened upstairs. "It went all right—there were some good parts and some not so good." The jury wanted to hear from her and she had wanted to testify, he said. "I think that she got across to the jury that she didn't do it."

The problem with the letters was that she had been fed so much information by family and friends, that she built up her hopes, drawing pictures around imaginary facts that came to her as she sat in jail.

"We think she held up very well—she answered truthfully and forcefully," he said. Anyway, that was besides the point, he said. In his view, the bottom line was that the state really had no case.

Greg Davis gave it a different slant. "I think her tears were pretty genuine there toward the last, when she realized she'd been caught."

31

WITH THE END of Darlie's emotional testimony, the
state now had a final chance to bring on more witnesses,
as the trial moved into the rebuttal phase.

Bill Parker, a private investigator since 1985 when he
left the Dallas Police Department after twenty years, has
a reputation as a wizard at questioning suspects. When
Darlie Routier was about to be arrested, one of the first
things Rowlett officials did was put her into a chair opposite Parker, who read her the Miranda warnings again
and set about picking her brain. He then presented a copy
of her ten-page statement and she spent a few minutes
reading it. When he asked if she wished to make changes,
she replied, "No, that's exactly what happened."

For the next three hours, Parker questioned Darlie in
detail and, a dozen times, confronted her with the bald
accusation that she killed her kids. He testified carefully
that she never denied committing the act, but would say
only, "If I did it, I don't remember." Once, she shrugged
her shoulders.

Doug Mulder cross-examined Parker, a longtime personal friend. In contrast to the high hourly prices of
expert witnesses, Parker said he did the job for the Row-

lett cops for only one dollar, but had not yet billed them. His comment drew laughter.

Prior to meeting Darlie, he went to the scene, spoke with various investigators, and examined photos and the written statement. Greg Davis' thrust was simply, "Did Ms. Routier ever deny killing her children?" Parker replied unequivocally, "No, sir, she did not."

Doug Mulder used the rare tactic of building up Parker's qualifications as a "skilled interrogator," then queried why the expert did not record his interview, made no notes and no official report. Again, everything was verbal, leaving no risky paper trail for defense attorneys to follow in questioning witnesses. Mulder's spin was, "If Darlie were guilty, Bill Parker would have gotten a confession from her."

Dr. Richard Coons was the lone rebuttal witness for the defense. A psychiatrist in Austin for more than twenty-two years, he was an expert in criminal forensic psychiatry, and took the court on an in-depth examination of the human memory. He hit the high point immediately, testifying that "in response to extremely overwhelming trauma, a person may have amnesia—they do not store memory properly, like abused children block things out" and auto accident victims forget details of the crash, for to remember everything might "overwhelm" the victim. He testified that Darlie, traumatized by the attack and seeing her kids dying, might very well believe she slept through events she could not recall, blocking what really happened from her memory. The mind, he said, is not a vacuum cleaner that sweeps up every morsel of reality and stores it forever.

And Coons reflected back on Parker's long interview. "If a person is trying to fill in the gaps, they might entertain suggestions made by a detective of twenty years' experience," he said, including the possibility of "false

memories'' that were created in the mind to answer some
question. In other words, Darlie, trying to please the police by dredging up details, may have been led down a
specific path by Parker's precise questions. "As the traumatic effects on her diminish, you would expert her
memory to get better,'' he said.

To diminish the impact of the responses Darlie made
to Parker, the psychiatrist said, "If I'm saying an attacker
did it, then saying I didn't do it would be redundant.''

Toby Shook, on cross-examination, belittled the doctor's comment, although Coons has, in the past, testified
in cases for the Dallas County District Attorney. Shook
pointed out that Coons had not interviewed Darlie, read
the statements, seen police reports or medical records, or
watched the Silly String tape. "You're not telling the
jury she is suffering from traumatic amnesia?'' he asked.
"I don't know her,'' Coons replied. It was a neat bit of
questioning, for Coons had centered his testimony on
overall, general reactions of a person to certain trauma,
a glove that would fit Darlie as well as anyone else. Turning that generality into a specific point reduced Coons's
effectiveness.

When Coons stepped down from the witness stand on
a bright Thursday afternoon, the testimony in the trial,
which had lasted almost four weeks, came to an end.

Closing arguments were heard on Friday, the final day
of January. The trial had lasted all month and for those
involved, it felt even longer, like maybe a couple of life-
times.

Toby Shook, representing the prosecution, addressed
the weakest point of the state's case, saying, "We may
never know the true motive,'' but added that the state
was not required to prove motive and it didn't change
the evidence in this "brutal, vicious murder of a child,
of two children.'' He told the jury that when they put to-

gether the evidentiary jigsaw puzzle, the result would point to Darlie as the killer, not an intruder.

Concerning the lengthy medical testimony of the first week, Shook said the doctors had no reason to lie when they pronounced the deep cut to be "a superficial wound." He liked the sound of that term, which he repeated several times with heavy emphasis. Shook stated she suffered no major trauma to her arm and did not see the big bruises "because it didn't happen." The nurses also had no reason to lie and Darlie had volunteered her story to them.

Then he underlined the conclusions of Jim Cron, the crime-scene analyst, saying "it didn't take him long to figure out" what happened. No disturbed dust on the windowsill; no blood in the window or garage or outside; the closed gate; and other points. Charlie Linch's investigation determined the bread knife found in the butcher block had cut the screen. The bloody knife print on the carpet, containing Darlie's and Damon's blood, was inconsistent. "What intruder would stab her and Damon and then lay the knife down?" Shook asked. The FBI profiler, Allen Brantley, had declared the attack was "personal" and that the crime scene was staged.

The prosecution attorney took a leap, however, when he said Barbara [Basia] Jovell also had no motive to lie, but what the jury didn't know wouldn't hurt him. He took another stretch when he said that "I don't think the defendant was going to kill herself [on June 6]. She loves herself too much." This was an ironic statement from a prosecutor that had put so much emphasis on Darlie's alleged suicide attempt.

Then he took a swat at the cemetery party, specifically the Silly String. "I think it gives you a lot of insight into this woman. She's having fun. She likes the attention. She said, 'He went to them first.' She's enjoying it." And he pointed to inconsistencies in the statements she gave police. Darlie, Shook claimed, set it up by making certain Darin went to sleep upstairs with Drake, while she was downstairs with Devon and Damon. "She killed those boys and she faked that scene." Yes, he said, the intruder was lucky. "Lucky for him that Darlie gets amnesia."

Shook recalled for the jury how Darlie had almost gone to pieces on the witness stand when she was questioned about her letters from jail. "Those tears started rolling down, that voice started shaking, those hands started shaking," he said. "Those tears were for herself."

The prosecutor wrapped up. "Damon opened his eyes and he saw who was murdering him. . . . He saw his mother!"

Curtis Glover responded to Shook, beginning the defense closings, and reminded the jury there was no requirement for the defense to prove anything at all. But there were clearly holes in the state's case, he said. Confusion reigned at the crime scene, there was reasonable doubt about the evidence and James Cron's "waltzing through there and says there was no intruder" was the trigger for the police to pursue Darlie.

Countering Shook, Glover said a neck wound that comes within two millimeters of killing someone cannot be called "superficial." Serious, he said, is a better word.

He reminded the jurors of the large window that was wheeled into the courtroom and how large Detective Frosch had ducked through it with ease, putting his hands "exactly" where fingerprints were found that were never identified. In addition, "They want you to infer through all this melee that Darlie runs out and plants the sock with her children's blood on it," Glover said.

"Use your common sense," Glover said. "This woman didn't kill her two little children."

*   *   *

Richard Mosty continued for the defense, the good-ole-boy demeanor gone and the experienced lawyer standing before the jury promising to "spend every ounce of my energy to defend a person I believe in."

He pointed out that not one witness had said Darlie was not a good mother, and none of the witnesses could really tell the jury what happened that night. "It makes no sense that this lady would change from a good mother, a doting mother, to a psychotic killer.

"Darlie Routier was in the [police] cross-hairs immediately," he asserted with anger in his voice. "I want to get Cron in a room and say quietly, 'Who do you think you are? Judge, jury, and executioner?' " The state, in the absence of facts, relied upon Cron's opinion. "What's the one word that never came out of his lips?" Mosty asked. "Sock. In the entire time he testified, he never said the work 'sock.' Do you know why? Because he can't explain it."

Mosty did his own run through some of the evidence, saying Linch had an opinion that was "not scientifically verifiable" because the amount of sample he used for testing conveniently left none for the defense to test in comparison. Mosty said it was very ironic that, with Cron and Linch using hypothetical conclusions, and police and other experts changing and updating their own reports, "The only person who has to have a perfect story is Darlie Routier."

He was scathing in attacking Brantley, the FBI profiler. "All he did was get up under oath and deliver the state's closing argument for them." But just as Cron did not mention the sock, Brantley didn't talk about the black car that showed up near the crime scene at least four times, including being parked in the alley behind the house.

Touching on the lack of a clear motive, Mosty said, "It makes no sense that this lady could change from a good mother to a psychotic killer" for no reason. And the state's claim that the family was broke was simply wrong. The cash flow was sufficient to pay all of the bills, including the bills that police found in the trash can.

On details, Darlie's blood was found by Devon's body, blood was on the kitchen towel drawer and a white towel was near Devon's hand, and all of these things could not be explained by the prosecutors. The wounds, he said, were defensive in nature and "that's medical opinion, not witchcraft." He scalded the police, too, saying they knew she was drugged when she was questioned at the hospital, and went too far by placing listening devices at the grave. "The only person who needed a lawyer was Detective Patterson," he said, claiming the investigator illegally bugged "a prayer service for those children."

According to the defense attorney, the prosecution had no choice but to intercept Darlie's mail from jail because they were still hoping she might confess something to someone.

The state, Mosty said, had failed miserably in its job of explaining what happened. "They don't like Darlie Routier, they don't like the lifestyle she led, they have to trash her because they can't explain [the crime]," he declared. "She had the audacity to express herself in the way she really is and to be the victim of a crime that doesn't fit what somebody in Washington thinks it ought to look like."

Now Doug Mulder rose to walk a tightrope. He was the third defense lawyer to speak that day and he had to be wary of saying too much, pushing too hard. Glover and Mosty had done the detail work, and he wanted to both wrap it up and paint the overall picture, without drawing the jury's animosity. Darlie watched timorously, chewing her lips.

"There was no death being contemplated by her," he said of his client. The police had befouled the case from the start, because "there were some leads out there that they should have pursued," and the prosecution had certainly agreed that the police were a weak link because "I had to call [Patterson]. Can you believe the lead detective was not called by the state?"

Fingerprints of potential suspects went unchecked and interviews about the black car were ignored. Patterson interviewed a neighbor named Nelda Watts, who said when she heard a scream that night, she looked out her window and saw the car parked by her mailbox. But the cops focused on Darlie, and that didn't make sense because she was a "rose garden and picket fence" parent, who "just doesn't, out of the blue, go haywire and kill her children."

She had been under extraordinary scrutiny by the state, which had "unlimited funds" for its investigation, but still "can't come up with a single witness who will say anything bad about her as a mother."

Then he waved his hand toward the prosecutors, sitting three abreast at their table. "They have a duty and responsibility to tell you how it happened," he said. Instead, there was Jim Cron, a fingerprint man who "grew himself a beard and calls himself a consultant." And Detective Frosch put his hand exactly where unidentified prints were found on the screen. Bill Parker? Well, "If Bill Parker can't get a confession out of someone, then they haven't done anything." The lawyer said Officer Waddell froze and didn't help the kids.

None of Darlie's blood was found outside the house. "Do you really believe [that] she is sophisticated enough to put a smidgin of blood on the sock and put it down the alley and depend on Patterson and his crew to find it?" Mulder asked.

Addressing the weak point of his own case, Darlie's own nervous testimony, he said that, although she did not have to testify, "I called Darlie Routier to the stand because I thought you had a right to hear her account.''

Then, joined by Richard Mosty, Mulder spelled out the timeline for the crime, using the exact times cited by officials. He pointed out the emergency police call was made at exactly 2:31 A.M., and Darlie was on the line for five minutes, therefore the crime had to happen before she made the call. According to medical experts, based upon the wounds and rate of bleeding, Damon was stabbed sometime about 2:29 A.M. and died about nine minutes later at 2:38, after the paramedics arrived.

Therefore, he said, Darlie had to stab both children multiple times, get ''a smidgin of blood'' from each onto the sock, go out the window, kick the gate open while she was barefooted, run some seventy-five yards down the alley and return in the dark, come back into the house, take the knife and cut herself five times, carefully pulling her shirt out to make additional cuts that don't touch her. Then she had to lay the bloody knife down carefully, go over and bleed on the sofa pillow, and lay a blood trail to the utility room, ''slowly, the state says.'' After that, she must go back to the children because her blood was found there, and move the vacuum cleaner around over the blood she spilled on the floor.'' Not to mention dialing the telephone.

''All of this has to happen in two minutes,'' Mosty said, disbelievingly, if Damon was wounded at 2:29 and Darlie made her call at 2:31.

Assistant District Attorney Greg Davis, who had lived with the case since a few days after the boys were murdered, was the last to speak. The jury, pondering that incredibly busy time line drawn by the defense, appeared eager to hear Davis answer it. He simply brushed it away, like shooing a fly, a standard prosecution tactic but effective with the jury. ''I daresay you aren't surprised that none of the defense attorneys are satisfied with the state's case. In nineteen years, I've never seen it happen.''

Davis denied there was ''some sort of conspiracy,'' and said if there was, he would personally instruct the jury to write NOT GUILTY on the verdict sheet. He said he was ''not ashamed'' to represent the Rowlett police and was proud ''to represent the voices of those two little boys, who never had a chance to talk as their mother slaughtered them.''

He played the home field card, saying this was exactly the kind of trial that could be expected when ''a guilty woman . . . comes down here to trial in Kerr County.'' Davis almost sneered. ''And as she sits there with a plaintive little look on her face, she's trying to mislead you.''

Moving beyond rhetoric, he turned to the evidence. The defense was wrong in claiming she was a suspect before a thorough investigation was made. ''If the Rowlett Police Department had put her in the crosshairs, why was Hamilton still lifting fingerprints five hours later?'' he asked. As for Jim Cron, her story simply didn't match the evidence and the difference ''stuck out like a sore thumb.''

He asked about the contention that state experts were wrong. If that were so, then where were the defense experts to contrast the bloodstains and blood-splatter theories? As for the critical piece of evidence, the sock, he said Linch identified it as Darin's and Darin had said on the stand it was his sock and it came from the utility room.

As for the claim of ''traumatic amnesia,'' Davis almost laughed. ''I call that the 'I-can't-remember or the I-won't-remember' defense.'' The forensic opinions of Dr. Coons were also sideswiped. ''Is there a doctor in the house? The defendant has mortally wounded her case and we need a doctor,'' Davis chided. Then he listed conditions he said just could not happen. An innocent woman wouldn't sleep through her children being stabbed or her own attack, not immediately call her husband on seeing an intruder, or worry about leaving fingerprints on a knife while her children were bleeding to death. "You have a very simple choice. Either this woman, Darlie Lynn Routier, or some mysterious lucky intruder" killed the boys. He picked up a pen and pointed it at the defendant, but kept his eyes on the jury. "All the evidence points very clearly at this woman and only at this woman."

He also skated by the motive, saying the jury knew "the pressure" she was under, but "only God and she know why she did it."

Davis called her a murderer again, this time right to her face. "The very last thing that each of those two children saw was their killer."

Darlie barked at him. "Liar," she said. "You're lying. I didn't kill my kids."

It was just the response any prosecutor would love to have a jury watch. The defendant, needled with in-your-face confrontations by an aggressive prosecutor, loses control and snaps, just as she may have snapped in an instant on a dark night six months ago. Davis, victorious, grabbed the moment like a golden apple. He paused for dramatic effect, shoulders almost slumping. "Now she says I'm a liar . . ." and he let that hang in the air before concluding.

"They saw this woman in a rage coming down on them with a knife," he said, and sat down, ending the four-week trial.

32

JUDGE TOLLE, ACCORDING to Darin Routier, made a prediction to Doug Mulder and Richard Mosty late Friday afternoon after charging the jury with the exact laws to apply to the case. Darin said His Honor confided that, in his own opinion, "You established reasonable doubt." If this was the view of the judge, it was irrelevant; he was not on the jury, and his personal opinion didn't count.

The long trial was finally in the hands of the jury of seven men and five women. They deliberated for six hours, into the night on Friday, and the passing time boosted the spirits of the defense team. Darlie's chances improved with each tick of the clock, for it indicated there was disagreement in that secluded room.

Saturday dawned cloudless and beautiful, with a strong sun warming the town that had been so frigid when the trial began four weeks earlier. Darin showed up in high spirits, telling reporters, "I slept like a baby last night. I know it's not going to be a hung jury, and I know they're not going to find her guilty. They can't convict her, not on what they got. They got nothing." He showed off his tattoo, a picture of Devon and Damon.

Darin could actually communicate with his beloved because Darlie, being held in a second-floor cell of the courthouse, could look out a narrow window at the crowd gathered in the sunlight on the lawn below. Television cameras surrounded Darin as he smiled up, jerking a thumb toward the street like a hitchhiker and mouthing the words, "Come on. Let's go!"

Almost every relative wore a T-shirt that bespoke their support, with pictures of Darlie and the boys. Dana, her sister, had one that also bore the inscription from Proverbs: "Save me, O Lord, from lying lips and deceiving tongues." They borrowed pens and paper to draw up signs to hold up to Darlie: BE STRONG, and WE ALL LOVE YOU. She wrote an I LOVE YOU and held it up in return.

Darlie smiled and waved and drew letters in the air with an uplifted finger. D-R-A-K-E. Authorities had refused to let her see the child, but Darin held up a large color photograph of their son. "One more day!" Darin said in pantomime. She had been in jail for seven months, and he wanted to take her home.

The jurors signaled shortly before noon, after a brief lunch, that they had reached a verdict, and everyone filed back into court, through a cordon of extra deputies pulling weekend duty for the controversial trial. Mulder's face was a mask of dismay. The verdict, he said, had come too soon. "It ain't looking good," he told someone. Family members, ebullient only moments before, now gathered nervously in a prayer circle in the little anteroom before entering court.

Darlie was distraught when they entered, her face in her hands, sobbing. Mulder looked to the family and covertly gave a negative sign. Thumbs down. It was as if an electric current paralyzed the entire group, and the young sisters Dana and Danelle dissolved into tears. None of the jurors looked at the defense table when they filed in.

The verdict, read by Judge Tolle at 12:40 P.M., confirmed their worst fear. Darlie was found guilty of capital

murder. She looked up, then quickly back down, squeez-
ing her eyes closed and bringing a clenched fist to her
mouth, and whispered to Richard Mosty, "I did not kill
my babies."

The family erupted in protest, with a shout of "Killers!" Stunned jurors looked at them. "Goddammit, you
are killers!" Darin folded over in his chair, drained and
stunned, his head in his hands. Sarilda was crushed, her
eyes wet from crying. Danelle screamed, "They're all
lying. Greg Davis is a killer!" Mama Darlie swept an
arm around Danelle and remained quiet, but pure fire
flashed in her eyes. The weeping rose in volume as the
jurors rose, one by one, and raised a hand to denote
agreement with the verdict. A burly bailiff finally ordered
the family to be quiet or leave.

Once outside, Darin raced through a turbulent sea of
television cameras. He was stunned and his comments
did not vary from everything he had said from the moment Darlie was arrested. "You keep on and on and on
until you're dead. I'll never quit," he said. "We've got
a lot of fight left." Then he ran across the street and
disappeared around a corner.

Greg Davis told the crowd that, even with the guilty
verdict, this wasn't over yet. "Our only regret is we cannot bring those boys back," he said. "We will be seeking
the death penalty. I think she is a future danger." Asked
about the verbal abuse heaped on him by the family,
Davis said he understood their feelings. "They've been
through a hard time in the last year or so, losing those
boys. But, again, they have only one person to blame,
and that's Darlie Routier."

The jury was back at work Monday morning to determine
whether Darlie should become part of one of the most
exclusive clubs in Texas. Only six other women were on
death row. They would have to decide two things. First,

if Darlie posed a continuing threat to society. If so, they would have to consider the second point, whether anything in her background might mitigate or lessen her moral responsibility for the crime.

Prosecutors hauled out the dirty laundry to assail Darlie's character.

Eileen Schirmer testified that, at a party, Devon squirted Darlie with a water gun and Darlie smacked him in the face with a piece of birthday cake. "Everybody stopped laughing" and Darlie told the boy he got what he deserved.

Allison Hennessey of Rowlett, a friend of one of the Routier baby-sitters, said she complained when Darlie offered her sixteen-year-old friend marijuana, wine coolers and beer, but Darlie laughed off the criticism. Hennessey also said the boys played unsupervised on busy streets and rode their bikes several blocks away from home, and that, when told, Darlie "didn't seem concerned."

Kay Norris, who worked in a pawnshop, said Darlie was a rude customer who came in every week, cursed at her children and forced Darin to buy her jewelry. Norris, whose own dress had wowed policemen in the witness room, said Darlie dressed "very tacky [and] everything was showing." Norris didn't challenge her customer, however, because "I got commission. I made money off the woman."

Melanie Waits, a friend of Darlie's torn by having to testify, described the two Mother's Day get-togethers in 1994 and 1995. A male stripper was hired to perform at Darlie's house the first year, and the next year, the group of women held a slumber party at Loew's Anatole Hotel in Dallas and went to the LaBare, a male strip club. "It was more or less a Mother's Day out. We had a good time," said Waits.

But the key witness was none other than Halena Czaban, who had not been allowed to tell her strange story to the jury during the trial. Now she was back to drop the full load, still working through a translator.

While she worked for Darlie a few days as a maid, she said Darlie told her she was in financial trouble and needed $10,000 to get out of debt. And when Halena tried to console Darlie as they stood beside the casket at the memorial service, she told Darlie: "I am so sorry for what happened. You had so many problems and now the expensive funeral." Darlie, she said, responded, "I am not worried because I will get $5,000 apiece" from insurance policies. Court watchers gasped.

Against such testimony, the tearful pleas of Darlie's relatives had little chance. Mama Darlie asked, "If you have any compassion, do not put her to death, because she did not do this."

Sarilda Routier came to the witness stand again and said, "I think you're dead wrong. . . . You have to live with that. I lost those two grandbabies and they're never coming back. Dig down deep in your soul and don't make it any worse."

And Darin's plaintive testimony fell on deaf ears. "I've lost everything," he said, but added that he still believed in Darlie's innocence.

Final closing arguments followed on Tuesday morning, terse this time, with Assistant District Attorney Sherri Wallace asking for the death penalty, the prosecution using a tactic of having a woman, not a man, seek the execution of another woman. "You know she's a threat. She's a threat to anything that gets in her way," Wallace told the jurors. "As long as you don't cross her, everything's fine. But if you get in her way, God help you."

Greg Davis put the jury on the side of the angels. "We don't like to think that evil exists, but ladies and gentlemen, there is evil in this world, and today that evil goes by the name of Darlie Lynn Routier." Bringing back a death-penalty sentence would not be an act of hatred toward Darlie, he said. "That's justice."

Defense attorneys took one look at the jury and knew they didn't have a chance. Doug Mulder reviewed critical points and said the jurors should have lingering doubt about the evidence, enough to question handing down a death sentence. "If they expect you to answer the ultimate question, then you're entitled to some answers and some explanations," he said.

Richard Mosty, who had become emotionally wrapped up in the trial and the verdict, spoke quietly with Darlie when the jury went into seclusion to make its decision. "Darlie," he said, "I don't think we've got a chance in the world of a life sentence. There's no way we're going to sway this jury." She looked at him and nodded agreement. "I looked at that jury while we were arguing," he said. "They just weren't listening to what we had to say."

It took four hours for the decision to be made, during which time Darlie looked one last time out of the window of her second-floor cell. As always, Darin was down there for her. Both were totally drained, numb and spent. There was no strength left, no money, no hope. Nothing but the way they felt about each other. He mouthed to her the silent words, "I love you."

An hour later, Darlie Lynn Routier was sentenced to die by lethal injection.

AUTHOR'S NOTE

This was a disturbing case. As an author, I have come to learn that each book presents a set of unique circumstances, and this one was in a class of its own.

A courtroom is not necessarily a place where truth emerges. It is a place of firm rules, mutual agreements, and written law in which opposing arguments are made before a jury that doesn't necessarily hear everything related to the people and situations involved.

One of my decisions was to let the trial unfold on its own, allow the lawyers to do their jobs and let them stand on the results. I found out that would be impossible, for what was happening around and beyond the courthouse became central to the story.

Is Darlie Routier guilty of murdering her children? Certainly the prosecutors solidly convinced the jury of her guilt, and played by the rules in so doing. Legal appeals of the verdict, automatic with a capital murder conviction, are in process.

But in covering the case, arriving in Rowlett the week that Darlie was arrested and making several subsequent visits to Rowlett and Dallas prior to the trial, I formed opinions that run contrary to the public perception of two very important questions:

Did she deserve the death penalty? *No.*

Was her trial really fair? *Probably not.*

The reasons are the same for both of these personal conclusions. The prosecutors played to fear and emotion with a jury that was very conservative, drawn from a pool in a small town that has now seen its last four capital murder cases end with death penalties. After the trial, one juror appeared on national television and said she voted to convict because the defense didn't prove that Darlie was innocent, directly contrary to the "innocent until proven guilty" maxim of American law.

The jury should have been sequestered, because the tight confines of the courthouse and the physical small-ness of Kerrville made it impossible for jurors to be divorced from outside influences. One was often seen reading newspapers, others dined at tables adjacent to trial participants or family members, and, worst of all, they constantly overheard comments from observers at the courthouse while they moved to and from the court-room without a shepherd.

They were also the product of their surroundings, and in Kerrville that means a staunchly conservative political viewpoint and deeply fundamentalist religious belief. So when prosecutors had Darlie admit she didn't regularly go to church, watched male strippers on Mother's Day, bought jewelry at a pawnshop, and let her kids listen to African-American rap music, the jurors were jolted, al-though none of that had anything to do with murder.

The constant mention of "Gangsta's Paradise" was particularly questionable and obviously tuned to racial prejudice. It was an unfair portrayal of a song that begins with a Bible verse, "As I walk through the valley of the shadow of death . . . ," points out the dead-end life of an urban street tough, and contains not a single obscenity. Instead of being a bad influence on children, the popular song is a cry to end gang violence. It was unlikely any of the jurors ever listened to it, and the tactic was akin to preachers four decades ago railing against Elvis Pres-ley and rock-and-roll. Norman Kinne calling Darlie Kee "trailer trash" was totally out of line and indicative of a narrow mindset within the District Attorney's Office.

The same conclusion can be reached with the unexpected mention of marijuana in the early part of the trial. The police officer who made the statement had been taken through his testimony repeatedly in practice sessions.

Rowlett police issued a news release after the trial, praising the work of its investigators and other officers. Actually, the work was very questionable in many aspects from the very start. In a thirty-year career in which I have reported on hundreds of trials, it is very rare that the lead investigator, his partner and his boss are not called as the primary witnesses by the prosecution, for they know the case best of all. Or should. Patterson, Frosch, and Grant Jack were shelved in favor of paid experts from out of town. One prosecution witness described the Rowlett police in the waiting room at the trial as ''arrogant.''

Of equal importance was the way that police notes either were updated, vanished, or were never made at all. Law enforcement agencies around the country usually insist on clear notes and, in many places, the use of tape recorders to assure valid statements in court. That is not the case in Rowlett.

Had they kept adequate notes, however, they might have been in the same awkward position as Baylor hospital staff members, whose comments on the stand directly contradicted what they had written about Darlie's condition months before, when they thought she was the victim of an attack.

Police efficiency was a sometime thing, from Sergeant Tom Dean Ward saying an alley gate was closed and locked when it actually stood open, to evidence collection specialist David Mayne not logging the pictures he shot and then choosing, seemingly at random, which documents and rags to collect and how to preserve them. That question could be mitigated by the fact that a representative of the Dallas County District Attorney was not on the scene to guide the earliest stages of the investigation, also a routine procedure on high-profile crimes in many states.

The very important moment of when Darlie became a suspect was another troubling point, and the prosecution argued that perhaps more than a week had passed after the June 6 murders before that decision was made. Countering that was Jim Cron's testimony that he decided at dawn of the first day, after only thirty minutes on the scene, that there was no inturder, and had told police that. Cron made his decision without knowledge of the bloody sock and incorrectly assuming that Darlie did not bleed on the sofa, because he did not see the blood-splotched pillow that had been knocked to the floor.

The following decision to withhold the 911 tape would confirm they thought pertinent information was on it, which would point to Darlie. And police had Darlie sign a Miranda warning on June 8 as soon as she got out of the hospital, meaning that, if not before, she was certainly a suspect at that early point.

After the June 26 preliminary hearing, it was plain that prosecutors didn't want to pin their case on the testimony of Patterson and Frosch. Instead of relying on the Rowlett police, the investigation went for outside specialists, for more and better evidence and for witnesses who would not crumble under the questions of defense lawyers. DNA expert Judith Irene Floyd, Oklahoma forensic specialist Tom Bevell, and FBI profiler Allen Brantley started work not in the summer of the crime, but rather in September. Charles Linch was back at the house looking for clues as late as November 21, and forensic expert Robert Poole was brought on board only a month before the start of the trial.

And still there was no explanation on how the sock stained with the boys' blood was found so far from the crime scene, or why it had a deer hair on it. The experts blandly said the sock was planted there, without explaining how it might have been done, or even proving whose sock it was.

Likewise, the reason that Darlie may have killed her children remained so elusive that prosecutors just waved it off, with Toby Shook saying they didn't have to prove motive. Their scenario of money problems and depression was an extreme attempt to force facts to fit an idea. That left the state in the ironic position of trying to demonstrate Darlie's state of mind at the time of the murders without calling an expert psychiatric witness of their own. I spent many hours interviewing the members of the Routier family and found not a single instance of Darlie being violent.

Nevertheless, most of Darlie's problems were self-inflicted. She talked to police too much without legal advice; she wrote too many letters, not realizing they would be read by her jailers; she disregarded Mulder's advice not to testify; and she tried to argue with Toby Shook, a skilled attorney, who shattered her on the witness stand.

The jury simply didn't like Darlie, and so disregarded much of what was said in her defense and ignored the holes in the prosecution's case. The conviction was a surprise to many, possibly even the judge. However, the die was cast. They barely listened to testimony about the death penalty. Even if Darlie was totally guilty of everything and every instance alleged by the prosecution and the witnesses, nothing was said to prove she posed a continuing threat to society and deserved a death sentence instead of a lengthy, even a life, prison term. The Routier family said post-trial interviews showed that four jurors originally voted in Darlie's favor. If true, that makes the shift to a unanimous death sentence even more extraordinary.

It is unfortunate that this trial was decided by emotion, not fact, and was lost when it was moved from Dallas to Kerrville.